INDEPENDENT AS F***

UNDERGROUND HIP-HOP

FROM 1995-2005

BEN PEDROCHE

Ben Pedroche fell in love with hip-hop in 1993 and has been listening non-stop ever since. He has written about and documented the genre for decades, including as a regular contributor to the groundbreaking rap magazine, Hip-Hop Connection, and various other titles. He has also written extensively for online gaming magazines, and more recently, Ben has contributed to websites such as Albumism, and since 2014 has been the editor of his own hip-hop culture platform, Grown Up Rap. He has published three books about his other passion, London history, and has appeared in TV documentaries for the BBC and Channel 5. In 2016, a short story Ben wrote was performed on BBC Radio 4.

For Florence and Frances...
just don't repeat the name of the book out loud.

First published by Velocity Press 2025

velocitypress.uk

Printed and bound in Great Britain by Clays Ltd, Elcograf S.p.A. GPSR

Cover design: Hayden Russell

Mika Väisänen: mika-photography.com
Mika Väisänen collection on Wikipedia: https://commons.wikimedia.org/wiki/Category:Photographs_by_Mika_V%C3%A4is%C3%A4nen

Typesetting: Paul Palmer-Edwards

PHYSICAL ISBN: 9781913231873

EBOOK ISBN: 9781913231880

Publisher: Velocity Press, London, United Kingdom

EU Authorised Representative: Easy Access System Europe
Mustamäe tee 50, 10621 Tallinn, Estonia

CONTENTS

ENTRODUCTION...

The ancient streets of London allow you to take many different routes when walking from A to B, the result of a dense hotchpotch of main roads and labyrinth backstreets connected over centuries of time. It helps to keep things interesting, especially when faced with doing the same boring walk each day to your place of work. I don't have to use the side street that connects Great Marlborough Street to Oxford Street, but I choose to everyday. The side streets are quieter, where even in one of the world's busiest cities at rush hour you can still find pockets of peacefulness that help before facing another banal eight hours at the day job. There's also another reason why I take this particular street, Poland Street to be precise. At number 44 there's an unassuming shop front, currently a confectionary shop. Years before, however, and until it closed in 2003, this was home to the greatest hip-hop record store in the world.

Mr. Bongo still lives on today as a boutique record label specializing in reissues and world music, but the physical retail store in London is long gone. The shop was a modest affair, away from the footfall and the tourists despite being just seconds away from London's most famous retail zone. But IYKYK, and those of us who did know were rewarded handsomely once we stepped inside. It was only a small shop, with an upper floor for Latin music, which I personally never had cause to venture up to. The ground floor was my spot, where every available inch of space was packed with hip-hop vinyl.

I only moved to London in 2008, and so my trips to Mr. Bongo were few and far between, and like a special pilgrimage each time. I was born and raised in Nottingham, way up North from London, and although the UK is only small, the divide between London and the rest of the country can be vast. My older brother, Nico, went to university in the town of Luton from 1995 to 1998, and after that moved to London for work. My parents and I would come on occasional weekends to see my brother, and it was on these trips that I'd get to visit Mr. Bongo. I had my go-to record shops back home in Nottingham (RIP to the now defunct Selectadisc, where me and my friend Shaun used to shop at every Saturday, me buying hip-hop, him buying house), but the London weekends were when I got to stack up on wax I couldn't get up North, back when the internet wasn't quite yet a big thing.

The London trip ritual included going to the flagship branch of HMV on Oxford Street, Tower Records in Piccadilly Circus – where they stocked lots of import-only rap albums on CD (at dumb high prices) and the latest issues of the smaller US rap magazines that covered underground hip-hop, like Mass Appeal, Urb, Complex and Scratch – and to Mr. Bongo.

It could be an intimidating shop to step inside. At peak times the small space would be jam packed with rap heads. Claustrophobia aside, this suited me best, because it allowed me to blend in with the crowd. Slower times were more daunting, paranoia setting in that the judging eyes of the staff behind the counter would laugh at me if I was seen to be looking at a record they deemed to be wack.

I'm sure the workers were all friendly really, but they gave off an air of the snobbery you often get in record stores. If you didn't know your shit they could be brutal, and I once witnessed this first hand. On a visit to the store in 1999 I was browsing the racks when a man came in and excitedly asked the guys behind the counter if they had the "Zam Zany" song. I knew right away he was talking about the "Slim Shady" song, meaning "My Name Is" by a then largely unknown Eminem. The song was getting a lot of traction at the time, and tons of people who didn't usually buy rap music now wanted it. Not only did I know he meant Slim Shady, the guys behind the counter did too, but instead of helping they feigned confusion, claiming not to know the record. Dejected, the man left the store empty-handed. It was painful to watch, not to mention bad for the prospects of the store, because I'd bet good money that man never again set foot inside Mr. Bongo.

Experiences like this made me scared to ask questions like the names of songs being played over the speakers, meaning I missed out on adding some killer records to my collection. I'd typically leave the store with three or four new 12"s, and then it was back to Oxford Street to rejoin my parents who had been patiently waiting for me in the cafe of the also-now-defunct Borders book shop, bemused as to why their teenage son had been buying hip-hop records again. By the time I finally migrated to London to live, Mr. Bongo was no more.

Ask most underground hip-hop aficionados which record store was their favorite and they'll probably say Fat Beats, the famed outlet in New York City, located first in a basement on East 9th Street in Lower East Side Manhattan, and later relocated to 6th Avenue. There were also branches of Fat Beats in Los Angeles, Atlanta, and even Tokyo and Amsterdam, but the 6th Avenue location in New York is the one people remember as the mecca of indie rap record stores.

I only managed to get to Fat Beats one time, on a trip to New York in 2002. It was an experience I'll always remember, and I'm forever glad I got to go before the store closed in 2010.

Fat Beats was sacred ground in the world of independent hip-hop, but for me personally, it still came a very close second to Mr. Bongo. Ultimately, however, it didn't matter if the shop was in London, New York, Japan or anywhere else in the world. Mr. Bongo, Fat Beats and other similar hip-hop record stores all shared the same aesthetic and essential characteristics. The walls had to be covered in graffiti tags, event flyers, promo stickers and record sleeves signed by any artist who had passed through. The older records needed to be in shelving bins on the shop floor, while the newest releases were to be found in racks on the walls. The 12"s with plain white or black sleeves needed to be labeled with stickers written in tag writing. There had to be a turntable where customers could listen to wax before they buy, and that turntable better be a Technics SL-1200. And last but not least, the music needed to be constantly blasted loud. If you got these elements correct you had yourself a quintessential hip-hop vinyl record emporium.

Record shopping today is different. Sales of vinyl have inexplicably boomed again in recent years, but most of this is done online. There are still physical record stores, and the new lease of life that records have experienced has seen new shops open in cities around the world. It is all very sanitized now, however, and the place people buy records from is often primarily a clothes shop or an artisan coffee joint with a token vinyl section thrown in for good measure, because why the fuck not. Come for the chai latte, stay for the over-priced special editions of Taylor Swift and Chappell Roan albums on vinyl. I can walk two minutes from where Mr. Bongo used to be located to Urban Outfitters on Oxford Street – a clothes shop – and buy a copy of Kendrick Lamar's *DAMN.* or The *Miseducation of Lauryn Hill* on wax. It is good that a new generation of listeners can discover these two albums on a record, or at least purchase them, seeing as lots of people buying new vinyl do so as a collection item and not to actually listen to, but it's all a far cry from what record shopping used to be like.

Some of this is false nostalgia. The classic era of underground hip-hop covered in these pages was fuelled just as much by online sales as it was by purchases at physical stores, when primitive e-commerce sites like Sandbox Automatic, UGHH and Hip Hop Site sold copies of the latest releases from labels like Rawkus Records, Fondle 'Em Records and Hydra Entertainment, and shipped them to places across the world. No website purchase, digital download or play on a streaming service can match the feeling of going into a record store and touching vinyl, however, and for me the experience was a big part of what made underground hip-hop so exciting, especially during a golden age when there was something new, fresh and utterly dope to purchase every week. *Independent as F**** is an attempt to describe everything that was great about the period from 1995-2005, and the artists and records that made it memorable.

Author's Notes

This book focuses on the decade in question (1995-2005), with time periods before and after that only covered for context and history. Some of the most important underground albums are therefore only discussed briefly, because they were not released in the focus period. The book also does not necessarily give a fully exhaustive account of each artists' discography, even if an album was released in the period.

There are a selection of key artists from the era not being covered in detail in this book because of their actions, regardless of how much good music they made during the period. Some have espoused opinions in recent years that are hateful and extreme right leaning, or that veer wildly towards the promotion of dangerous, and thoroughly debunked, conspiracy theories. Others have been accused of harassment, bullying, or horrendous physical and sexual abuse, including one artist who at the time of writing is serving a prison sentence for felony rape. Some of these artists are mentioned briefly but not celebrated or discussed at length, unless this is required for context.

1

FROM 93 TIL

T he shining lights of what would become the golden era of indie rap were without doubt influenced by those that flourished in the first half of the 1990s, with 1993 and 1994 particular years of major significance. The rappers and producers from this generation – themselves influenced by the first golden era of the late 1980s, when innovative acts like Public Enemy, BDP, NWA, Ultramagnetic MCs, Run-DMC, Ice-T, the Juice Crew and others all released classic albums – advanced the genre further still, creating, among other things, boom-bap, 'jazz rap', and G-funk.

These artists may not have been signed to indie labels – although some labels did start out independently, or operated as such, with distribution via major labels, such as Loud Records, Relativity, Rap-A–Lot Records, and others – but the music they made matched the sentiments of the future underground era in many ways: neither era was concerned with following the conventions of 'popular' music, they didn't need huge recording budgets to make breathtaking music, and they were not willing to compromise their integrity by being forced to make certain types of records just because they would sell lots of CDs.

There were exceptions. The RnB crossover song, the inevitable 'ladies' track, and the much-maligned hip-house cut were staples you'd often find on albums where the record label had insisted on an attempt to make an impact on the charts. But even when a record by a group like A Tribe Called Quest or Pete Rock & CL Smooth did become a modest hit, or even a big hit in the case of a group like Naughty by Nature, the authentic, street-level aesthetic of such artists made them too raw and unpolished to ever be considered 'pop stars'.

The following is a potted, non-exhaustive history of the kind of hip-hop released between 1990-1995 that had a lasting impact on the underground artists from the second half of the decade.

THE ORIGINATORS

In Brooklyn, Queens and the Bronx, a mixed group of emcees and producers were honing their skills, and eight of them came together to form the Diggin' In The Crates (D.I.T.C.) crew. Various albums followed, starting with *Funky Technician* by Lord Finesse and DJ Mike Smooth in 1990; *Stunts, Blunts & Hip Hop* by Diamond D, Showbiz & A.G.'s *Runaway Slave*, and *Return of the Funky Man* by Lord Finesse, all in 1992; Fat Joe's *Represent* in 1993; O.C.'s *Word...Life* in 1994; and Big L's *Lifestylez ov da Poor & Dangerous*, Fat Joe's *Jealous One's Envy*, and Showbiz & A.G.'s *Goodfellas*, each in 1995. Between them, the producers in D.I.T.C. – Diamond D, Lord Finesse, Showbiz and Buckwild – helped to create the sound of boom bap, as did Large Professor, DJ Premier, Q-Tip, Pete Rock, Da Beatminerz, The Beatnuts, Easy Mo Bee, EZ-Elpee, and others, themselves inspired by the likes of Marley Marl, DJ Prince Paul, Rick Rubin and the 45 King.

DJ Premier was responsible for a string of early 90s New York classics as one half of Gang Starr with his partner Guru, despite the kicker that neither were from the city (DJ Premier is from Texas, and Guru originally founded Gang Starr in Boston in the mid 80s with rapper Big Shug and DJ Suave D). The DJ Premier and Guru incarnation of Gang Starr actually dropped their debut in 1989, but it was on *Step In the Arena* (1991), *Daily Operation* (1992) and *Hard to Earn* (1994) where they became boom bap icons. They also developed a group of emcees under the banner of the Gang Starr Foundation, resulting in albums by Jeru The Damaja (1994's *The Sun Rises in the East*) and Group Home (*Livin' Proof* in 1995). In 1993, Guru introduced the first volume of his *Jazzmatazz* series, and volume 2 arrived in 1995. Gang Starr also helped to bring other artists to wider attention, including M.O.P. Group members Billy Danze and Lil Fame debuted with *To The Death* in 1994.

Pete Rock debuted in full in 1991 when he and CL Smooth released *All Souled Out*. This was followed a year later by the masterful *Mecca and the Soul Brother*, and *The Main Ingredient* in 1994. After learning his craft while producing for Eric B. & Rakim and Kool G Rap, under the tutelage of Paul C, Large Professor introduced his group Main Source with the release of *Breaking Atoms* in 1991, although he had already left by the release of the group's next album in 1994, *Fuck What You Think*. In addition to producing for their own groups, DJ Premier, Pete Rock, Large Professor, Diamond D, Buckwild and Lord Finesse also earned respect for production on other people's records, each one building a solid reputation as a go-to New York beatmaker for original songs and remixes.

In Brooklyn, Black Moon's *Enta da Stage* and Smif-N-Wessun's *Dah Shinin'* hit hard in 1993 and 1995. Both were soundtracked by Da Beatminerz, and laid the foundations for the Boot Camp Clik. Other key Brooklyn releases included records by X-Clan (*To the*

East, Blackwards in 1990 and Xodus: *The New Testament* in 1992); Jaz-O (*To Your Soul* in 1990, featuring a young Jay-Z); Original Flava, whose line-up included future acclaimed producer Ski Beatz (their *This is How It Is* album came in 1992, and *Beyond Flavor* in 1994, again featuring Jay-Z); and Digable Planets (1993's *Reachin' (A New Refutation of Time and Space)* and 1994's *Blowout Comb*).

In Queens, Pharoahe Monch and Prince Po combined to form Organised Konfusion and dropped an album of the same name in 1991, and then *Stress: The Extinction Agenda* in 1994. Onyx then introduced a new, rowdy style with their debut *Bacdafucup* in 1993, and *All We Got Iz Us* in 1995. There was also a strong debut in 1995 by Mic Geronimo with *The Natural*.

Elsewhere in New York, in 1991, Tim Dog released the incendiary *Penicillin on Wax*, Nikki D released *Daddy's Little Girl*, Staten Island group The U.M.C.'s debuted with *Fruits of Nature,* and Bomb Squad proteges Son of Bazerk dropped *Bazerk Bazerk Bazerk*; in 1992 Positive K released *The Skills Dat Pay da Bills*, and Hard Knocks dropped *School of Hard Knocks*; in 1993 Da King & I released *Contemporary Jeep Music*, and Akinyele released *Vagina Diner*; and in 1994 Kurious released his debut, *A Constipated Money*, while his fellow CM Mob members Hard 2 Obtain released *Ism & Blues*. Kurious would later become a key player in the indie rap scene thanks to his close friendship with one of its biggest stars.

Although they continued to release records throughout the 90s, bitter fighting between Erick Sermon and Parish Smith meant that EPMD broke up and reformed more than once during the decade. This caused a split between several artists the duo were working with, creating two separate factors. On one side was the Hit Squad, led by Smith, maintaining the name used by the entire collective pre-split. The line-up of this splinter cell included K-Solo

– who released *Tell the World My Name* in 1990 and *Time's Up* in 1992 – and the duo Das EFX. With a novel way of rapping – the so-called 'iggedy' style of flow – Das EFX scored some success with *Dead Serious* in 1992, *Straight Up Sewaside* in 1993 and *Hold It Down* in 1995.

On the other side was the Def Squad, led by Sermon. Their ranks included the late Hurricane G, and Keith Murray, who debuted in 1994 with *The Most Beautifullest Thing in This World*. The jewel in the Def Squad crown, however, was New Jersey rapper Redman. After gaining recognition on tracks with EPMD, Redman released his debut in 1992, *Whut? Thee Album*, and followed it with *Dare Iz a Darkside* in 1994. Sermon and Smith also each released their own solo albums during the period: Sermon's *No Pressure* came out in 1993, and *Double or Nothing* arrived in 1995. Smith released *Shadē Business* in 1994.

Redman was far from the only New Jersey artist earning critical acclaim with a sound similar to the boom bap beats coming from across the Hudson River. The group Lords of The Underground – for whom Redman used to deejay – came out with *Here Come the Lords* in 1993, trailed by *Keepers of the Funk* a year later. Both albums featured production by Marley Marl and one of hip-hop's most underrated producers, DJ K-Def. El Da Sensei and Tame One formed the Artifacts and released *Between a Rock and a Hard Place* in 1994, and both would later become stalwarts of the indie scene in the next half of the decade and beyond. In Trenton, the Poor Righteous Teachers released a run of albums starting with 1990's *Holy Intellect*. Meanwhile, the Fugees released *Blunted on Reality* in 1994, two years before they would reach megastardom with their next album.

A member of the 45 King's Flavor Unit, Apache released his

debut in 1993, the self-deprecatingly named *Apache Ain't Shit*. When the Flavor Unit morphed from being a crew of artists into a management company headed by Queen Latifah, they continued to support artists from their native New Jersey. Their clients included the group Channel Live, who came out with *Station Identification* in 1995, but the biggest hitter for Flavor Unit Management was Naughty by Nature. The group scored genuine hits with tracks from *Naughty by Nature* in 1991 and *19 Naughty III* in 1993, and to a lesser extent on 1995's *Poverty's Paradise*. It was far removed from when Naughty By Nature first attempted to break through in the late 80s under the name New Style. The group used their new found success to develop other artists, including the Rottin Razkals with their *Rottin to da Core* album in 1995.

The Native Tongues collective had a degree of success in the late 1980s with the first albums from De La Soul and the Jungle Brothers. By the turn of the decade, the various members and artists in their wider circle were ready to unleash their own high quality albums. A Tribe Called Quest moved into the spotlight in 1990 with *People's Instinctive Travels and the Paths of Rhythm*, and went on to release two masterpieces with *The Low End Theory* (1991) and *Midnight Marauders* (1993). Monie Love dropped her debut, *Down to Earth*, in 1990, and her sophomore album with *In a Word or 2* in 1993, and Chi-Ali released *The Fabulous Chi-Ali* in 1992. Queens based Dres and Mista Lawnge formed Black Sheep and released *A Wolf in Sheep's Clothing* in 1991, followed by *Non-Fiction* in 1994. Dres also helped introduce the group The Legion, whose *Theme + Echo = Krill 94* album came in 1994. And plenty more crucial releases emerged from artists on the periphery of the Native Tongues, most notably Brand Nubian and The Beatnuts. Brand Nubian debuted in 1990 with *One For All*, and although Grand Puba left soon after, the group continued with *In God We Trust* in 1993 and *Everything is Everything* in 1994. Grand Puba's solo run began in 1992 with *Reel to Reel*, and the *2000* album three years later. Juju and Psycho Les (plus original third member Fashion (later known as Al Tariq)) released the first The Beatnuts project in 1993, named *Intoxicated Demons: The EP*. This was followed by their self-titled full length debut album in 1994 with fourth member The Mighty V.I.C. Other Native Tongues affiliated acts to release records in the era were the groups Da Bush Babies (*Ambushed* in 1994), the Fu-Schnickens (*F.U. Don't Take It Personal* in 1992 and *Nervous Breakdown* in 1994), and the Leaders of the New School. The latter released *A Future Without a Past...* in 1991 and *T.I.M.E. (The Inner Mind's Eye)* in 93, on which the world got to witness the coming out of a major new talent in Busta Rhymes.

The rich, diverse amount of good hip-hop coming out of New York and New Jersey in the early-mid 90s helped the east coast reclaim its luster and respect after having lost ground to the mega rap hits that were being released on the west coast. All of the aforementioned albums helped, but there were several marquee releases from 1993-1995 that really made an impact. When the RZA formed the Wu-Tang Clan he had a fully-sketched out plan for how his group would take over the rap game, starting with the release of their classic debut in 1993, *Enter the Wu-Tang (36 Chambers)*. Solo debuts were the next part of the plan, starting with Method Man's *Tical* in 1994, followed by a bumper year in 1995 which saw the releases of albums by Ol' Dirty Bastard *(Return to the 36 Chambers: The Dirty Version)*, Raekwon (*Only Built 4 Cuban Linx...*) and the GZA (*Liquid Swords*). The latter album was not actually GZA's debut – that came with the pre-Wu-Tang era *Words from the Genius* released in 1991, the same year that RZA released his debut

EP as Prince Rakeem, *Ooh I Love You Rakeem*. The success of the Wu-Tang Clan also created an entire cottage industry of albums by Wu-affiliated artists, starting in 1994 with *AKA the Rugged Child* by Shyheim, and the release of *6 Feet Deep* by RZA's side-project the Gravediggaz, with former Stetsasonic members DJ Prince Paul and Frukwan, and Too Poetic of the group Brothers Grym.

Nas and The Notorious B.I.G. released their classic debuts in 1994, *Illmatic* and *Ready to Die*, marking the official arrival of two major new talents. B.I.G.'s label mate Craig Mack also did good numbers with 1994's *Project: Funk da World*. In 1995, Mobb Deep released *The Infamous* (very different to their 1993 debut, *Juvenile Hell*); Nas' partner-in-rhyme AZ released *Doe or Die*; and The Notorious B.I.G. helped establish the group Junior M.A.F.I.A. with their debut, *Conspiracy*.

Outside of New York and New Jersey, Black Thought and Questlove started their long and celebrated career with The Roots on 1993's *Organix* and 1995's *Do You Want More?!!!??!*, and fellow Philadelphia group Da Youngstas released three albums between 1992-1994 (*Somethin 4 Da Youngstas*, *The Aftermath* and *No Mercy*). In Boston, Edo.G debuted in 1991 with *Life of a Kid in the Ghetto*, and followed up with *Roxbury 02119* in 1993, both with his group Da Bulldogs. In the Midwest, Chicago's Common (then known as Common Sense) released *Can I Borrow a Dollar?* in 1992 and *Resurrection* in 1994.

On the west coast, the explosion of gangster rap and G-funk opened the floodgates for important releases from across the state of California. Compton's Most Wanted released their debut in 1990, *It's a Compton Thang*, and then *Straight Checkn 'Em* in 1991 and *Music to Driveby* in 1992. Group leader MC Eiht also released his solo debut in 1994 with *We Come Strapped*. Fellow Compton emcee DJ

Quik – for many years a rival to MC Eiht in a vicious beef – kicked off his lengthy career in 1991 with *Quik is the Name*, *Way 2 Fonky* in 1992, and *Safe + Sound* in 1995. DJ Quik also featured on albums by his proteges AMG (*Bitch Betta Have My Money*) and the self-titled debut by 2nd II None, both in 1991. Yo Yo, another Compton native and a protege of Ice Cube, was introduced in 1991 with *Make Way for the Motherlode*, followed by *Black Pearl* (1992) and *You Better Ask Somebody* (1993), while the Ice Cube-affiliated Da Lench Mob released *Guerillas in tha Mist* in 1992. Kid Frost released *East Side Story*, also in 1992; South Central Cartel released several projects, including 1994's *'N Gatz We Truss*; and although she was from Detroit, Bo$$ transplanted to Los Angeles, resulting in her one and only album, *Born Gangstaz* (1993).

In other parts of the state, Above The Law impressed with *Livin' Like Hustlers* (1990), *Black Mafia Life* (1993) and *Uncle Sam's Curse* (1994); Kokane made his debut in 91 with *Addictive Hip Hop Muzick*: Mack 10 debuted with his self-titled album in 1995, and WC left the duo Low Profile, releasing *Ain't a Damn Thang Changed* in 1991 and *Curb Servin* in 1995 with the Maad Circle. That group also featured Coolio, who released his debut in 1994, *It Takes a Thief*, and then found huge success with 1995's *Gangsta's Paradise*.

There was also much good music coming out of the Bay Area. E-40 began what is now one of the largest bodies of music from any hip-hop artist with a flurry of albums and EPs, including *Mr. Flamboyant* in 1991, *Federal* in 1992, *The Mail Man* in 1993, and *In a Major Way* in 1995, plus two projects with his group The Click (*Down and Dirty* and *Game Related*, in 1992 and 1995 respectively). Richie Rich came out with *Don't Do It* in 1990; Spice 1 broke through with a self-titled debut in 1992, and then *187 He Wrote* (1993), *AmeriKKK's Nightmare* (1994) and *1990-Sick* in 1995; Dru Down released *Fools From the*

23

Streets in 1993 and *Explicit Game* in 1994, the same year that Celly Cel came out with *Heat 4 Yo Azz*; Seagram debuted in 1992 with *The Dark Roads*, The Conscious Daughters dropped *Ear to the Street* and producer Ant Banks made *Sittin' on Somethin' Phat*, both in 1993; Luniz released *Operation Stackola* in 1995; Sway & King Tech released *Concrete Jungle* in 1991; and although he later moved the operation to his native New Oreleans, Master P started his No Limit Records empire in the Bay, releasing solo albums, including 1994's *The Ghettos Tryin' to Kill Me!*, and projects by his group Tru.

Eclipsing all of these gangster rap albums, however, was one by a skinny kid from back down in Los Angeles, Long Beach more specifically. Snoop Doggy Dogg's *Doggystyle* became one of the biggest albums of the 90s, and set him on the journey towards being the cultural icon Snoop Dogg is today. Snoop Dogg was also heavily involved with another big hit for Death Row Records, 1995's *Dogg Food* album by the Dogg Pound, and Snoop's fellow 213 member Warren G also achieved major success with *Regulate... G Funk Era* in 1994. Warren G additionally has his own artists in development, including Twinz, who released *Conversation* in 1995.

Adjacent to this, away from gangster rap, various other west coast acts were making hip-hop that was either politically charged, weed-infused, alcohol soaked, or just straight up fun. In Los Angeles Cypress Hill scored major success with their eponymous debut in 1991, *Black Sunday* in 1993, and *III: Temples of Boom* in 1995; Funkdoobiest debuted in 1993 with *Which Doobie U B?*; House of Pain had a huge hit with their self-titled debut in 1992; Tha Alkaholiks impressed with *21 & Over* in 1993 and *Coast II Coast* in 1995; and Kam unleashed *Never Again* in 1993.

Back up in the Bay Area, Paris made hard-hitting albums with *The Devil Made Me Do It* (1990), *Sleeping with the Enemy* (1992) and *Guerrilla Funk* (1994), as did The Coup with *Kill My Landlord* in 1993 and *Genocide & Juice* in 1994. The late Shock G and his group Digital Underground burst onto the scene with *Sex Packets* in 1990, and then *This Is an EP Release* and *Sons of the P* in 1991, and *The Body-Hat Syndrome* in 1993. Group member Money B, meanwhile, collaborated with DJ Fuze to form Raw Fusion, releasing *Live from the Styleetron* in 1991 and *Hoochiefied Funk* in 1994. Digital Underground also helped introduce the world to 2Pac, who released *2Pacalypse Now* in 1991, *Strictly 4 My N.I.G.G.A.Z...* in 1993 and *Me Against the World* in 1995. He also introduced his crew with *Thug Life, Volume I* in 1994.

Indie rap pioneers Freestyle Fellowship, Pharcyde and Hieroglyphics were also releasing music during this time on the west coast, but we'll hear more about that later in the book.

———

Away from the established centers of rap, local scenes were emerging in other large cities and regional markets. In Houston, a new line-up of the Geto Boys was bringing success for Rap-A-Lot Records thanks to *We Can't Be Stopped* (1991) and *Till Death Do Us Part* (1993), and solo albums by Scarface: *Mr Scarface is Back* in 1991, *The World is Yours* in 1993, and *The Diary* in 1994. There were also albums by the other two Geto Boys members; Willie D (*I'm Goin' Out Like Soldier* and *Play Witcha Mama* from 1992 and 1994, respectively), and Bushwick Bill (*Little Big Man* in 1992 and *Phantom of the Rapra* in 1995). Other key Rap-A-Lot Records releases of the time included *Ghetto Dope* (1993), *Gangsta Funk* (1994) and *Rated G* (1995) by the 5th Ward Boyz, and *Convicts* by the duo of the same name, in 1991. Convicts and peripheral Geto Boys member, Big Mike, released his own debut in 1994, *Somethin'*

Serious. In Port Arthur, Texas, UGK introduced themselves to a wider audience in 1992 with *Too Hard to Swallow*, and *Super Tight* in 1994.

In Memphis, Tennessee, Eightball & MJG put the Suave House label on the map with *Comin' Out Hard* (1993), *On the Outside Looking In* (1994), and *On Top of the World* (1995). Also from Memphis, Three 6 Mafia debuted in 1995 with *Mystic Stylez*. In Cleveland, Ohio, Bone Thugs-N-Harmony released the *Creepin on ah Come Up* EP in 1994, and hit pay dirt a year later with the successful *E. 1999 Eternal*.

In Flint and Detroit, Michigan, MC Breed dropped a bevy of albums as a solo artist (*20 Below* in 1992, *The New Breed* in 1993, *Funkafied* in 1994, and *Big Baller* in 1995), and with the DFC, also in 1991 (*M.C. Breed & DFC*). DFC later released *Things In Tha Hood* without MC Breed, in 1994.

In Atlanta, Georgia, Outkast started their soon-to-be-legendary run in 1994 with *Southernplayalisticadillacmuzik*, and fellow Dungeon Family group the Goodie Mob debuted with *Soul Food* the following year. Also coming out of Atlanta were Arrested Development, who in 1992 found success with singles from their *3 Years, 5 Months and 2 Days in the Life Of...* album, and also released *Zingalamaduni* two years later.

———

Coming just a few years after the late 80s classic era, several artists from that generation were also still making albums between 1990-1995. In New York, Kool G Rap released two additional albums with DJ Polo (1990's *Wanted: Dead or Alive* and 1993's *Live and Let Die*), and then branched out on his own with his full solo debut in 1995, *4,5,6*. Kool G Rap's fellow Juice Crew members were also still active in this timespace. Big Daddy Kane released *Taste of*

Chocolate in 1990, *Prince of Darkness* in 1991, *Looks Like a Job For...* in 1993, and *Daddy's Home* in 1994, and Roxanne Shante released her second (and as of yet final) album in 1992, *The Bitch is Back*. Biz Markie furthered his legacy with *I Need a Haircut* in 1991 and *All Samples Cleared* in 1993. Masta Ace came out with his debut, *Take a Look Around*, in 1990, and later released two acclaimed albums with his Masta Ace Incorporated crew (*SlaughtaHouse* in 1993, *Sittin' on Chrome* in 1995). Craig G released his second album, 1991's *Now, That's More Like It*, and extended Juice Crew members Grand Daddy IU and Intelligent Hoodlum released albums between 1990-94, while the collective's leader, DJ Marley Marl, dropped his *In Control Volume II* project in 1991.

Boogie Down Productions leader KRS-One – the Juice Crew's nemesis in the infamous Bridge Wars – released BDP albums in 1990 and 1992 (*Edutainment* and *Sex & Violence*), and then launched his solo career in 1993 with *Return of the Boom Bap*, followed by *KRS One* in 1995. Fellow BDP member D-Nice also went solo with *Call Me D-Nice* in 1990, and the follow up *To tha Rescue* a year later. Public Enemy dominated with *Fear of a Black Planet* in 1990 and *Apocalypse 91... The Enemy Strikes Black* a year later; and the Beastie Boys had hits with *Check Your Head* (1992) and *Ill Communication* (1994). Eric B. & Rakim were also still making records, bringing forth *Let the Rhythm Hit 'Em* in 1990 and *Don't Sweat the Technique*, as were EPMD, who released *Business as Usual* in 1990 and *Business Never Personal* in 1992. Slick Rick released albums in 1991 and 1994 (*The Ruler's Back* and *Behind Bars*), Stetsasonic dropped *Blood, Sweat & No Tears* in 1991, and LL Cool J regained his status as one of rap's biggest names with *Mama Said Knock You Out* in 1990, *14 Shots to the Dome* in 1993, and *Mr. Smith* in 1995.

27

The Native Tongues members who first came out in the very late 80s continued to release stellar albums, including Queen Latifah with *Nature of a Sista'* (1991) and *Black Reign* (1993), and the Jungle Brothers' *J Beez wit the Remedy* in 1993. De La Soul made the biggest critical splash, however, releasing two classic albums in *De La Soul is Dead* in 1991, followed by *Buhloone Mindstate* in 1993.

MC Serch and Pete Nice released one last 3rd Bass album in 1991, *Derelicts of Dialect*, and when the group broke up, MC Serch debuted as a solo artist on *Return of the Product* (1992), and Pete Nice released *Dust to Dust* in 1993 with the other former member of 3rd Bass, DJ Richie Rich (as Daddy Rich). 3rd Bass proteges KMD released their *Mr. Hood* album in 1991, and the Ultramagnetic MCs continued to put out albums with *Funk Your Head Up* in 1992, and *The Four Horsemen* a year later. The lead members of both groups would very soon become two of the most important figures in underground rap.

Special Ed released two albums in the period, *Legal* in 1990 and *Revelations* in 1995; Original Flava Unit member Lakim Shabazz dropped *The Lost Tribe of Shabazz* in 1990, and Mount Vernon's Heavy D & The Boyz released *Peaceful Journey* (1991), *Blue Funk* (1992) and *Nuttin' But Love* in 1994; DJ Jazzy Jeff & The Fresh became household names thanks to *Homebase* (1991) and *Code Red* (1993); as did Salt-N-Pepa with various albums, including the multi-platinum *Very Necessary* in 1993; Def Jef released *Soul Food* in 1991; Chubb Rock followed up his 80s work alonside Howie Tee by releasing three albums in the period, beginning with 1991's *The One*; King Sun released *Righteous But Ruthless* in 1990, MC Lyte continued her rise with *Act Like You Know* (1991) and *Aint No Other* (1993); the Tuff Crew released *Still Dangerous* (1991); there was a final Fat Boys album in 1991 (*Mack Daddy*) before Prince

Markie Dee went solo in 1992 with *Free*; Rob Base & DJ E-Z Rock put out their final album, *Break of Dawn*, in 1994; Nice & Smooth came with *Ain't a Damn Thing Changed* (1991) and *Jewel of the Nile* (1994), and there were several albums by 2-Live Crew and solo projects by frontman Uncle Luke. There were even albums released in the 90s by artists from an era before the late 80s, including *Funke, Funke Wisdom* and *Interlude* by Kool Moe Dee in 1991 and 1994 respectively, and *How a Black Man Feels* (1991), *Welcome to America* (1994) and *Reservoir Dog* (1995) by gangster rap originator Schoolly D.

On the west coast, Ice-T recorded some of his most well-received albums in 1991 and 1993 with *O.G. Original Gangster* and *Home Invasion*, King T released *At Your Own Risk* in 1990, *Tha Triflin' Album* in 1993, and *IV Life* in 1995, Too Short released *Short Dog's in the House* in 1990, *Shorty the Pimp* in 1992, *Get in Where You Fit In* in 1993, and *Cocktails* in 1995; and Mellow Man Ace released *The Brother With Two Tongues* in 92. N.W.A. released the *100 Miles and Runnin'* EP in 1990 and their second album with *Niggaz4Life* in 1991, albeit without Ice Cube, who went on a tear of a solo run with *AmeriKKKa's Most Wanted* and *Kill at Will* in 1990, *Death Certificate* in 1991, *The Predator* in 1992, and *Lethal Injection* in 1993. There were also albums and EPs by MC Ren (*Kizz My Black Azz* in 1992, *Shock of the Hour* in 1993) and Eazy E (*5150: Home 4 tha Sick* in 1992 and *It's On (Dr. Dre) 187um Killa* in 1993), but the N.W.A. member who eclipsed all of them was Dr. Dre. His debut *The Chronic* came out in 1993 to universal acclaim.

These pivotal releases opened doors for a tranche of important records in a similar vein throughout 1996 and 1997, and further beyond. Bahamadia, Mad Skillz, Blahzay Blahzay, Lost Boyz, Camp Lo, Cormega, Jay-Z, Cella Dwellas, Heather B, Big Noyd, Royal

Flush, Smooth da Hustler, East Flatbush Project, Capone-N-Noreaga, Miilkbone, Kwest Tha Madd Lad, Big Pun, dead prez, and Wu-Tang Clan affiliates Cappadonna, La The Darkman, Killarmy and Sunz of Man are just some of the solo emcees and groups introduced at the start of the second half of the 90s with direct ties to what came before, and heavily inspired by it.

More specifically, the many different influences from the early 90s blended together to form the foundation for a new breed of hungry artists from the underground ready to take hip-hop to new places. It would be a stretch to suggest that the indie movement would never have happened without what came before, but the echoes of the first five years of the 90s were definitely a powerful influence on what happened next.

2

STRESS RAP

The concept of independently-released music is not just confined to hip-hop, and far predates the ten-year period on which we'll be focussing here. Most listeners probably have a good sense of what being 'independent' means, but for those that don't, a basic definition is as follows: Being independent means that the artist or 'indie' label they are signed to is responsible for creating, manufacturing, promoting and selling their art outside of, and with no assistance from, the systems, processes and marketing channels of a major corporation. An independent film is a movie not made by a studio. An independent book publisher, like the one publishing the book you are reading right now, does so without the support and infrastructure of a large publishing house. And an independent musician is one who writes, records, presses and sells their music themselves, with no help from a record label. An independent musician can be signed to an independent record label, like many of the artists talked about in this book, but that record label is also still operating outside of the major label system.

All of this means the artist or independent label takes on every financial risk associated with releasing music, paying for everything from studio time (or the cost of building a bedroom studio at home), a producer, and mastering engineer, to the cost of manufacturing physical copies – very much a thing again since people have started buying CDs, vinyl, and even tapes once more, despite physical media having been all but killed off for many years, first by MP3 downloads and then by streaming services, with merchandise now one of the few reliable ways an artist can make money – distribution fees, marketing costs, and various other expenses.

For the listener, the promise of independent music is that it is often more organic and creatively daring than music produced and sold for a mass audience. This is not always true. Much of the greatest music ever recorded has been released on major record labels, and conversely, an independent artist can sometimes just be emulating the same kind of formulaic music often found on the radio, especially so in rap music. But in theory at least, independent music should be edgier and beyond the boundaries of convention.

The reasoning is simple and, at least from a financial perspective, purely transactional. A major record label is in the business of making money. They have a lot to lose if they sign and invest in an artist who fails to make music that the average person wants to hear, or who is too controversial. Hip-hop in particular has a long history of seeing first hand how risk-averse big labels tend to be when it comes to artists with an agenda, or who say and do things not everyone wants to see or hear, especially in a country like the US, where conservative-led morale panic and overt racism mean that rap music has historically been a convenient scapegoat on which to pin all of society's problems. In the late 1980s and early 90s there was outrage over N.W.A. telling the Police to go fuck themselves, Ice-T fantasising about killing one of those same cops, and the sex raps of 2-Live Crew.

A media backlash was enough to get an artist thrown off their label, copies of a single pulled from shelves, or an album canceled. It still happens now, hardly a surprise in the context of the neverending culture wars that dictate how anything even mildly controversial or different will cause a shitstorm, forcing major labels to be very cautious. Cardi B and Megan Thee Stallion know this for certain. In 2020, their song "WAP" (aka Wet-Ass Pussy) was catnip to pearl-clutching conservatives, and although the record never got banned and neither artist got dropped, it caused a headache for Atlantic Records. Incidentally, Megan Thee Stallion would later break ties with her label and management to become an independent artist.

This is not to say that the primary reason why an artist chooses to release their music independently in lieu of trying to get signed by a major is so they can say whatever they want on record. It's certainly a part of it, and similar to the punk movement of the 70s and 80s, there's a definite rebellious, anarchic and anti-establishment thread running through a lot of the independent hip-hop covered in this book. But the biggest advantage is on the creative side, where a lack of pressure from label executives laser-focused on trying to make money allows for freedom of expression, experimentation, and a safe space for unique voices to grow.

Consequently, being independent usually has its own aesthetic vibe, probably none more so than in hip-hop from the time period being discussed. A self-made, DIY approach to releasing music is also very much in rap music's blood. When the world decided that hip-hop music had reached the 50-years-in-existence milestone in 2024, it was mostly for vanity, with numerous media outlets covering various celebratory events, despite them having largely turned their nose up at rap music for most of those five decades. The 50 years was in reference to a party DJ Kool Herc and his sister threw in the Bronx on August 11, 1973. It's now considered to be ground-zero for when hip-hop was birthed, but it's actually a fairly arbitrary marker, as elements of what was soon to be officially called hip-hop certainly existed before August, 1973.

But what that party in the Bronx does represent is the resilience and determination that hip-hop artists have always had to have in order to be heard. DJ Kool Herc's sister, Cindy Campbell, threw the party because she needed money for school clothes before the new semester started. Early rappers began picking up the mic as a way of coming together in the face of the vicious gang wars, fire and poverty that had devastated several New York City neighborhoods in the 1970s. A lack of funds for decent equipment and electricity bills saw enterprising deejays plug their turntables and speakers into public street lamps. Budding producers unable to afford keyboards or other instruments raided their parents' record collection instead and sampled from the vinyl, making rudimentary beats using two tape decks. Those fortunate enough to get their hands on an actual sampler had to create workarounds for making the most of the tiny amount of memory early machines allowed for, being economical with how much they took from the original song, and by slowing down the record deck. Years later when digital software became the normal way to make music, hip-hop artists with no disposable income downloaded bootleg copies of programmes for free, or stretched the limitations of basic production software as far as they could. And when downloads, MySpace, SoundCloud and streaming sites came and changed the music business beyond all recognition, rappers and producers were the early adopters, showing that all they needed to get their music to people's ears was a computer and an internet connection.

It all adds up to more than fifty years of innovation born out of necessity. Add to that the generally accepted shittyness of the music industry, and the willingness of corporate America to exploit people of color as much as possible, and it's hardly surprising that so many rap artists choose to go the independent route. If a major record label gatekeeper won't even allow you to get a foot in the door let alone release your music, then why not just do it yourself. Not only do you get to stay in control of your own destiny, you also get the chance to send a big fuck you to those record label people who ignored you.

Before we dive deeper into the world of underground hip-hop we first need to set some parameters. The independent hip-hop we'll be focussing on was released during the period from 1995-2005, a time when a generation of rappers and producers, primarily from New York City and Los Angeles, emerged with a gritty new sound, raised on the classics of the late 1980s and early-mid 90s, but infused with something more urgent, fresh and raw, and nothing like what was happening on the popular music charts of the time, that were by now dominated by big name rap stars.

There are several other eras of rap history that have been equally as fertile and unique for independently-released music, but those won't be covered here. This is not because those periods and movements are not worthy of discussion – they are, and deserve their own books. In fact, there already are books and podcast series on these eras. They just don't have the specific aesthetic features of what we traditionally think of when we say 'indie' rap, or more specifically 'underground' hip-hop.

The book does not, therefore, talk about artists like west coast rap pioneer Too Short, who independently sold a lot of tapes out the trunk of his car in his native Oakland in the 80s for his 75 Girls imprint. Nor does it talk about DJ Screw, who built an entire indie rap empire selling his chopped and screwed tapes and CDs from his house and the Screwed Up Records and Tapes store in Houston, Texas. We won't be talking about how ambitious entrepreneurs like Percy "Master P" Miller, James "J. Prince" Prince, Michael "5000" Watts, and Ronald "Slim" Williams and his brother Bryan "Baby" Williams, built their own powerful independent record labels like No Limit, Rap-A-Lot Records, Swishahouse, and Cash Money Records, not just outside of the mainstream channels, but also outside of the traditional rap strongholds of New York and Los Angeles (several of these labels later signed distribution or partnership deals with major labels anyway, taking them out of the fully independent model). We also won't be covering periods like the 'mixtape era', where the lines got blurred between what constituted an album and what was just a bunch of songs strung together, and where artists employed deejays to mix collections of music to either give away for free, or sell independently of the major label deal many of the artists were signed too. We'll only touch briefly on the 'blog era', a time period where all the industry rules were thrown out the window as artists like Drake, Kendrick Lamar, Wiz Khalifa, Big K.R.I.T., J. Cole, and Curren$y started uploading their music to rap blogs such as NahRight, 2DopeBoyz, and Pigeons & Planes whenever they felt like it, no longer tied to traditional label release dates.

Lastly, the focus of this book is on North America, as it is from here where the most renowned and popular independent and underground hip-hop has emerged. The rich and exciting indie rap scenes that have blossomed across the world, in particular in the UK, France and other European countries, and Japan, are all therefore beyond the scope. The music of each of these countries deserves its own book, and the reader is encouraged to go explore these local scenes themselves.

———

There are lots of different reasons why someone wakes one day and decides they want to pick up a brush and paint, or a guitar to learn chords, or a microphone to start singing or rapping, or a pen to write a novel or a poem, or a book about independent hip-hop. Creative urges come from somewhere deep inside those of us who choose to recognise them and give them an outlet.

There are lots of reasons why someone might decide they want to become an underground hip-hop artist, and some of these are more unabashed than others. Not to stereotype or pigeonhole, or to claim that these are the only motivations for why they did it, but indie rappers from this era often tended to be making music for one of the following reasons. First, they had been chewed up, spat out and brutally fucked over by the mainstream music business, or had a little taste of it that wasn't what they expected. They were now looking to prove they could do it on their own terms, and perhaps take a little revenge on those that wronged them or failed to recognise their talent. MF DOOM, R.A. The Rugged Man and Masta Ace all fit this description, as do Blu and Little Brother, who each had bad experiences signed to majors.

Next there's the artists who never had a record contract with a big label, but knew all about how utterly horrible the industry can be, and were rebelling against it with anger. Company Flow, and especially their leader El-P come to mind here. Other underground artists had no choice but to put their music out independently because no one at a label would even consider giving them the time of day. This was especially true for artists who weren't from New York or California, instead from cities like Boston, Detroit, Columbus, Minneapolis, or further north across Canada.

Others saw themselves as outsiders, either unintentionally

because they were making music that a mainstream audience would not understand, or on purpose, because they had something new or different to say. Kool Keith, Del The Funky Homosapian, and others fall into this category.

But probably the biggest reason underground rappers in this era made music was because they had a deep love for hip-hop and wanted to make it good again, as in the late 90s, good hip-hop had become a rare commodity.

———

Tales about the awfulness of the music business are as old as time. It has been standard practice for decades for artists to be handed exploitative contracts that mean they see very little in the way of money from the sales of their creativity, or ownership of their master copies. If you happen to come from a poor background then you are even more susceptible to exploitation, especially since you'll be less likely to afford a lawyer to read the contract and explain the legalese. And if you are a Black musician, then you're also probably going to be fighting against racial inequity and a lack of respect from a major corporation who only sees you as a product ready to be appropriated.

In the major label system, an artist is only as useful as their last decent sales figures, a depressing and sobering fact all too familiar to Brooklyn's Duval Clear, better known as Masta Ace. Hip-hop's first golden era came in the late 1980s, when a young breed of artist launched onto the scene and broke new ground, taking rap music from a mostly single-based and live scene, to one of fully fledged albums, by a group of voices that rapped and made beats in a novel and different way. In 1988 alone there were milestone, genre-shifting albums released by Slick Rick, Boogie Down Productions, EPMD,

Public Enemy, Jungle Brothers, Ice-T, Ultramagnetic MCs, Biz Markie, Stetsasonic, King T, MC Lyte, Run-DMC, Big Daddy Kane, Audio Two, and many more.

Big Daddy Kane and Biz Markie were both part of the Juice Crew, a collective of artists under the mentorship of producer Marley Marl and radio DJ Mr. Magic, that also included Kool G Rap, Roxanne Shante, MC Shan, and the young Masta Ace. The crew were signed to Cold Chillin' Records, a label that in many ways resembled an independent but actually had the backing of distribution via Warner Bros. Records, at the time one of the major labels trying to capitalize on the growing popularity of rap music.

Masta Ace enjoyed some success with his first album, 1990's *Take a Look Around*. But when time came to make his next album, Warner Bros. Records squeezed Cold Chillin and made them reduce the size of their artist roster. Ace didn't make the cut and was dropped in a remorseless manner. Ace would go on to sign with Delicious Vinyl, a label that started as an independent in 1987, but had signed a joint venture agreement with Atlantic Records by the time Ace joined the roster and dropped his *SlaughtaHouse* album in 1993 with his group Masta Ace Incorporated. Years after taking an extended break from recording albums, Masta Ace reemerged as a fully-fledged independent artist with the release of *Disposable Arts* in 2001.

Richard Andrew Thorburn is another New York rapper who knows what it's like to get screwed over by a major label. In the early 90s, around the same time that Masta Ace was being messed around by Cold Chillin' and Warner Bros. Records, Thorburn, better known by his stage name R.A. The Rugged Man, was being courted by several majors and landed at Jive Records. Operated as an independent but actually part of the larger Zomba Group, Jive

Records had found success with hip-hop, releasing albums from the mid-80s by tentpole artists and groups such as DJ Jazzy Jeff & The Fresh Prince, Whodini, Schoolly D, Kool Moe Dee, Boogie Down Productions, Too Short, and A Tribe Called Quest. Perhaps looking to catch the wave of the white rapper craze at the time, Jive Records likely saw in R.A. The Rugged Man someone to attach a cheap gimmick to, but it wasn't to be. In retrospect, betting on a rapper who had a reputation for wild antics and a penchant for making songs with titles like "Cunt Renaissance" was never going to be a good fit for a major-label affiliated company like Jive Records. It was all too much for Thorborn, and an experience that was no doubt the inspiration for the song "Every Record Label Sucks Dick" (the elegantly-titled "Cunt Renaissance" and "Every Record Label Sucks Dick" can be found on an album R.A. The Rugged Man released under the name Crustified Dibbs. Titled *Night of the Bloody Apes*, it features tracks that would have been on his album with Jive Records. It does not currently appear to be available on streaming services, and physical copies are rare). R.A. The Rugged Man has been an independent artist ever since.

Then there's the sad story of KMD. After being taken under the wing of MC Serch, and being featured on the song "The Gas Face" by Serch's group 3rd Bass, KMD — which consisted of brothers Zev Love X and DJ Subroc, originally from the UK but by now representing Long Island, New York, and third member Onyx The Birthstone Kid — were signed to Elektra Records and released their first album, *Mr. Hood*, in 1991. What happened next has been told and retold many times already, but still deserves repeating because of what it led to. In a relatively short space of time, everything fell apart for KMD while they worked on what was to be their second album, *Black Bastards*. Onyx The Birthstone Kid left the group, DJ Subroc was killed in a tragic road accident, the new album was shelved, and the group, what remained of it, was dropped by Elektra. At the time, Elektra Records' owner, Warner Bros. Music was still dealing with the fallout from the controversial 1992 song "Cop Killer" by Ice-T and his rock group Body Count. That song – actually about the threat of police brutality, influenced by the Rodney King case – had sent the Bush administration into a frenzy, putting pressure on Warner to take some action. It was ultimately Ice-T himself who decided to pull the record from shelves, but the major company's reputation had still taken a significant hit. Warner Bros. Music's issue with KMD was not only the inflammatory album title, but also the artwork, which depicted a Sambo character being hung. Fearing another backlash, the exec team told Elektra to drop the album and the group, ending the short career run of KMD. The man behind Zev Love X would return years later and become one of the most important figures in underground hip-hop, full of disdain for how the industry had treated him, and boldly claiming on his breakthrough solo record that his new mission was to destroy the rap business.

Sometimes, artists who start off independently on the under-ground scene get noticed by a major and snatched up, only to find they lose the creative freedom they enjoyed when they were doing their own thing, coerced to go in different directions than they would have liked. Few groups represented underground hip-hop as hard as Los Angeles' Dilated Peoples. But after first receiving attention with 12" singles on the independent label ABB Records, they signed with Capitol Records for the release of their debut album, 2000s *The Platform*. Being on a major label didn't compromise their style at all at first, helping members Rakaa, Evidence and DJ Babu to become leading lights in the underground scene. They maintained this solid reputation with their second album in 2001, *Expansion Team,* but the sound had changed by 2004's *Neighborhood Watch.* Likely feeling the pressure to give Capitol a return on their investment, the group adopted a more commercial sound, especially with the single "This Way", which featured and was produced by Kanye West, still relatively up and coming at the time but getting white-hot on the strength of his recently-released debut album, *College Dropout. Neighborhood Watch* only served to isolate Dilated People's core fanbase, and ironically didn't bring Capitol major sales figures either. It was an all-round disaster that saw the group return to their familiar sound for 2006's *20/20* album, albeit still released on Capitol, but in association once again with ABB. After the deal with Capitol ended, Dilated Peoples signed with indie rap powerhouse Rhymesayers Entertainment, and remain proudly independent today.

ABB Records was also home in 2003 to North Carolina's Little Brother, releasing their first album, *The Listening.* By 2005 the group had been signed to Atlantic Records for the release of their second album, *The Minstrel Show.* It was another strong album, but Atlantic's marketing department didn't know what to do with it, finding it getting rejected or misunderstood by mainstream magazines and TV networks who assumed their readers and viewers would probably not be interested in hip-hop that carried a message. It is hardly shocking to hear that the group has released most of their music independently since.

———

For others, the need to prove themselves independently was about rebellion. If the industry movers and shakers were not interested in them, they'd do it themselves, a narrative that tapped into the classic David vs Goliath, us-versus-them mentality. There were few artists that pushed this angle harder than Brooklyn's El-P and his group Company Flow, who wore their independence proudly as a badge of honor. The group's mantra and rallying cry of "independent as fuck" succinctly captured the spirit of underground hip-hop in the mid-late 90s, and is the inspiration for this book's title. We'll dive more deeply into the story of El-P and Company Flow later, but the abridged version is that on their debut album, *Funcrusher Plus*, the group spend a lot of the runtime personifying the music industry as the evil nemesis of quality hip-hop, a dastardly machine that chews people up, spits them out, and leaves them for dead.

Company Flow's depiction of the state of affairs was mostly accurate, although in an ironic twist, the independent label under which Company Flow released their music would later be rumbled for having its own connections to mega-corporations, and for treating their artists badly. It was an unfortunate set of circumstances that afterwards culminated in El-P stating on record how he'd "rather be mouth fucked by Nazis unconscious" than be back on his former label, a sentiment not unlike the aforementioned one from R.A. The Rugged Man, who even more ironically also appeared on *Funcrusher Plus*.

An uprising against the ills of the music business was hardly a new stance for a rap group to take; Public Enemy, N.W.A. and others had been doing it for years. But Company Flow were amplifying the message loud and clear once again, as were other groups making underground hip-hop around the same time, from fellow New Yorkers Beans, M. Sayyid, High Priest and Earl Blaize – literally calling themselves the Antipop Consortium – to California's Lootpack, the message was clear: don't want to release our music? Fine. We don't need you, and we're also going to tell everybody about what scumbags you are. Today El-P is best known as a member of the group Run The Jewels, who have found a decent amount of crossover success. His anti-establishment philosophy is largely still intact, however, with Run The Jewels releasing their music independently, and rolling their albums out using methods outside of the promotional and distribution routes you'd typically find on a major label.

Independence allowed artists to rebel not just against the music industry but also politics and social norms, following a long tradition of rappers making bold and uncompromising statements about the world. While there were some mild references to politics and other serious issues in mainstream rap in the late 90s – such as artists naming themselves after political and military figures (Noreaga), and Busta Rhymes' preoccupation with the end of times in the albums he released around the turn of the millennium – these tended to be lite on context and meaning, with nothing that would actually challenge or disrupt the status quo. In contrast, with no corporate restraints to care about, artists like Jedi Mind Tricks, Immortal Technique and dead prez were free to say whatever the hell they wanted, and they did.

Underground hip-hop was also a safe space for rappers to say other types of controversial and scandalous things. It provided a group such as Non Phixion the platform to make a song like "I Shot Reagan" in 1998; an in-your-face track that not only references the assassination attempt on the former US President namechecked in the title – a sort of companion piece to Ice-T's "Cop Killer" from six years earlier – but also talks about everything else from war to corruption and the misuse of political power, peppered with references to divisive and polemic historical figures. The chances that the actual Ronald Reagan ever listened to "I Shot Reagan" are slim to none, and it was also way too low-key for anyone else in the Republican Party to kick up a fuss, but it's still a record that almost certainly could not have been recorded by a group signed to a major label. Incidentally, Nancy Reagan would also not have approved of Non Phixion had she known they even existed, as their heavy reference to drug taking was the antithesis to her misguided "Just Say No" campaign.

The underground was also a place where the darker side of rap could flourish, like the kind of music made by Necro, the brother of Non Phixion member Ill Bill. Necro specialized in horrorcore, a subgenre of rap that had bubbled just below the surface of mainstream rap music for years, thanks to artists and groups like the Geto Boys, Gravediggaz, Gangsta N.I.P. and Three 6 Mafia. Its heyday was over by the turn of the new millennium, but Necro, Cage, and a small selection of other underground emcees kept the spirit alive in a way that never would have been possible in the mainstream, where music about graphic murder, psychiatric wards, or entire albums dedicated to the consumption of angel dust were hardly the kind of thing A&Rs from the majors were after in their pursuit of the next big smash.

There's one additional act of defiance and rebellion that a lot of independent, underground hip-hop based itself on, one of the oldest and now very much-cliched concepts in the entire history of the genre: the need to prove that you are authentic and 'keeping it real'. Rappers have been obsessed with authenticity from day one. In the 1970s and 1980s, if you didn't wear the right clothes, or your dance moves were out of step, or you're hype man couldn't move the crowd, or if you didn't write your own raps, you were seen as fake.

Those same claims to authenticity were still just as relevant in the 1990s and 2000s, especially the part about a rapper not writing their own lyrics. It didn't matter that in every other genre of music it is accepted standard practice for an artist to not write their lyrics

45

entirely by themselves, or even at all. In hip-hop, where image is everything, if a rapper wasn't writing the words they committed to record, they were suspect. In reality – or at least in the faux-reality of commercial rap music, where the listener is usually asked to suspend disbelief and buy in to the idea that their favorite artist is living a life of absolute luxury, driving expensive cars, dwelling in expensive houses, surrounded by expensive women – it was actually a badly-kept secret that lots of famous rappers were not writing their own lyrics. Most of the words that came out of Dr. Dre's mouth during his time as a member of N.W.A. were written by either Ice Cube, MC Ren or The D.O.C., and when he ascended to mega-stardom status, his lyrics were written by a revolving door of ghostwriters that included Jay-Z, Snoop Dogg and Eminem. Nas, Kool G Rap, Rakim, Pharoahe Monch and Skillz are just a few of the masters of rhyming that also wrote for big name acts like Puff Daddy, Will Smith, and countless others. Today, the rise of AI-generated content means that ghostwriting a song can now be fully-automated, stripping out any last remnants of original skill.

The major-label stars didn't care much about any of this, choosing to use their clout and big budgets to pay someone else to do the heavy lifting that writing a successful song demands. For those who did take the art of rap seriously, however, the ghostwriting trend was seen as nothing but fakery, with any rapper that didn't write their own songs considered not 'real' enough. And no other faction of the rap world spent as much energy proving they were the realest of the real than in the underground. Coinciding with an overall sense that *all* things commercial rap were fake, writing your own lyrics, producing your own beats and designing your own artwork were considered to be pillars of the supposed 'real' underground artist, and reasons for them to wear their independence proudly.

As the second decade of the 21st century drew to a close, a new way of describing a certain strain of underground hip-hop started being used; 'art rap'. The supposed logic behind the descriptor was that some underground rappers were now making rap music that was more avant-garde than traditional, boombap-inspired hip-hop. First used by rapper Open Mike Eagle — who even named his 2010 debut album *Unapologetic Art Rap*, and was inspired by 'art rock' — it became shorthand for categorizing the music of some of the most talented rappers working right now, including Mike Eagle himself, Quelle Chris, Jonwayne, billy woods, Elucid, and several others on woods' own Backwoodz Studioz label.

The intentions were good, and the reasoning made sense in a lot of ways, but 'art rap' was arguably just another exercise in the pigeonholing of artists that people love to do, especially in music, where genres often get divided and splintered into sub-genres, sub-sub genres, and on and on. To label part of a music genre that is already divided by imaginary lines between mainstream versus independent, real versus fake, and drilling this down to an even more granular level risks further disenfranchising an artist and pushing them towards the fringes. A label like 'art rap' can also come across as pretentious if not handled right, as if to suggest that this music has more artistic value than non-art rap.

The artists labeled as art rap are also still making music that is unabashedly hip-hop, with all of the hallmarks of what makes it such an endlessly interesting genre, especially from those artists outside the mainstream. In an article about the art rap title published in 2017, writer Max Bell described the sub-genre as "left field, forward-thinking production, unconventional song structures and cadences, songs written from the perspective of fictional characters, explicit and protracted engagement with social and political issues, and absurdist metaphors and similes." So, basically, classic underground hip-hop. This is not to say that the 'art rap' rappers are not unique or offering a fresh perspective. They are, but there's no valid reason to label them in such a specific way, when it's all just good, quality hip-hop.

Back in the late 90s and early aughts, in addition to being labeled as 'independent', this form of rap music was tagged with the name 'underground'. The reasons were obvious and accepted, and you've probably already noticed the terms being used interchangeably in this book. But there were also other names by which people used to classify this music, including 'backpacker rap'. Unlike 'underground' or 'independent', which were both descriptive and complimentary, 'backpacker' ended up being derogatory, and not representative of the richness and depth of the culture. The 'backpack' part derived from the standard issue identikit of the average underground rap fan, including the wearing of a backpack. It became emblematic of a certain kind of rap, also often lumped together with the term 'conscious rap'. Both terms were used broadly to mean any artist that rapped about things those in the mainstream did not, from politics and spirituality, to positivity and culture. While the 'conscious rap' tag was also used to describe artists from earlier in the 90s, such as A Tribe Called Quest, Gang Starr, Brand Nubian and more, it was also given to artists who emerged from the independent scene in the late 90s and started to cross-over, including Mos Def, Talib Kweli, Common, and Kanye West. In just a few short years the 'backpacker' and 'conscious rap' labels became cringey, cliched and pejorative, and today both are used as a way to parody the period.

Arguably the worst label that underground rap of the time got lumbered with, however, was 'alternative' hip-hop. It was an appropriate name for how this type of rap was providing a different perspective to what everyone else was doing. It also accurately captured how a lot of indie rap crossed over into other subcultures not traditionally thought of as being associated with rap, like the skateboard scene. In actuality the term 'alternative hip-hop' was usually just subterfuge and a nicer way of saying "rap made by weirdos and freaks". It was more pointless pigeon-holing, not to mention degrading to those who were making it. The broad spectrum of artists who got tagged with the label included everyone from those who made music influenced by sci-fi, dystopia, and paranoia, like El-P and Mr. Lif, to those simply making music slightly left-of-centre, like MF DOOM, Del The Funky Homosapien or Quasimoto, and also as a general catch-all name for any kind of independent rap artist, providing a neat why for the wider music press to bundle what was actually a huge range of diverse artists into a tidy package.

For those immersed in the culture of underground hip-hop, 'alternative' often meant strange and weird, unique and surreal, in all the best ways. If the Ultramagnetic MCs paved the way for rappers to talk about sci-fi and abstract subjects in the 1980s, and 90s groups and collectives like Project Blowed, Souls of Mischief and The Pharcyde showed that it was acceptable for rappers to be their nerdy selves, a new band of rap acts took all of this and ran with it further as the 90s progressed and the new millennium began. In the process they made some of the most original and creative hip-hop ever heard. At the forefront of this new movement was a name with a big connection to those previous, groundbreaking eras; Ultramagnetic MCs front man Keith Matthew Thornton, better known as Kool Keith. Ultramagnetic's fortunes had faded by 1995, but Kool Keith rebounded to become an indie rap icon, releasing unique albums under his own name, and most memorably under a range of different alter egos, both solo and in groups.

Alter-egos in fact became a defining characteristic of underground hip-hop from the period, breaking new ground in a genre so obsessed with being authentically yourself. Between 1995 and 2005, Daniel Dumile released albums under the name MF DOOM – itself a comic book inspired alter ego – and also under the names King Geedorah and Viktor Vaughn, and as part of the duos Madvillain and Danger Doom. New York emcee Phillip Collington Jr. sometimes released music as Sir Menelik, sometimes as Cyclops 4000, and sometimes as Scaramanga, each one a different alter ego. Elsewhere, rappers like Edan and J-Zone were creating multiple variations of their own characters, often as exaggerated versions of their real selves.

The most critically acclaimed Kool Keith alter ego was Dr. Octagon, a collaboration with producer Dan The Automator, who similarly built his own reputation for off-the-wall hip-hop. In addition to his work with Kool Keith, Dan The Automator made clever hip-hop with another throwback from the late 80s and early 90s, Prince Paul, as the duo Handsome Boy Modelling School, and also as part of Deltron 3030. That group included another influential artist from an earlier generation of rap music, Del The Funkyhomosapien. It was fine to call these artists 'alternative', or weird, or nerdy, or whatever else people wanted, but ultimately they were just making hip-hop, different for sure, but still rooted in the principle elements, and still 'real' and authentic.

It was all way too kooky for the major labels, failing to see any sort of mass appeal for this kind of hip-hop, leaving so-called alternative artists to go the independent route by releasing music on their own labels, small experimental imprints, or in the case of Handsome Boy Modelling School, via an established independent label like Tommy

Boy Records. Interestingly, once it has picked up some traction beyond the underground, Dr. Octagon's *Dr. Octagonecologyst* album was reissued by a much bigger record label, DreamWorks Records, suggesting that at least some of the major labels saw commercial value in promoting a different brand of hip-hop, especially albums that garnered universal acclaim from critics.

Irrespective of whatever people decided to call it, artists on the fringes were making the most original rap on the independent music scene. Such artists have also undoubtedly had an impact on some of today's biggest stars. You only have to do a quick search on YouTube to find clips of Tyler, The Creator and Earl Sweatshirt giggling like children the time they got to meet their idol MF DOOM backstage at a festival. Danny Brown, Lil Yachty and countless others were also inspired in the same way, appreciative of the doors indie artists opened, allowing rappers to express themselves however they wanted.

———

If artists from New York City or Los Angeles – centers of hip-hop and home to the majors – needed to go the independent route because nobody at those labels would give them a shot, it was doubly-hard if you came from anywhere else. New York and L.A. have a lineage and pedigree for breeding talented rappers and producers, but opportunities were scarce for artists from cities like Detroit, Philadelphia, Boston, or Columbus, where there was a history of Black music but not necessarily hip-hop, or that had a degree of hip-hop credibility but merely on the strength of a few breakouts. The outlook was even bleaker if you happened to have been born and raised in a place no one associated with hip-hop at all; places like Providence, Rhode Island, Saint Paul, Minnesota, or Portland, Oregon.

The only choice for artists from these places was to do it them-selves. If hip-hop was born of a mentality of making the best of what was available out of necessity, this same work ethic was applied to those trying to break through from places well outside of the traditional centers of hip-hop. The problem was that these artists had an even bigger mountain to climb in order to get heard than the average underground artist from New York or LA. They were not only on or beyond the physical outskirts of the music industry, they were also fighting against the ingrained opinion of most hip-hop fans of the era, that if you were not from a respected hip-hop city, you were probably wack.

New Jersey already had a solid reputation for nurturing quality rappers and producers by the mid 90s, but it still took artists like El Da Sensei and Tame One, Heather B and Channel Live to put the Garden State's underground credentials on the map. Further up the Eastern Seaboard, artists and groups like Edo.G, Gang Starr, and The Almighty R.S.O. had pioneered a healthy hip-hop scene in Boston, but it was hard work for underground artists from the region to make an impact outside of the state, artists like Mr. Lif, Akrobatik, Edan (not actually from Boston, but studied there and became a fixture of the local scene), REKS, 7L & Esoteric and others. Over in Philadelphia, Vinnie Paz and his Jedi Mind Tricks crew helped people to think of more than just DJ Jazzy Jeff & The Fresh Prince and The Roots when the subject of Philadelphia hip-hop came up, as did Bahamadia, The High & Mighty, Grand Agent and Last Emperor. In Connecticut, rappers like Apathy managed to build a solid reputation, while local legend Dooley-O had a second-wind with several 12" releases. Not too far away, in Providence, Rhode Island, Sage Francis was making waves, and even way up in Maine, a place definitely not synonymous with rap music, Sole, Alias, and a selection of other rappers were building a local scene that eventually spread out far beyond the northeast.

South of New York, Washington D.C. was beginning to bubble with upcoming underground talent, and in Virginia, Mad Skillz and producer Nottz were gaining respect at the same time that fellow Virginians Timballand, The Neptunes and Clipse were fast becoming huge stars. Over in the midwest, regional underground rap scenes spawned across the biggest cities in Illinois, Michigan, Ohio, and further north to Minnesota. In Chicago, the foundations built by artists like Common and NO I.D. opened doors for Psalm One and Kidz in The Hall member Naledge, a generation of independent rappers such as Open Mike Eagle and Vic Spencer, not to mention huge future stars like Kanye West, Lupe Fiasco and Chance the Rapper. A few hours drive away over in Detroit, a young Marshall Mathers played his own part in the city's underground scene before he found megastardom as Eminem. And Detroit's other hip-hop icon, J Dilla, came from a sphere of independent artists that included his group Slum Village, plus Elzhi, Phat Kat, Frank-N-Dank and more, while artists like Guilty Simpson and Black Milk also made their own moves.

Cities in various different parts of Ohio proved to be fertile ground for good hip-hop. In the state's capital, Columbus, the MHz collective made some of the most memorable and hardest hitting music of the time, centered around rappers Copywrite and Camu Tao, and producer RJD2. Elsewhere in the city, Blueprint and Illogic were also making noise, as was J. Rawls. In the southwest of the state, Mr. Dibbs, Mood and producer Hi-Tek were also making a name for themselves. It was very different from the music being made by Ohio's biggest rap music export, Cleveland's Bone Thugs-N-Harmony.

In Minnesota Atmosphere were putting Minneapolis on the map, while close by in Saint Paul, rapper Eyedea and his partner DJ Abilities were building their own momentum.

The situation was tougher still for those coming from places in southern states. Atlanta, Houston, New Orleans and Memphis are respected hip-hop hubs today, but it wasn't always that way. It took the success of Outkast, Lil' Wayne, UGK, Lil Jon, T.I. and several others to break through before anyone outside of these locales put some long overdue respect on these artists' names. But if you were making underground hip-hop instead of crunk, club tracks, or anything else classed as 'dirty south' rap, which was dominating radio and Billboard in the early 2000s, you were still going to be mostly unnoticed.

Fortunately, by 2001 the blog era was in full swing, as were the vibrant message boards on websites like Okayplayer. These new, fledgling channels gave underground artists a place to build a fanbase and spread their music, regardless of where they were from. It's how Little Brother first appeared on people's radar and staked a claim for North Carolina as an outpost for the kind of hip-hop beloved by underground rap fans. Their sound was boombap-inspired hip-hop, albeit with a soulful twist thanks to producer and group member 9th Wonder, and the smooth vocal hooks of rapper/singer, Phonte. Little Brother still had to look far beyond the borders of North Carolina to drop their first proper releases, however, hooking up with the mostly LA-underground-centric indie label ABB Records, a business relationship that would later turn sour.

In Georgia, groups like Mass Influence were showing a side of Atlanta hip-hop beyond Andre 3000 and Big Boi of Outkast, Lil Jon and TI, and deeper south still, in Lexington, Kentucky, CunninLin-guists were also able to build a solid reputation. To paraphrase that well-worn but still prophetic statement from Andre 3000 himself, the south did indeed have something to say, and it was deeper and more complex than most people probably realized.

Even being a native New Yorker was not always enough, especially if you didn't come from one of the renowned boroughs or neighborhoods, despite being close to the right people, record shops, shows and ciphers. Places like Mount Vernon, Amityville and New Rochelle had expanded the New York hip-hop map beyond Brooklyn, the Bronx, and Queens, thanks to breakout stars like Pete Rock, De La Soul and Brand Nubian, but any artist from the underground from such a place still had to prove their worth. If you came from somewhere further out, like producer Danger Mouse, who represented White Plains, you'd inevitably find yourself having to take frequent trips to the city if you wanted to get a foot in the door.

The situation could be even worse in a state as vast as California. The underground scene that flourished in the Bay Area was able to leverage the area's proven reputation for creating rap stars like E-40 and Too Short, and pioneers of the indie rap sound Souls of Mischief. In and around Los Angeles the groundwork laid by Freestyle Fellowship, and influential venues like the Good Life Cafe had already demonstrated throughout the 90s it was a breeding ground for underground rap. It was a different story in other parts of the state, a scene made up of regional pockets dotted across the map. Blackalicious plied their trade in Sacramento, 130 miles away in San Jose, Peanut Butter Wolf and his partner Charizma hustled hard to be heard, and in Oxnard, Madlib began his long and illustrious career as part of the group Lootpack, in parallel with his brother Oh No, MED, Dudley Perkins, and various others. Out in Fresno, Planet Asia built his own cottage industry, as did later talents like Fashawn.

Regardless of wherever these artists came from, they all had to do it themselves, building a local fanbase, putting on their own shows, and financing their own records, some even starting their own independent labels. It was the only way these disparate outliers had any chance of someone actually getting to hear their music and what they had to say.

———

There is one thing all underground artists could probably agree on; the notion that mainstream rap was in a terrible state by the end of the 90s. The enshittification of hip-hop, if you will. It's easy to blame everything about the decline in quality on Puff Daddy, but we'll do it anyway, because it is mostly true. After the death of the Notorious B.I.G. in 1997, Puff's popularity exploded as he became a major star on his own, no longer just the guy who dropped adlibs under the vocals of better rappers while taking credit for producing many of the tracks he appeared on, when in fact he did not. Ever since disturbing allegations of horrific sexual and physical abuse by Puff Daddy have come to light in recent years he is now a pariah and well and truly canceled, and rightly so. Any prison time he serves will be justice for the victims of his abuse, and satisfying for the many recording artists he treated like shit.

The music Puffy made alongside collaborators like Ma$e was popular but lacked originality, lyrical prowess or skill, all hallmarks of what makes good hip-hop so great. Sampling – a key element of rap production since the beginning – is often looked down on by music purists who argue that taking elements of an existing song to make a new one is unoriginal. It's a dated and condescending opinion that completely ignores the creative ways in which a skilled producer is able to make something different and fresh, reimagining the original source material and breathing new life into it. But Puffy came along and undid decades of good work, handing those same snobby detractors more ammunition to bemoan the use of sampling. The big hits that Puff found fame with didn't simply take subtle snippets from the source, they took everything wholesale, and the sources also happened to be huge records known by everyone. The songs used were also often by successful white pop stars, like Sting, David Bowie and Lisa Standsfield, adding insult to injury by denying Black artists the chance to benefit from their songs being used with a career revival and some royalty earnings.

Commercial rap music also underwent a complete image change to go with the music. And for this we have a second industry figure to blame; video director Hype Williams. A talented visualist for sure, his oeuvre for rap videos was to make them as big, brash and flamboyant as possible. Budgets could be as high as a million dollars, an obscene amount of money to be thrown at a music video by any metric. William's visual style and Puffy's music coalesced to shape a new, excessive era of rap music obsessed with wealth and luxury, subsequently dubbed the 'shiny suit' era. The name was a nod to the aesthetic and style of the typical Hype Williams video, where shiny cars and literal shiny suits were a common feature. Bragging about money and material possessions had been cannon in hip-hop since before Big Bank Hank boasted of his Lincoln Continental, Cadillac and color TV on "Rapper's Delight" in 1979, through to the first golden era, and basically every other era since. The key difference between then and the shiny suit era was that even though Big Daddy Kane, Rakim, Slick Rick and Special Ed wore gold chains and expensive clothes and talked about such excesses on wax, they counterbalanced this with more meaningful and important subject matter. They also had the skills

57

to do it well, writing complex and expertly-structured rhymes full of wit and tricky wordplay. Puffy and friends, on the other hand, made records with basic, shallow lyrics that talked about wealth and partying, and not much else.

It was a significant departure from rap that crossed over into mainstream territory in the first half of the decade, when all that artists like Pete Rock & CL Smooth, Wu-Tang Clan, A Tribe Called Quest, Dr. Dre, Das EFX, Smif-N-Wessun, Gang Starr and others needed to get signed to a major label was hard beats that sampled snippets of jazz and funk to rap over, spitting lyrics that had depth, integrity and a message. Videos tended to consist of scenes shot on location in the ghetto or an abandoned building, with the artist's real crew, friends and family waving their arms in the background. The fashion choices were simple; oversized jerseys and Timberland boots as far as the eye could see. The era of the shiny suits changed all previous definitions of what a rapper needed to look and sound like to be a major star.

There are a lot of obvious parallels to be drawn between the worlds of rap music and pro-wrestling. The competitiveness, the larger-than-life personalities, and the mostly manufactured animosities and beefs are just some of the elements they share. Many rappers are wrestling superfans, there have been several rapping wrestler characters, John Cena has released actual rap albums, and Snoop Dogg has a history of making appearances in the WWE. Westside Gunn has even taken it a step further with his own wrestling promotion.

Any wrestling scholar worth their salt will tell you that pro-wrestling lost its way for a while in the 90s thanks to an overload of silly gimmicks. Wrestling always had gimmicks (and still does), and when they are well devised and executed, they work. But for every successful long-term gimmick like The Undertaker, there's 10 others that are ill-conceived, embarrassingly bad, or just straight up offensive, racist, xenophobic or misogynistic. And it's here where the parallels between wrestling and hip-hop continue. The shiny suit era meant that every commercially-aiming rapper was now trying to emulate the same look and sound, becoming their own version of a WWE gimmick. Some embraced it by choice, but others were forced into it, and it often didn't work out the way they intended. Consider Nas, for example. After breaking through with his perfect debut, 1994's *Illmatic*, by his second album he began to change his style and subject matter, and by album number three, *I Am...* – released in 1999 and as such very much in the shiny suit era – he morphed into a gimmick character, leaving behind his former credibility for a good few years. It was similar to a classic heel turn in wrestling, industry-fuelled kayfabe that hurt Nas' reputation for a long time before he turned face again.

Some wrestling gimmicks fizzled out because those pulling the strings didn't know how to make them work. Take Doink The Clown, introduced to the WWF in 1993 as an evil clown character, portrayed by wrestler Matt Borne, who had a real-life troubled personality that helped enhance the gimmick. But it didn't take long for management to notice that kids loved Doink because they saw him as a funny, regular clown, and changed the gimmick to be a harmless good-guy prankster. This is not unlike what happened to The Lox. After gaining minor buzz under the name the Warlox, the group was signed to Puff Daddy's Bad Boy Records and repackaged with a new name and a new image. A new gimmick, essentially. It worked on a commercial level, but The Lox always looked uncomfortable with the shiny suits, the bling and the excess, and Puff didn't seem to know what to do with them. Unlike Doink – whose career fizzled, Matt Borne later dying of an overdose – The Lox managed to survive the fallout, de-gimmick, and have made decent music ever since.

There are some personas and gimmicks from the shiny suit era that were very good, like Jay-Z and his drug-dealer-turned-rap-mogul schtick, and the Notorious B.I.G.'s Frank White phase, both of them maintaining credibility by always sticking close to the roots of the classic hip-hop sound. And some of the most gimmickiest rappers of the time, like Busta Rhymes and Missy Elliot, who both had their own extravagant, expensive, and very shiny-suited Hype Williams videos, did it all with flair and creativity, always making sure to entertain first and foremost.

On the whole, however, the 90s ended with a lot of substandard commercial rap music dominating the charts, massively widening the gap between the music that was considered to be 'real' hip-hop versus 'pop rap'. It remains to be seen just how real the culture gap actually was behind the scenes. Mainstream and underground rappers often frequented the same spaces, and artists like Talib Kweli have stated how most indie artists like him did in fact like a lot of commercial rap, they just didn't want to admit it.

Nevertheless, the division felt very genuine to fans and artists in camp 'real' hip-hop, and it gave the underground a cause to rally against and prove that they were making something way more authentic, the latest version of the old "keeping it real" debate. If an underground rapper was to be locked out of the mainstream industry, they could at least make hip-hop culture better and more meaningful again, by making rap music that was creative, new and innovative, pure and classic all at the same time. It is for this reason why so many underground artists felt inspired and compelled to create their own movement.

Interestingly, the mass popularity of shiny-suit rap pushed

artists who had experienced commercial success in the early 90s to the fringes. The solution for De La Soul, Q-Tip, DJ Premier, Pharoahe Monch, Sadat-X, Common, and others was to embrace the burgeoning underground scene, integrating themselves to join the rebellion, and in the process helping to legitimize the movement.

As we've seen, attempting to capture the myriad reasons why someone creates indie hip-hop is a difficult endeavor, but defining the actual aesthetic quality, musical dynamics and atmosphere of underground hip-hop is a lot easier. This is not because indie rap from 1995-2005 was narrow minded or limited in scope. It wasn't. On the contrary, the era offered up a broad spectrum of different types of lyrical delivery and production. It is also not because indie rap is a simple artform that can be distilled into a neat, succinct description. It isn't, and it can't. It is a hugely complex and varied sub-genre of an already complex and varied genre. There are, however, some similarities and threads running through every type of indie rap from this period, because ultimately, it is all just hip-hop, and based on the same fundamentals of every other era or movement in the fifty-plus years of the genre's existence. That said, there are nuances and niche sounds, often reflected by geography.

In his 2011 memoir *Root For The Villain: Rap, Bullshit and a Celebration of Failure*, Jay 'J-Zone' Mumford – an emcee and producer who released several acclaimed solo albums on his Old Maid Entertainment indie label, and contributed to albums by several other artists – talks about going crate digging in the basement of a record shop so infested with damp and mold that customers should probably have been wearing hazmat suits when they went inside. That same anecdote could also be used to accurately describe the typical indie rap sound, in particular what was created in New York City.

The exact timeframe of when people first started to use the term 'boom bap' is as hazy as the weed-filled studios where the many songs and albums given that tag were recorded. What is certain is that this style of hip-hop production – created and perfected by Marley Marl, Da Beatminerz, DJ Premier, Large Professor, The Beatnuts, Pete Rock, Diamond D, Showbiz and others – shaped the sound of rap music through the 90s. The sound is characterized by the use of a thick, bass-heavy kick drum followed by a neck-snapping snare, with samples laid on top, and cuts and scratches added for extra flash and flare.

The spirit of the sound was kept alive by the indie producers who started to develop their own sound from the mid-90s onwards, taking something that already made windows rattle and the ground vibrate even deeper underground. Records by boom bap luminaries like Gang Starr, Diggin In The Crates, Black Moon, Smif-N-Wessun, Nas, Pete Rock & CL Smooth were rugged, raw and dusty, but producers like El-P, DJ Spinna, Ge-Ology, Nick Wiz, Alchemist, Madlib, Ez Elpee, Shawn J Period and Hi-Tek came along and somehow made beats that sounded even dustier, like what might happen if you made a recording of a DJ Premier beat on a cheap cassette, left it in the basement J-Zone described, came back in ten years, dumped the drums into a sampler and chopped them up without even bothering to clean the scum and mildew off the tape first. It is a sound that evokes not just imagery of the grimy, graffiti covered walls in record shops like Mr. Bongo and Fat Beats, but also the subway tunnels deep below them and the train cars riding through, with even more graffiti tags and the sound of train wheels grinding against the hot steel of the tracks. If this kind of rap was a movie it would be a gritty flick shot in 1970s New York, a Taxi Driver or a French Connection, or any blaxploitation film made when Times Square was still the place to go for porno movies and peep shows.

The aesthetic was typically then enhanced by the choice of samples laid on top of the thick beats, and various elements added or left in on purpose that you would never find in 'clean' pop music made in a professional setting, like vinyl crackle and static, distortion, and roughly truncated samples and vocal snippets. Sometimes these elements were due to the limitations of the basic equipment being used, like on MF DOOM's *Operation: Doomsday*, where beats were made in places as unsophisticated as Bobbito Garcia's bedroom. J Dilla later perfected the art of intentional imperfection, knowingly producing music that was off-beat or oddly structured, creating a unique sound that author Dan Charnas calls Dilla Time in his book of the same name.

All of this was then complemented by the lyrics sitting on top of the music. The rugged, post-boom bap beats worked as the ideal soundtrack to rhymes about everything from standard hip-hop discussion points like 'keeping it real' and being a better emcee than your opponent, to more abstract, sci-fi inspired tales, drug-fuelled nightmarish worlds, economic and social struggle and everything in between.

The subject matter and vibe of underground hip-hop from New York City and other major cities was not all doom and gloom, however. Some of it was also infused with a sense of soul and positivity, leaning more towards spirituality, politics and love than towards grimy streets and abandoned buildings. That sense of positivity could certainly be found in the sound of California's underground scene. Los Angeles, the Bay Area and the many other enclaves of indie rap across the state are huge, expansive places, and this seeped into the music. The beats were still hardcore, but often with more openness and sparsity than New York drums, evoking a freer, less claustrophobic vibe. Whereas New York rap was frequently about hopelessness, California rap seemed to have at least some hope, even if the stories being told were still bleak. The music from California is also arguably a lot more fun to listen to, be it the throwback feel of Jurassic 5 or Ugly Duckling, the witty wordplay of Saafir or Freestyle Fellowship, or the party life of People Under The Stairs.

Conversely, the vastness of open space could also evoke feelings of isolation and desolation, especially when you subtract the sunny blue skies of California and replace them with gray clouds and a colder climate. Against this backdrop, it's easy to understand why the aesthetic of indie rap made in states like Minnesota and Maine, where the weather can be harsh in the winter months, could sometimes be darker, moodier and more depressive compared to what was coming out of New York or California.

Each one of these elements and conditions added to the low-tech, unpolished feel of underground hip-hop, united by the ultimate goal of making the listener nod their head to the beat.

3

THE FIRE IN WHICH YOU BURN

NEW YORK

At the 2023 GRAMMY awards, as a star-studded, Questlove-curated line-up of rappers from different decades of the genre performed on stage, a screen at the back listed the names of hundreds of artists. Scattered among the names of hugely successful artists on the list was a respectable number of indie rappers and groups, many from New York City, including Mos Def, MF DOOM, Arsonists, Aesop Rock and Screwball. It was a commendable gesture, and recognition of the impact underground hip-hop has had on the culture. For New Yorkers, many who had rallied against the mainstream music business by defiantly putting out music on their own terms, it was also validation, confirmation that the approach they had chosen was correct. The journey had not been easy.

Long before he lost his mind and credibility using up all his time and money trying to prove dumb political conspiracies on behalf of an orange-faced demagogue, Rudy Giuliani was Mayor of New York City. He briefly became a national hero in the wake of 9/11, but outside of that he wasn't a very good mayor, and his 'broken windows' policy of trying to reduce crime levels and clean up the streets had a devastating and disproportionate impact on the poor and people of color.

It was this tension-filled environment under which New York underground hip-hop came of age, and this wasn't the only flash-point. The World Trade Center bombing of 1993, the killing of 23-year old Amadou Diallo in 1999 at the hands of cops, and their subsequent acquittal, the falling of the Twin Towers and the beginning of the war on terror were all pivotal NYC events that influenced how and why the city's rappers and producers expressed themselves. Add to that a deep seated resentment towards the music business and the degradation of commercial rap, and what resulted was a rich melting pot of styles, sounds and personas.

KOOL KEITH

There was underground hip-hop coming from everywhere across the map of New York City by 1995. Much of that was being made by someone from the recognised birthplace of hip-hop, the Bronx. This was not a new upstart emcee, however. In fact, they had been making music since the mid-80s. By 1995, the Ultramagnetic MCs had had their day, seven years on from the release of their genre-defining *Critical Beatdown*, and three years since the less-well-received (but still very good) *Funk Your Head Up*. On their third album, 1993's *The Four Horsemen*, the group had begun working with emcee/producer Godfather Don, a relationship that kickstarted a new creative era for the veteran Kool Keith, one that would help define the New York underground.

The Four Horsemen was an Ultramagnetic MCs album, but some of the recording sessions were originally meant to be for an aborted Kool Keith solo album he intended to release under the name Rhythm X, the first of many aliases Kool Keith would use in subsequent years. The album never saw the light of day, but Kool Keith and Godfather Don instead used the tracks on an EP they released in 1995 as the group the Cenobites, on Bobbito Garcia's indie label Fondle 'Em Records, along with other tracks intended to be skits and promos to promote Bob's radio show.

The following year Kool Keith created a new alias named Dr. Octagon and recorded the second classic album of his career, *Dr. Octagonecologyst* (1996). The album was a collaboration with Dan the Automator and DJ Qbert, and proved to be a critical success that helped shine a light on what was happening on the fringes of mainstream, commercial rap music. *Dr. Octagonecologyst* also marked the start of Kool Keith's relationship with another producer he'd go on to work with extensively, KutMasta Kurt. Kool Keith rounded off 1996 with the release of an album with another rap veteran, Tim Dog (best known for the 1991 diss record "Fuck Compton", he died in 2013 under a cloud of mystery and court cases), who had been a peripheral member of Ultramagnetic MCs since the early days. *Big Time*, released under the name Ultra, was their one and only album together, mostly produced by KutMasta Kurt. Forever the horny freak, 1997 saw Kool Keith drop the *Sex Style* album, again produced by KutMasta Kurt, except for three tracks produced by T.R. Love from Ultramagnetic.

That same year Fondle 'Em Records released a fuller version of Kool Keith and Godfather Don's Cenobites project, titled the *Cenobites LP*. Kool Keith developed two new aliases in 1999, recording weird and wonderful concept albums for each of them. The first was as the character Dr. Dooom for the album *First Come, First Served*, where Kool Keith's switched back towards a more straight up hip-hop sound, and even included a track on which the Dr. Octagon character is killed off (and then brought back to life on later projects). Then came the release of *Black Elvis/Lost in Space*, ostensibly billed as being by Kool Keith, but really the debut of his latest persona, Black Elvis. Notably, the album was produced by Kool Keith himself, as was his next album, 2000's *Matthew*, with one track by KutMasta Kurt. That same year saw Kool Keith debut a new alias and concept, this time as a member of the group the Analog Brothers, which also featured Ice-T (as Ice Oscillator). They released the *Pimp To Eat* album, with Keith taking on the character of Keith Korg.

Later in 2000 Keith and KutMasta Kurt connected with the rapper Motion Man to form the group Masters of Illusion, releasing a self-titled album. There was a return to *Sex Style* territory with *Spankmaster* in 2001, before a few increasingly obscure and now largely forgotten projects. In 2002 Kool Keith released an album named *Game* as part of the group KHM alongside fellow Analog Brothers members Marc Live and H-Bomb. A few years later in 2004, the group changed their name to the Clayborne Family for the release of a self-titled album. Also in 2004 was the release of an album as part of an even more obscure group called Thee Undatakerz, this time with Kool Keith using the alias Reverend Tom, and a return to more familiar ground with KutMasta Kurt for an album named *Diesel Truckers*.

With the exception of *Dr. Octagonecologyst*, which was given a major label re-release a year after the first version, all of the Kool Keith albums listed were released on indie labels, including several on two different labels that KutMasta Kurt had a hand in running; Threshold Records, and the very Kool Keith sounding Funky Ass Records. Keith has released a huge amount of music since 2005, with varying degrees of quality, but his legacy is strong, and he is one of the few rappers able to say they have been influential in two different eras of rap history.

EL-P

While Bronx originator Kool Keith was making the transition from one era of hip-hop to another, similar things were happening across New York City. In Brooklyn, Jaime Meline was learning studio engineering and the legal side of the music business by day and making plans to be a rapper at night, calling himself El-P. At the same time, not far away, Leonard Smythe was honing his skills as a deejay by the name of Mr. Len. The emcee and the deejay crossed paths in 1993 and started the group Company Flow, later adding Justin 'Bigg Jus' Ingleton as the third member. Passionately independent right from the jump, the group released their debut EP, *Funcrusher*, on their own under the guise of Official Recordings. Company Flow then signed a deal with Rawkus Records, who in 1997 released an extended version of the EP as a fully-fledged album, *Funcrusher Plus*. It proved to be a game-changer that helped inspire the next couple of decades worth of underground hip-hop. But as impactful as *Funcrusher Plus* was, Company Flow came and went in the space of just a few years.

The group finished the 90s with several appearances and contributions to other people's records – including a track on 1998's Rawkus compilation *Lyricist Lounge, Volume One* ("Weight"), "Jonny Rookie Card" from the *Sut Min Pik EP* by Boulevard Connection, and on "Bladerunners" from Mike Ladd's *Welcome to the Afterfuture* album – but Bigg Jus had already left the group by the release of their second and final album, 1999's *Little Johnny from the Hospitul:*

Breaks & Instrumentals Vol.1.

Bigg Jus went on to launch a consistently good albeit obscure solo career, releasing the *Plantation Rhymes EP in 2001, Black Mamba Serum*s in 2002, *Black Mamba Serums v2.0* in 2004, and the *Poor People's Day* album in 2005. He also forged a partnership with Orko Eloheim as the duo Nephlim Modulation Systems, releasing the *Woe to Thee O Land When Thy King Is a Child* album in 2003, and *Imperial Letters of Protection* in 2005. Several of these releases were on UK indie label Big Dada, itself distributed by the larger but still independent Ninja Tune label.

Mr. Len, meanwhile, started his own post-Company Flow solo run, releasing several projects oftentimes as eclectic as those from Bigg Jus. His debut came in 2001 with the snappily titled *Pity The Fool (Experiments In Therapy Behind The Mask Of Music While Handing Out Dummysmacks)* album, where the cream of the underground rapped over his production. It was released by renowned indie label Matador Records, who by the turn of the millennium had branched out from their traditional focus on rock to embrace hip-hop. Mr. Len followed this up with several releases on his own indie label, Smack Records, including *Beats and Things, Vol. 1*, and the throwback to his old group, *Class X, A Tribute to Company Flow*, both in 2004. He also formed a duo named Roosevelt Franklin with Kimani Rogers from the group Masterminds, releasing *Something's Got to Give* in 2003. In 2005 Mr. Len was also part of an intriguing doo-wop parody album and mockumentary named *The Art of Picking Up Women* by the fictional group The Dix, which also featured DJ Prince Paul and his longtime collaborator, the late Don Newkirk.

The Company Flow member who has gone on to have the biggest impact is El-P. After the group went their separate ways, and their deal with Rawkus had gone south, El-P founded his own indie rap label, Definitive Jux. Over the course of the following decade, the label went on to become one of the premier underground labels, releasing important albums by Aesop Rock, Cannibal Ox, Murs, Cage, Camu Tao, and El-P himself, among others. El-P delivered his first solo album in 2002 with *Fantastic Damage*, followed by guest vocals and production for many Definitive Jux artists and beyond, most notably producing the entirety of *The Cold Vein* album by Cannibal Ox. Later in 2002 El-P released an instrumental/extended version of his debut, *Fandam Plus: Instrumentals, Remixes, Lyrics & Video* (the 'plus' part perhaps a callback to the *Funcrusher Plus* days). El-P then released two albums in 2004, a jazz-fusion project named *High Water* with the The Blue Series Continuum, and a collection of his lesser-known works, *Collecting the Kid*. He also collaborated with Camu Tao as Central Services.

There was sadly no crossover between the former Company Flow members on any of these albums, but the group toured for a few years after they stopped making music together, and still appear to be on amicable terms today. New music by Mr. Len or Bigg Jus has been less forthcoming in recent years, but El-P went on to release more acclaimed solo albums, before finding his biggest fan base yet as one half of the group Run The Jewels with Killer Mike.

MOS DEF

Dante Terrell Smith was always destined to do big things. Born in Brooklyn, he acted in a number of commercials, TV shows, movies and plays as a child and early teen, and by 1996, having pivoted to music, was fast-becoming a star, capable of stealing attention from rap's biggest names each time he was given the chance to touch a mic. Today he is known as Yasiin Bey, but back then he called himself Mos Def, and it is no overstatement to suggest that in the mid-late 90s he had the potential to become one of the most renown emcees of all time, equipped with the skills, confidence, looks and everything else needed to reach that level. It didn't fully turn out that way and likely never will (Bey still raps today, but sporadically), but the music we got from Mos Def's heyday is some of the best.

Mos Def's debut came in 1994 when he recorded *Manifest Destiny* as part of the group UMD (Urban Thermo Dynamics, which also included DCQ, who is Mos Def's brother, and Ces). The album, which didn't actually get a release until a decade later in 2004, is mediocre, but provided a glimpse at what was to come from the young and hungry Mos Def.

His true breakout came in 1996, starting with appearances on two tracks from the *Gravity* album by fellow Brooklynites Da Bush Babees. One of those tracks, "The Love Song," was produced by De La Soul member Posdnous, putting Mos Def on the radar of the revered group. Clearly impressed, De La Soul then featured Mos Def on the track "Big Brother Beat" from their *Stakes Is High* album, and on a remix of the title track as a b-side to the single "Itzsoweezee (Hot)." Like the original, the remix was produced by J Dilla (then still going by Jay Dee), therefore placing Mos Def in the same orbit as not just the Native Tongues but also the Soulquarians collective, leading to later collaborations with A Tribe Called Quest in 1998 ("Rock Rock Y'all" from *The Love Movement*), The Roots in 1999 ("Double Trouble" from *Things Fall Apart*), and Common in 2000 ("The Questions" on *Like Water For Chocolate*).

By 1997 Mos Def was ready to make his official solo debut, and did so by forging a relationship with Rawkus Records, which by now was fast becoming New York's most important indie rap label. He released the "Universal Magnetic" 12", which also featured on the Rawkus compilation album, *Soundbombing*, as were several other tracks with him on. By this time, Mos Def had also formed a relationship with fellow Brooklynite Talib Kweli, and featured on the track "Fortified Live" by Kweli's group with DJ Hi-Tek, Reflection Eternal, which was also on *Soundbombing*. The 12" singles continued into 1998, including tracks with Mike Zoot, "Crosstown Beef" (as part of the group Medina Green, which also included DCQ from UMD), and "Body Rock" from *Lyricist Lounge, Volume One*, on which Mos Def got to share the microphone with two hip-hop legends from the previous era, Q-Tip and Tash.

Mos and Kweli then solidified their partnership with the release of a collaborative album under the name Black Star, *Mos Def & Talib Kweli Are Black Star*, which put both emcees in the realm of 'conscious rap'. Mos Def finally released his actual solo album, *Black on Both Sides*, in 1999 to much acclaim, and also continued to record guest vocals for a varied list of artists in the years that followed, including The High & Mighty, DJ Honda, DJ Shadow, and N'Dea Davenport. He scored a crossover record in 2000 when he collaborated with Pharoahe Monch and Nate Dogg for "Oh No" from *Lyricist Lounge 2*, although by now Mos Def was focused on acting. He released his second solo album in 2004, *The New Danger*, a messy, self-indulgent mix of different genres and sounds. It took until 2009 before Mos Def was able to return to form on *The Ecstatic*, but his musical output has been sporadic since then.

Talib Kweli released the debut album from Reflection Eternal with Hi-Tek in 2000, *Train of Thought*, before then dropping his own solo debut, *Quality,* in 2002. The album spawned the single "Get By", produced by Kanye West who at the time was really starting to take off. There was also a high profile remix that paired Talib Kweli with major stars including Jay-Z, Snoop Dogg and Busta Rhymes.

It came at a time when Rawkus was desperately trying to become a mainstream label, much to the disappointment of listeners used to them releasing records with a harder, underground style. Kweli released his second album in 2004, *The Beautiful Struggle,* his final on Rawkus, with a much more commercial sound. He has had several albums since, but his career has sometimes been mired in controversy.

MF DOOM

When things fell apart for his group KMD, life looked bleak for Zev Love X. Years in the wilderness followed, as the man born Daniel Dumile struggled to work out what to do next, and how to feed his family. The logical solution was to return to what he did best, only this time things would be different. The comeback started slowly, making incognito appearances at New York City open mic nights with his face hidden by pantyhose like Ghostface Killah in early Wu-Tang Clan videos.

Then, like a lot of things related to the New York underground in the 90s, Dumile's return to the rap scene was facilitated by radio deejay and label owner Bobbito Garcia. First on the agenda was some unfinished KMD business, and so Bobbito's Fondle 'Em Records released an EP named *Black Bastards Ruffs + Rares* featuring tracks that would have been on *Black Bastards* had it been released as planned in 1994. The EP no doubt gave Dumile some closure on the demise of KMD, but it was now time to move on, right some wrongs, and get his own back on an industry that deserted him.

After putting out a few 12"s on Fondle 'Em Records, Dumile and Bobbito set about releasing a full album. The result was *Operation: Doomsday*, created in a matter of weeks in Bobbito's apartment.

Raw and unpolished, the production is basically nothing more than familiar instrumentals, often used wholesale, with beats and cuts laid on top. Lyrically, the album is a masterclass in the art of rhyme. It was also most people's official introduction to the MF DOOM character, a supervillain ready to destroy all enemies in the vein of the comic book bad guys it was inspired by.

MF DOOM had arrived, heralding a new era of indie rap. What followed was a creative streak of solo albums, collaborations, instrumental projects and reissues that few in any musical genre can rival, solidifying DOOM as an iconic, god-like figure to fans of indie rap and beyond that has only grown stronger since the death of the real man behind the mask in 2020.

The new millennium of DOOM began with an EP recorded with MF Grimm. DOOM and MF Grimm's friendship went back years, and Grimm is featured on *Operation: Doomsday*. More of a collection of tracks than a cohesive project, the *MF EP* features songs by both artists, plus remixes and instrumentals.

The choice to put on a mask was more than just a way to keep Zev Love X as a relic of an earlier chapter, or a way to protect whoever the real Daniel Dumile was. It was also a way for him to express a fascination with comic book characters and a love of pop culture in general. MF DOOM was just one of several alter egos that would emerge after *Operation: Doomsday*, starting in 2003 with *Escape from Monsta Island*; a group album by the Monsta Island Czars – a loose collective of regular Dumile collaborators including Jorge 'Kurious' Alvarez, and MF Grimm – released on Dumile's own imprint, Metal Face Records. Each member rapped under a name inspired by monsters from the original Godzilla movies produced by Japan's Toho company. Dumile performed as King Geedorah, based on the King Ghidorah monster.

The King Geedorah character was carried over to Dumile's next album, 2003's *Take Me To Your Leader*, released via UK independent label Big Dada. Although it is not quite a full solo album – he only actually raps on a handful of the 13 tracks – *Take Me To Your Leader* is among Dumile's best work.

For his next album, also released in 2003, Dumile returned to the realm of comic book bad guys with the *Vaudeville Villain* album, this time under the guise of Viktor Vaughn (a riff on Marvel character Victor Von Doom, who becomes Dr. Doom after an accident scars his face). Released on the New York indie label Sound-Ink Records, the album is notable for being one of the few Dumile solo projects produced entirely by outside beatmakers. The year ended with the release of the *Best of KMD* compilation, via Nature Sounds.

Dumile headed into 2004 with his reputation already secured as the new king of underground rap, but with the release of the highly acclaimed *Madvillainy* album with producer Madlib as the duo Madvillain, his star would ascend further than just fans of hip-hop. After the critical highs of *Madvillain,* Dumile followed up with arguably the only album in his entire discography that isn't universally loved. *VV:2* was another Viktor Vaughn project, but is uneven and largely forgettable. It does, however, feature Kool Keith, pairing up two of hip-hop's most eccentric artists. Next came a return to solid form with the release of *Mm..Food,* this time via Rhymesayers Entertainment. It's another stellar album, and another for the comic book heads, filled with Doctor Doom soundbites from episodes of *Spider-Man & His Amazing Friends*.

The following year Nature Sounds released a live MF DOOM album, *Live From Planet X*, recorded in San Francisco. On that occasion it *was* actually Dumile performing, unlike at several other infamous shows, where so-called 'DOOM imposters' would be deployed to perform in Dumile's absence, to the disappointment of fans. Next came another ambitious concept album, this time a collaboration with producer Danger Mouse as the duo Danger Doom. Essentially an extended promo for TV shows produced by Cartoon Network's Adult Swim, *The Mouse and The Mask* sees MF DOOM drop some of his most humorous bars, and started a long-running relationship with UK indie label Lex Records, a sub-label of Warp founded in 2001 by Tom Brown. Dumile released other acclaimed projects post-2005, including *Born Like This* in 2009, *Key to the Kuffs* in 2012 as JJ DOOM with Jneiro Jarel, *NehruvianDoom* in 2014 with Bishop Nehru, and *Czarface Meets Metal Face* in 2018 with Czarface.

Throughout his reign Dumile was also able to carve out a respectable side hustle as a producer, releasing many instrumental albums under the name Metal Fingers, including several volumes of the *Special Herbs* and *Special Blends* series between 2001-2005, some released on Metal Face Records, some on Nature Sounds, and others on more obscure labels. Many tracks from these albums were used by Dumile on his own vocal albums, and by other artists for their own projects. Among the highest profile artists to reuse Metal Fingers instrumentals was Ghostface Killah, on his 2006 albums, *Fishscale* and *More Fish*. MF DOOM and Ghostface Killah collaborated several more times in the following years, although their much-hyped and somewhat mythical joint album will never now see the light of day.

GODFATHER DON

An affiliation with a prominent rapper can be a gift and a curse. The career arc for a rapper down with someone already well known usually goes like this: the understudy artist shines bright on a song or two, and is then never heard from again. But sometimes the artist is able to run with the opportunity and build a strong career of their own. It helps if you also made music before you connected with the renowned artist, like Godfather Don did. In 1991, a few years before he produced for Ultramagnetic MCs and released the *Cenobites LP* with Kool Keith, Don dropped the *Hazardous* album. Post-Cenobites, Godfather Don forged a relationship with indie label Hydra Entertainment and released many 12"s for the label, including the much loved "Properties of The Steel". Several of these releases today command high prices on vinyl resale sites. Hydra was also where he released his second album, *Diabolique*, in 1998, including a guest appearance by Kool Keith on "Voices". Godfather Don was additionally in the duo Groove Merchantz alongside The Mighty V.I.C.

There were also several editions of the acclaimed Hydra Beats instrumental series released between 1997 and 2005. The series was a showcase for Godfather Don's exquisite production work, earning him several high-profile placements, including a track on Cormega's 2001 *The Realness* album, and two tracks on the 2003 mixtape by Mobb Deep, *Free Agents: The Murda Mixtape*. He was also a prominent producer for the group Screwball, joining the list of esteemed beatmakers who contributed to their 2000 debut, *Y2K: The Album*, released via Tommy Boy, that also included Marley Marl, Pete Rock and DJ Premier. He also produced their next album, *Loyalty*, which came out on Godfather Don's home label, Hydra. Godfather Don has released several more albums and EPs since, and is still active today. As of yet, there has never been another official Cenobites album with Kool Keith (the *Demented Thoughts* EP from 2008 doesn't count. It is very much unofficial, and essentially just a collection of unreleased tracks recorded years before).

MF GRIMM

Having been on the scene since the early 90s also helped MF Grimm to be thought of as something more than an artist living in the giant shadow of MF DOOM. Fondle 'Em Records released a run of MF Grimm 12"s before and after his work with Dumile on *Operation: Doomsday* and the *MF EP*, but MF Grimm released his debut album in 2002 via his own small label, Day By Day. *The Downfall of Ibliys: A Ghetto Opera* is a dark but rewarding listen, and his best work. Most of the production is by Dumile under his Metal Fingers name, continuing their long-running partnership. For his next album in 2004, *Digital Tears: E-Mail from Purgatory*, MF Grimm used both a new alias, and a reference to an old one. The album is listed on the artwork as being by 'GM Grimm as Superstar Jet Jaguar', the GM bit being used for the first time, and Jet Jaguar being the name MF Grimm used as a member of the Monsta Island Czars. Unlike his previous work, this time MF Grimm enlisted various different producers, of which J-Zone was the only one with any name recognition.

Sadly, MF Grimm's career has been marred by bad choices that have impacted his life. He served time in prison in 2002, and *The Downfall of Ibliys: A Ghetto Opera* is said to have been recorded in just 24 hours while he was on bail. His involvement in the world of drug dealing saw him almost get killed twice, first in 1986 and again in 2004, taking multiple bullets each time. The latter incident did the most damage, paralyzing MF Grimm and confining him to a wheelchair. His friendship with Dumile also soured in later years, culminating in a diss track named "The Book of Daniel" on MF Grimm's triple album from 2006, *American Hunger*. It is unclear if he and Dumile reconciled before Dumile's death.

JUGGAKNOTS

Another group who benefitted from being down with artists getting rave reviews at the time was the Juggaknots, who joined Company Flow and rapper J Treds to form the short-lived supergroup, Indelible MC's. All members appear on "Fire In Which You Burn" from *Funcrusher Plus*, and on the track "Weight" from the *Lyricist Lounge, Volume One* album. But similar to Godfather Don and MF Grimm, the Juggaknots had actually been making music for years before they connected with Company Flow, and like Daniel Dumile, their early career suffered from record label drama.

The group is made up of brothers Breeze Brewin (sometimes misspelled as Breezly Brewin on earlier records) and Buddy Slim (aka Kev Fevr), with their sister Queen Herawin also joining in later years, who were raised in the Bronx. They were recording music as far back as the late 80s (a compilation of their very early work named *Baby Pictures (C. 1989-1993)* can be found online), and by 1993 had signed a deal with Elektra Records thanks to Buddy Slim's industry connections, and in part due to having been championed by Bobbito and 3rd Bass member Pete Nice. Then, around the same time that Elektra dropped KMD, the label dropped the Juggaknots as well, having not liked the direction the group was going in with their debut album, *Clear Blue Skies*, and the group sticking to their vision about not wanting to veer towards a more commercial sound. Bobbito put the album out via his Fondle 'Em Records instead, as a vinyl only release in 1996.

An extended version of the album named *Re: Release* came out in 2003, with all tracks from the original *Clear Blues Skies* plus several extras. It is today considered to be one of the most significant indie rap albums from the era. In between these releases, Breeze Brewin featured as the protagonist on DJ Prince Paul's acclaimed

1999 concept album, *A Prince Among Thieves*. Breeze Brewin was also a member of The Weathermen collective (more on them later), and made guest appearances on various records in the years after his group debut. One particular highlight was when he and the Juggaknots reunited with fellow Indelible MC's member Mr. Len on *Pity The Fool*. A second Juggaknots album came out in 2006, named *Use Your Confusion*, and Brewin finally released a solo album named *Hindsight* in 2021. There have also been sporadic albums from Queen Herawin.

The Juggaknots other Indelible MC's partner, J Treds, seemed to disappear without much of a trace, dropping one 12" on Fondle 'Em, and not much since. There was, however, a compilation of his work released in 2018, named *The Unstoppable Album*.

ARSONISTS

In the opening bars of the 1997 Wu-Tang Clan song "Reunited", the GZA spits a line about how the group struck a match to the underground and lit up the entire music industry. Igniting the underground rap scene is also what a crew of emcees from Brooklyn hoped to do when they formed a group a few years earlier and branded themselves with the incendiary name of the Arsonists. With a core lineup of Q-Unique, D-Stroy, Jise One', Freestyle, and Swel Boogie, the Arsonists may not have been as impactful as GZA and the Wu, but they still left a sizable scorch mark on indie rap.

The Arsonists have their foundations in two previous groups. In 1994, Q-Unique was making music as one third of The Nomaads. D-Stroy, meanwhile, had been making demos with a pre-famous Tony Touch. He was also a member of a battle rap crew named Bushwick Bomb Squad, but when this and Q-Unique's group both fizzled out, they regrouped and became the Arsonists. Fondle 'Em Records put out the group's first 12"s between 1996-98, but for the release of their debut album, 1999's *As The World Burns*, they landed on an independent label not known for hip-hop, the aforementioned Matador Records, signing at the same time as Non Phixion. The album continues the fire theme (track names include "Backdraft", "Pyromaniax" and "Blaze"), but ultimately the experience likely left the group themselves burned out.

By the time Arsonists released their second album, *Date of Birth*, D-Stroy and Freestyle had left the group. It's another good record, but not as strong as their debut. The album also hit an unexpected snag due to having the unfortunate release date of September 11, 2001. While the hip-hop world remembers Jay-Z's *The Blueprint* having been released that fateful day as a quirky footnote of history, *Date of Birth* is sadly less remembered. The Arsonists still exist as a group today, including the original full line-up. *As The World Burns* was re-released in 2018 as part of a package named *Lost In The Fire* that also included previously unreleased tracks.

NON PHIXION

While the Arsonists were making moves in Bushwick, two brothers were establishing themselves in a different part of Brooklyn, this time Canarsie. Ill Bill and his younger brother Necro came from a death metal background, but had become enamored with hip-hop by the start of the 90s. Whereas 3rd Bass member Pete Nice played an early role in the career of the Juggaknots, it was his bandmate MC Serch who was influential in founding the group in which Ill Bill would gain indie rap fame, Non Phixion. It was Serch who connected his occasional deejay, DJ Eclipse, with rappers Sabac Red and Ill

Bill, who were later joined by Goretex to complete the line-up of what would become the four-man Non Phixion.

Serch's industry clout secured the group a record deal with major label Geffen Records, but early Non Phixion 12"s in 1996 and 97 were actually released on MC Serch's own imprint, Serchlite Music. Ill Bill and Goretex very briefly founded a label named Hebrew National, which put out one of the group's most remembered 12"s, "I Shot Reagan". Like the Arsonists, Non Phixion also briefly had a deal with Matador Records, but after years of never-ending record label frustration, Non Phixion's debut album was released independently on a label founded by Ill Bill himself, Uncle Howie Records (named after Bill and Necro's uncle). *The Future Is Now* came out in 2002 and featured production by DJ Premier, Pete Rock and Large Professor, plus a track with MF DOOM – each a sign of how much respect Non Phixion had at the time. Two years later the group released a collection of new and unreleased tracks with an accompanying DVD, packaged as *The Green CD/DVD,* but by 2006 Non Phixion had officially broken up.

Ill Bill released his solo debut, *What's Wrong With Bill* in 2004 before the group split, this time on his brother Necro's own indie label, Psycho+Logical-Records. He's released a ton of work since, including more solo albums, mixtapes, projects with Vinnie Paz and DJ Muggs, and as part of the group La Coka Nostra. Sabac Red released his debut album in 2004 named *Sabacolypse: A Change Gon' Come*, the same year as Goretex released his first album, *The Art of Dying*, both via Psycho+Logical-Records. Necro also has an extensive solo discography. His music is squarely in the horrorcore subgenre of hip-hop, and is an acquired taste that often skews back towards his death metal roots. There hasn't been new Non Phixion music for years, but the group has been touring together since 2014. After years of feuding, Ill Bill and Necro have also recently put aside their differences.

R.A. THE RUGGED MAN

The major label frustration suffered by Long Island emcee R.A. The Rugged Man didn't end after his time on Jive Records in the early 90s, and the aborted release of what would have been his first album, *Night of the Bloody Apes*. By 1999 he was signed to another major, this time Capitol, and yet again the net result was another unreleased album. That one would have been titled *American Lowlife*, but it never materialized. Fortunately, R.A. The Rugged Man was by now well known on the New York underground scene on the strength of being in the orbit of Rawkus Records, making a brief contribution to Company Flow's *Funcrusher Plus* album in 1997, and full tracks on *Soundbombing* (1997) and *Soundbombing II* (1999).

We finally got a fully available album by R.A. The Rugged Man in 2004, ending over a decade's worth of record industry drama. *Die, Rugged Man, Die* was released by Nature Sounds, a label who at the time was fast becoming one of underground hip-hop's most respected indie brands. Production on *Die, Rugged Man, Die* includes contributions by J-Zone and Ayatollah, plus some unexpected names. "How Low" is produced by Darryl Jenifer of the hardcore punk band Bad Brains. It's not the kind of fit you'd usually find on a hip-hop album, but years before Jenifer founded the group The White Mandingos with rap journalist Sacha Jenkins, they mooted starting a different group with R. A. The Rugged Man providing raps. The White Mandingos eventually went with Los Angeles indie rapper Murs instead, but the back story at least explains the Bad Brains connection on *Die, Rugged Man, Die*.

"Casanova (Fly Guy)", meanwhile, is produced by Nat "Gizmo" Robinson. Although known today more for his work as an engineer for major R&B artists, Gizmo is also one half of 80s rap group Audio Two. As a big fan of hip-hop from that era, R.A. The Rugged Man's work with Gizmo on *Die, Rugged Man, Die* provides a satisfying bridge between two golden eras of the genre.

R.A. The Rugged Man can also claim to be part of an exclusive group of indie rap artists to have a certified gold-selling album. Continuing the long tradition of rap and pro wrestling crossovers, in 2000 the WWE (still named the WWF at this point) released an album named *WWF Aggression*, via Priority. Sprinkled among the tracklist of big name rappers were indie artists Kool Keith, Peanut Butter Wolf, and R.A. The Rugged Man, whose track "Break Down The Walls" is themed around wrestler Chris Jericho. R.A. The Rugged Man has continued to release albums since *Die, Rugged Man*, and today is a wise veteran in the world of indie rap.

SIAH AND YESHUA DAPOED

Another Brooklyn based group on the come-up in 1996 was the duo Siah and Yeshua DapoED (aka Yesh). And as with so many others, it was through Bobbito and his Fondle 'Em Records that the group found their feet. The label released *The Visualz EP* to a hungry fanbase desperate to hear everything Fondle 'Em had to offer, despite Siah and Yeshua DapoED being almost completely unknown at this point. Over a decade later, the EP was given a re-release as *The Visualz Anthology*, with several extra tracks added. Siah released one 12" on Fondle 'Em in 1997 ("Repetition" b/w "Pyrite") before later exiting the hip-hop industry for good, but Yesh continued recording, dropping the acclaimed 12" "Directions" b/w "The Head Bop" in 1998 via Raw Shack Productions, the latter of which featured Siah. Siah and Yesh also appeared on several tracks on the *Unleashed* album by UK production outfit Unsung Heroes (Insight and Shiver), released domestically on Scenario Records, and in the US via 75 Ark. Yesh then released his first, and so far only album, *Into Fresh Things*, in 2002, this time on Ill Boogie Records, as part of their *Earplug* series.

He also went on to have a second wind as a member of the group Wee Bee Foolish alongside DJ Bless, and brothers Ken Boogaloo and Xtraordinaire. The group released the *Brighton Beach Memoirs* album in 2002, on the indie label Head Bop Entertainment, which Yesh had a hand in running. Yesh still performs live today, and in recent years has been connecting with his family roots in Colombia, working with some of the nation's up and coming rappers.

ATOMS FAMILY

Rap crews with multiple members is nothing new. Sometimes the strength in numbers approach can work, like with the nine-man Wu-Tang Clan. But more often than not, too many big personalities trying to grab the spotlight is too much. This is probably why New York's Atoms Family ended up thinning down their numbers from over 30 to a more reasonable eight. The collective formed in 1994, headed by Harlem emcees Vast Aire and Vordul Mega, who together made up the duo Cannibal Ox. The rest of the core group consisted of Alaska, Cryptic One, DJ Cip One, DJ Pawl, Jest, and Windnbreeze. Combined, the group has a dense catalog of releases, although hardly any of it is actually credited to the 'Atoms Family'.

When his former group Elite Bomb Squad broke up, Cryptic One and wider Atoms Family members Whichcraft and Molecule (not to be confused with Molecules from the group The Legion) formed a new group named Centa of Da Web, and released an EP in 1996 titled *Beyond Human Comprehension* on Cryptic One's Centrifugal Phorce label. The label then released the first product under the banner of the Atoms Family, a 2000 compilation album called *The Prequel*, with tracks from all of the emcees in the group.

When various label deals that Cryptic One had been working on fell apart, El-P stepped in and released music by the crew via his Definitive Jux label, including the highly acclaimed *The Cold Vein* album by Cannibal Ox, complete with guest features by Alaska and Cryptic One. A second Atoms Family compilation was released in 2002 by Centrifugal Phorce, *Atoms Archives Volume 1*. As with *The Prequel*, Volume 1 used the Atoms Family name as a banner for the collective as a whole, and no actual tracks are credited under that name.

Next it was time for Alaska and Windnbreeze to step up. Their group, Hangar 18, actually predated the formation of Atoms Family, but they joined the fold in 1994 and later added DJ Pawl to the group. The release of their debut, *The Multi-Platinum Debut Album*, was delayed by label issues, but eventually came out in 2004 via Definitive Jux. Cryptic One's first album also came out that year, *The Anti-Mobius Strip Theory*, as well as solo projects from both members of Cannibal Ox. Vast Aire released his debut, *Look Mom... No Hands*, featuring contributions by many of the most prominent underground rappers of the era. This was followed a few months later by Vordul Mega's first album, *The Revolution of Yung Havoks*. The various members of the Atoms Family also had a busy 2005, including the release of a live Cannibal Ox album (*Return Of The Ox (Live At CMJ)*), an album named *The Best Damn Rap Show* by Vast Aire and producer DJ Mighty Mi (via Mighty Mi's Eastern Conference label), and one final crew compilation, *Atoms Archives Volume 2*.

Today, most members of the Atoms Family collective still make music, although the chances of a future new group project now feel slim.

AESOP ROCK

A 2014 study by a data analyst named Matt Daniels found Aesop Rock to have the widest vocabulary of any rapper. It was hardly a surprise for fans of the Northport, Long Island raised emcee born Ian Bavitz, who had been dropping dense, word-heavy songs for many years.

Aesop Rock's long discography goes back to 1998's *Music for Earthworms*, a self-released collection of tracks from older sessions. The following year saw the release of his first EP, *Appleseed*, on which Aesop started collaborating with producer Blockhead, a working partnership that is still going strong today. He reached a wider audience and critical plaudits with the release of *Float* in 2000, and it was on this album Aesop began to crossover with other factions of the underground, including Slug of the group Atmosphere, Vast Aire from Cannibal Ox, and Doesone from the Anticon collective.

Aesop Rock's career then entered the Definitive Jux phase, signing for El-P's fledgling label and helping to elevate its reputation. The first fruits of the partnership came with the acclaimed *Labor Days* album in 2001, and an EP the following year based around one of the album's tracks, *Daylight*. Next came *Bazooka Tooth* in 2003, which also featured Blockhead's group Party Fun Action Committee (a duo with Jer), who released their own album on Definite Jux that same year, named *Let's Get Serious*. A new Aesop

Rock EP named *Fast Cars, Danger, Fire and Knives* emerged in 2005, featuring production by Rob Sonic, who Aesop would later partner with alongside DJ Big Wiz to form the group Hail Mary Mallon. Rob Sonic released his own Definitive Jux debut in 2004, *Telicatessen*, and four albums and two EPs as a member of the group Sonic Sum.

Aesop Rock would go on to release one more album on Definitive Jux (2007's *None Shall Pass*) before falling out with El-P, and would later sign with Rhymesayers Entertainment, who he is still with now. Today Aesop Rock is considered one of the brightest lights from the indie rap era, and has achieved cult status among his many followers.

CAGE

If the theory of the so-called tortured artist argues that said artist can only create something after they have experienced pain and suffering, then Christian 'Cage' Palko would make for a good case study. An unstable childhood, drug addiction, physical abuse, and an extended stay in a psychiatric unit are just a few of the traumas experienced by Palko, who somehow survived all of this to make a name for himself as a rapper who has worked with the best of underground rap from across New York, New Jersey and Ohio, releasing music on the four most important indie labels of the era.

Cage is another product of the Pete Nice and Bobbito talent pipeline, who were shopping him around and trying to get him a deal in the early 90s. Pete also put Cage on a track from his 1993 *Dust to Dust* album with Daddy Rich, which means that Cage's first significant placement was on a record released by one of hip-hop's most celebrated labels, Def Jam. After a few false starts under different names (including 'Cage Kennylz' and 'Keige'), short stints in a couple of groups, and a botched deal with Columbia Records, Cage regrouped with Bobbito, releasing 12"s on Fondle 'Em Records from 1997-98.

Cage then connected with The High & Mighty (Mr. Eon and DJ Mighty Mi) and together they started the group Smut Peddlers. A series of 12"s followed, some via Eastern Conference, some via Rawkus, culminating with the *Porn Again* album, released in 2002, which saw Cage collaborate not only with rising underground stars like R.A. The Rugged Man, but also legends such as Kool G Rap and Kool Keith.

The connection with Eastern Conference paved the way for Cage to sign with the label, dropping his debut album in 2002, the highly regarded *Movies For The Blind*. In addition to previous collaborators, the album saw Cage work with members of Columbus' MHz crew, including Camu Tao. A few months after *Movies For The Blind*, Cage and Camu released the *Nighthawks* concept album as a duo. More releases via Eastern Conference followed, including the *Weatherproof* EP in 2003, and the angel dust-themed *Waterworld* album in 2004, recorded as a duo with Artifacts rapper Tame One, under the name Leak Bros. *Movies For The Blind* also saw Cage work with El-P, and it was via his Definitive Jux label through which Cage released his second album, 2005's *Hell's Winter*.

There were more albums by Cage in the preceding decades, often in musical directions away from a traditional hip-hop sound. He has been less active in recent years, but still sometimes tours.

THE WEATHERMEN

Cage's ability to work with multiple crews across various different labels helped when it came time to pull together a dream team supergroup in 1998, gathering up members of Artifacts, Company Flow, the Juggaknots, Cannibal Ox, and MHz, plus several solo artists. They called themselves The Weathermen, and although accounts vary, the official line-up included El-P, Breeze Brewin, Aesop Rock, Vast Aire, Cage, Tame One, Masai Bey, Camu Tao, Copywrite, Tage Future, Jakki The Motamouth, Metro, and Yak Ballz.

There's only been a handful of tracks credited to The Weathermen ever released, and no one song that featured the entire collective at once. Some of these tracks appeared on 12"s and compilation albums from Definitive Jux and Eastern Conference, like "Same As It Never Was" (released in 2001 as a 12", and on the *Definitive Jux Presents 2* album), "Dead Weathermen" (a b-side to El-P's 2002 "Dead Disney" 12"), "Five Left In The Clip" (released in 2003 on 12", and on the *Eastern Conference All Stars III* compilation, which also included another The Weathermen track, "Gut You"), and "WMR (Weathermen Radio")" by El-P and Camu Tao (released on 12" and on the *Definitive Jux Presents III* compilation in 2004). Other songs appeared only on compilations; "Weatherwhatevermen" & "Let The Games Begin" on *Eastern Conference All Stars IV* in 2004, and "Reports Of A Possible Kidnapping" from 2009's *Definitive Jux Presents IV*.

The closest thing to a proper The Weathermen album was *The Conspiracy* mixtape released in 2003, on which various members appear on original songs, and freestyle over a bunch of well known beats. Yet even this release didn't represent the whole group, with no input from Aesop Rock, Masai Bey, or Tage Future. An unreleased track from 2001 surfaced online several years ago, named "The ONLY Weathermen Song", but this too is missing several members, this time Aesop Rock, Breeze Brewin, Tame One, Masai Bey, Camu Tao and Metro.

As everybody knows, rappers are very good at beefing with each other, and The Weathermen were no exception, despite the perceived camaraderie and compatibility. There are plenty of online rabbit holes to be traveled down for those who care, with old message board posts from years ago uncovering a lot of discord between the various members, much of which seems to boil down to people having issues with Vast Aire.

Whatever the reasons for in-fighting and the subsequent demise of the crew, all members can likely agree that things would never have been the same again after Camu Tao died in 2008. Cage has officially stated how Tao's death was why he personally wanted The Weatherman to end, although his turbulent relationship with Eastern Conference was also possibly a factor. The Weathermen remains as one of hip-hop's biggest what-ifs, but in this instance the sum of all parts is greater than the whole, thanks to the crew having left a huge body of collaborations between the various members.

ANTIPOP CONSORTIUM

DJ Vadim set up the Jazz Fudge label in 1994 as a platform to release experimental music by himself and similar like-minded artists. And few groups on the New York underground hip-hop scene were as experimental as Antipop Consortium, who released *The Isolationist* album with DJ Vadim in 1999. The group saw their music as avant garde, but it was polarizing for some listeners, who considered it to be too electronic and too weird, not only 'anti pop' but also anti rap.

Antipop Consortium became a group in 1997 with three emcees (Beans, High Priest and M. Sayyid) and a producer, Earl Blaize. The group started by self-distributing mixtapes and bombing the city with stickers of their logo on a scale large enough for High Priest to catch a vandalism charge that landed him in jail.

After *The Isolationist*, the group signed to Dan The Automator's 75 Ark label and released their debut in 2000, *Tragic Epilogue*, and *Shopping Carts Crashing* in 2001. Antipop Consortium then signed with British indie Warp Records, releasing an EP named *The Ends Against The Middle* in 2001, and then their most critically lauded album, 2002's *Arrhythmia*. The group broke up before the release of their next album, *Antipop vs. Matthew Shipp*.

A 2009 reunion project and several tours have happened since, but thus far Antipop Consortium have been unable to recapture the excitement of their first run, regardless of how divisive they were at the time.

J-ZONE

Hip-hop is a form of expression that often covers uncomfortable and serious subjects, violence and politics, and also a forum for a lot of posturing about being tough or authentic. Consequently, there's never been much space for comedy or not taking yourself seriously. But comedy is very hard to do right, and those who do try tend to come off as gimmicky and tacky. Done correctly, however, with skilful delivery, witty bars and punchlines, and it can be very powerful. The music of Jay 'J-Zone' Mumford was somewhere in the middle: straight up hip-hop with lots of posturing, but very much tongue in cheek, with everybody who listened fully in the knowledge that J-Zone was a character and a satire of rap, not a real person. And it worked perfectly.

In the span of just a few years, J-Zone went on a tear of album and EP releases that were wildly entertaining and creative, each one well written and produced, despite the (intentionally) dumb titles. First came *Music for Tu Madre* (complete with a photo on the cover of Mumford's real grandmother flipping the bird to the camera) in 1998, followed by *A Bottle of Whup Ass* in 2000, *Pimps Don't Pay Taxes* in 2001, *$ick of Bein' Rich* in 2003, *A Job Ain't Nuthin but Work* in 2004, and *Gimme Dat Beat Fool: The J-Zone Remix Project* in 2005. All of these releases were on Mumford's own Old Maid Entertainment label, which also put out 12"s by two of his frequent collaborators, Huggy Bear and Al-Shid.

During the period, J-Zone also became a sought after producer, providing beats for many of the underground's biggest names, including MF Grimm, Cage, Prince Po, R.A. The Rugged Man and 7L & Esoteric, and for veteran emcees such as Casual and Biz Markie.

Mumford has been very open about the struggles of being an independent artist, including the need to maintain day jobs, and the humiliation of performing to just a handful of people at live shows. It makes for a refreshing change from the standard braggadocious persona of most rappers, and you can read about his journey through the rap game in his brutally honest 2011 book, *Root For The Villain: Rap, Bullshit and a Celebration of Failure*.

Mumford has distanced himself from the J-Zone character in recent years. The last album under the name was *Fish-n-Grits* in 2016, and since then Mumford has been focused on his work as a professional drummer, and as one half of group The Du-Rites.

J-LIVE

East Harlem born J-Live is a rapper's rapper, and this is evidenced by the huge number of artists who invited him onto their records as a guest emcee during the period. The list includes not just contemporaries such as El Da Sensei, J Rawls and DJ Nu-Mark, but also legendary figures like DJ Jazzy Jeff and DJ Prince Paul.

For a lot of rap heads, the gateway drug into New York's underground scene was provided when DJ Premier, Payday Records and Eric Haze released the compilation album *New York Reality Check 101* in 1997. Among the many influential 12" singles included on the playlist was J-Live's "Braggin Writes", which had been released two years previous via Raw Shack Productions. By 1999 J-Live was ready to release his first album, *The Best Part*, but an end to his deal with Raw Shack, and a later deal with Payday going nowhere, meant that it wasn't released until 2001, this time via J-Live's own label, Triple Threat Productions. It was worth the wait, as *The Best Part* garnered much praise.

The critical success inspired J-Live to keep the momentum going, and a year later in 2002 he released the *All of The Above* album, two EPs in 2003 (*Always Has Been* and *Always Will Be*), and his third album, 2005's *The Hear After*. Appearances on important albums like Handsome Boy Modelling School's *So... How's Your Girl?* in 1999 and DJ Jazzy Jeff's *The Magnificent* in 2002 further boosted J-Live's profile. Incredibly, much of this music was created at the same time that J-Live was employed as a teacher in Brooklyn.

Several albums have been released since, and J-Live is still releasing music today. It is generally an accepted fact that he has never made a bad album.

DJ SPINNA

Few artists in the indie rap era were as prolific as Brooklyn's DJ Spinna. The multi-hyphenate producer has worked across many different genres over several decades, but his hip-hop productions are among his most renowned creations, providing beats for many artists. His official debut, *Heavy Beats Volume 1*, came out on Rawkus Records in 1999, followed by several more albums and compilations, including two acclaimed editions of the *Beyond Real Experience* compilations, Beyond Real Recordings being the indie label he co-founded. In addition to his work as a producer for other artists, DJ Spinna was also a member of two influential groups, Jigmastas, and the Polyrhythm Addicts.

The Jigmastas was a duo in partnership with rapper Kriminul. They released a steady stream of 12" singles from 1996, some via Tommy Boy Black Label (a sub-label of the larger Tommy Boy Records), and some on Beyond Real Recordings. The duo released their debut album in 2000, *Grass Roots: Lyrical Fluctuation*, and another in 2002, *Infectious*.

Polyrhythm Addicts saw DJ Spinna join together with three emcees: Apani B. Fly, Shabaam Sahdeeq, and Mr. Complex. Their *Rhyme Related* album arrived in 1999 on Nervous Records/Wreck Records.

Queens based Apani B. Fly was a guest emcee on some of the era's most important albums, both before and after her work with DJ Spinna, including Black Star's *Mos Def & Talib Kweli Are Black Star* in 1998, Pharoahe Monch's *Internal Affairs* in 1999 (a relationship forged when Apani B. Fly provided additional vocals on 1997's *The Equinox* album by Monch's group, Organized Konfusion), Da Beatminerz's *Brace 4 Impak* in 2001 (all three of which came out on Rawkus), J. Rawls' *The Essence of J. Rawls* in 2002, and Viktor Vaughn's *Vaudeville Villain* in 2003. She also continued to work with DJ Spinna, and he produced on her 2003 album, *Story 2 Tell*.

Mr. Complex, also from Queens, had a run of 12"s, including some on Rawkus. He released *The Complex Catalog* in 2000 and *Hold This Down* in 2001, both on his own CoRecords label. This was followed by *Twisted Mister* in 2004, with all three albums including DJ Spinna productions.

Like DJ Spinna, Shabaam Sahdeeq hails from Brooklyn. And like his fellow Polyrhythm Addicts members, he had a relationship with Rawkus, who released his "Side 2 Side" b/w "Arabian Nights" 12" in 1997, and "Sound Clash" b/w "5 Star Generals" in 1998. The DJ Spinna produced "5 Star Generals" is significant for featuring Eminem just before he hit the big time a year later with *The Slim Shady LP*.

MASTA ACE

A few years after Kool Keith and Daniel Dumile had made the transition from 80s and early 90s artists to indie rap darlings, it was now time for another rapper from that same era to do the same, Brooklyn rhyme veteran Masta Ace.

After his original solo run ended, and his group Masta Ace Incorporated split up in 1996 – one year after the release of their final album, 1995's *Sittin' on Chrome* – Masta Ace spent several years consistently touring but not releasing any new music, save for a few stray singles here and there. He finally felt ready to release a new album in 2001, kicking off a string of expertly written and structured concept albums, and giving him a second career phase that is still going strong today. The first came in 2001 with the release of *Disposable Arts*, a narrative album with Masta Ace meeting many different characters played by several emcees. Masta Ace followed with his next concept piece in 2004, *A Long Hot Summer*.

Both of the albums were well received and brought Masta Ace to a new generation of fans. He was still intrinsically connected with the first golden era of rap, however, and this was celebrated with the release of *The Best of Cold Chillin: Masta Ace* in 2001, part of a series of compilations from Ace's former label that also included editions for fellow Juice Crew emcees Roxanne Shante, MC Shan, Kool G Rap, and Biz Markie. *A Long Hot Summer* had been released by Masta Ace's own indie label, M3 Records. The label released two compilations, first *Hits U Missed* in 2004, featuring songs from Ace's time away from the spotlight, followed by *Hits U Missed Vol. 2* in 2005, including unreleased tracks and mixtape cuts. During the promotional run for *Disposable Arts* in 2001, Masta Ace joined Wordsworth, Punchline, and Stricklin to form the group eMC, and their *The Show* album came out in 2008. Masta Ace still releases new music at a steady clip today, and tours around the world, making him one of only a few hip-hop artists to stay relevant for so many decades.

MIKE ZOOT

Most of the indie artists discussed here are still around in some capacity, while others seem to have disappeared entirely. Mike Zoot regrettably falls into the latter category. The Brooklyn emcee was a key name on the roster of Guesswhyld Records, dropping some memorable 12"s, chief among them the "High Drama" songs released between 1997-98. The "High Drama, Pt. 3: The Search For 2" installment is especially notable for featuring Mos Def, Talib Kweli, and Consequence, just two years on from his breakthrough appearances on A Tribe Called Quest's *Beats, Rhymes and Life*, and years before he started an up and down working relationship with Kanye West.

Other highlights of Mike Zoot's all too brief career include appearances on the acclaimed *Superrappin (The Album)* and

Superrappin (The Album Vol II) compilations on Groove Attack, and the "B-Boy Document" 12" by The High & Mighty, alongside Mos Def and El-P.

There are collections of Mike Zoot's Guesswhyld Records tracks available on streaming services today, but he no longer appears to be in the music business.

PUNCHLINE AND WORDSWORTH

The date of September 29, 1998, is celebrated by fans and hip-hop historians alike as the most significant album release date in the genre's lifetime, as Outkast's *Aquemini*, Jay-Z's *Vol. 2...Hard Knock Life*, Brand Nubian's *The Foundation*, A Tribe Called Quest's *The Love Movement* and *Mos Def & Talib Kweli Are Black Star* all came out on that day. Perhaps even more impressive is that Brooklyn emcees Wordsworth and Punchline appear on two of those classic albums (*The Love Movement* and *Mos Def & Talib Kweli Are Black Star*). They formed a duo in 1998 and featured on *Lyricist Lounge, Volume One* before releasing the *Punch N' Words* EP in 2000. That same year they then appeared separately on *Lyricist Lounge 2*.

Wordsworth and Punchline also started a long-running collaboration with Masta Ace when they featured on his 2001 *Disposable Arts* album, and a few years later all three became members of the aforementioned group eMC (Punchline left in 2014, however). Wordsworth then branched back out on his own, featuring on Prince Paul's *Politics of the Business* in 2003, and on Masta Ace's *A Long Hot Summer* in 2004, among several other records. His solo debut came in 2005, named *Mirror Music*, and there have been multiple albums since.

PUMPKINHEAD

When Park Slope, Brooklyn emcee Robert 'Pumpkinhead' Diaz died in 2015 at just 39 years of age, it cut short the brief but impactful career of one of the underground's best battle rappers. After getting some traction with the "Dynamic" 12" in 1997, Pumpkinhead released his debut album in 2001, *The Old Testament*. Next came an EP named *Beautiful Mind* and a few self-released mixtapes between 2002-2004, before he broke through on a wider level with his second album, 2005's *Orange Moon Over Brooklyn*. Benefitting from the backing of label Soulspazm and distribution via Rawkus Records, the album received positive reviews across the board. *Orange Moon Over Brooklyn* is also notable for being one of the first significant albums produced by Marco Polo, who has since gone on to be a prolific producer. Pumpkinhead later released more albums and collaborated several times with Immortal Technique and Jean Grae.

His death, just a decade on from the release of *Orange Moon Over Brooklyn*, is said to have been caused by complications during preparation for surgery. It was a heartbreaking loss, and another example of a rapper being gone way too early.

SEAN PRICE

One could easily write an entire book about the life and music of Sean Price. In addition to being a highly skilled emcee, everyone who ever worked with Price seems to agree he was a funny, eccentric character and a great human being, all of which makes it even more sad he is no longer with us. Brooklyn through and through, Price was a member of the Boot Camp Clik – alongside Black Moon's Buckshot, both members of the group Smif-N-Wessun

(Tek and Steele), Rock, and all three members of the Originoo Gunn Clappaz (Starang Wondah, Louieville Sluggah and Top Dog) – and landed on most radars when he appeared on Smif-N-Wessun's 1995 album, *Dah Shinin*. The following year Price released his debut album *Nocturnal* with Rock as the duo Heltah Skeltah, with Price using the name Ruck.

The debut Boot Camp Clik album came out in 1997, named *For The People*, followed by Heltah Skeltah's second album, 1998's *Magnum Force*. It would be a decade before another Heltah Skeltah album arrived, but Price used the hiatus to launch a solo career.

After Boot Camp Clik released *The Chosen Few* in 2002, Price dropped the Ruck name and started recording simply as Sean Price. The first of several mixtapes came in 2004 (*Donkey Sean Jr.*), and his official solo debut, *Monkey Bars*, was released in 2005.

Several more albums followed before Price's death, including *Random Axe* in 2011, released as part of a group of the same name with Detroit's Black Milk and Guilty Simpson.

Sean Price died in August 2015. Since then, his widow Bernadette has worked hard to keep his legacy alive, giving her blessing to several posthumous albums.

SCREWBALL

Rappers going to great lengths to prove how tough they are is a staple trope in hip-hop, but some come across as more genuine than others, with street credentials to back it up. You would not want to fuck around, for instance, with Bumpy Knuckles or either member of the group M.O.P. if their music and reputation is anything to go by. Screwball, hailing from the infamous Queensbridge Houses, were also in this category, especially since their breakout 12" is named "F.A.Y.B.A.N. (Fuck All You Bitch Ass Niggas)". That record, along with the equally hard hitting "H-O-S-T-Y-L-E", came out in 1999 via Hydra Entertainment, who had been releasing Screwball 12"s since 1996. Hydra was also the home of Screwball members KL and Solo's previous group, Kamikaze.

Screwball's debut, *Y2K: The Album* (2000) instead came out on Tommy Boy Records, providing budget for several high profile producers, and features from many of the most respected emcees from Queensbridge Houses.

By the time Screwball released their next album in 2001, *Loyalty*, they were no longer signed to Tommy Boy Records. The new album came out instead via Hydra Entertainment, with distribution by Landspeed Records. It is another Queens-heavy affair, but this time had more significant input from Godfather Don.

A compilation of old, unreleased and remixed tracks came out in 2004 named *Screwed Up*, as did the *One Eyed Maniac* album by group member Hostyle, both on Hydra. Screwball is sadly another group that has faced tragedy. Two of the four members have since passed away: KL in 2008, and Hostyle in 2020. Of the surviving members Blaq Poet has released many projects since, but Solo appears to have called it quits.

INI

Despite its close proximity to the Bronx, there are not many rap industry people from Mount Vernon, New York. The few there are, however, have made a big impact. Puff Daddy and Heavy D were both raised there, as was Heavy's cousin, Pete Rock. Had it not been for some typical industry bullshit, more people would also remember another hip-hop act from Mount Vernon, Ini. The group was formed early in the 90s with a line-up of Grap Luva (Pete Rock's brother), Rob-O, DJ Boodahkan, Ras G, and Marco Polo (this Ras G is not to be confused with the late producer of the same name from Los Angeles, and the Marco Polo here is a different person to Canadian producer Marco Polo). Grap Luva and Rob-O both appeared on Pete Rock & CL Smooth's seminal *Mecca and the Soul Brother* album in 1992, and the group was briefly signed to Rock's Soul Brother Records.

When Rock left Elektra Records (who were set to distribute his label) after a falling out, it scuppered the release of InI's debut album, *The Life I Live*, irrespective of the moderate success achieved by the single "Fakin Jax". The album eventually came out years later as a bootleg under the name *Centre of Attention*, first in 2003 as part of a collection of unreleased Pete Rock works named *Lost & Found: Hip Hop Underground Soul Classics*, and finally in 2016 as a standalone album. It still stands today as the one and only InI album.

Most of the group subsequently disappeared from rap. Rob-O released several singles and an album (*Superspectacular*) before becoming a fireman. Grab Luva is still active, with a sizable catalog of music across various labels.

JEAN GRAE

Being the daughter of two renowned musicians and having formal performing arts training, Cape Town born, New York raised Tsidi Ibrahim was well positioned to make it in the music business, but you don't need prestigious education or nepotism when you are as naturally multi talented as Ibrahim, who hip-hop heads know better as Jean Grae.

After gaining minor buzz as a member of the groups Ground

Zero and Natural Resource, back when Grae rapped under the name What? What?, Jean's full debut came with *Attack of the Attacking Things* in 2002 on Third Earth Music. Jean Grae followed up a year later with *The Bootleg of the Bootleg* EP, featuring a rapper who would go on to collaborate with Jean several times, Pumpkinhead.

Wider attention and acclaim was received for *This Week* in 2004, this time released by the larger indie outfit Babygrande. The album connected Jean Grae with producer 9th Wonder, who by now was running hot thanks to the success of his group Little Brother and high-profile placements on albums by Jay-Z and Destiny's Child. Jean Grae and 9th Wonder then made a full album together, *Jeanius*, but record label issues and several rounds of leaked unfinished versions meant that the final product didn't materialize until 2008.

There hasn't been much new music from Jean Grae in recent years (apart from the *Everything's Fine* album with Quelle Chris in 2018), and today the artist is mostly focused on acting and stage performance. Jean's presence on the microphone is missed, but Jean is adamant they won't return to rap.

NATURAL ELEMENTS

If rap was originally a singles-led genre, then Natural Elements were a throwback, having never released a proper album. The difference is that for Natural Elements it was unintentional. Although at first consisting of multiple members, the group is most remembered for the line-up that still exists today: L Swift (later known as Swigga), Mr. Voodoo, and A-Butta, raised in the Bronx, Brooklyn, and Harlem respectively.

The main producer of the group was Charlemagne (a different person to the radio personality), who put out the first Natural

Elements record in 1994, *The EP*, via his Fortress Entertainment label. Then, after a short stint on Dolo Records, the group signed to Tommy Boy Black Label and started recording their first album. It wasn't to be, however, with delays and creative differences between them and the label eventually leading to the group walking away. Some years later, a selection of tracks that would have been on the album appeared as part of a 2009 compilation named *1999: 10 Year Anniversary*.

Another of the original members of the wider Natural Elements crew was Brownsville emcee Ka. He left the group in the mid-90s, but then reemerged with a solo album named *Iron Works* in 2008. From then on, Ka became one of rap's most beloved artists, an enigmatic talent who every couple of years dropped a brilliant new album almost unannounced, before disappearing back into the wilderness. He died unexpectedly in 2024.

X-ECUTIONERS

The history of turntablists The X-Ecutioners goes back to the late 80s. Known then as the X-Men, it was more a collective than a group, with many different members. By the mid-90s the name had been changed to The X-Ecutioners (because no one wants get sued by Marvel Comics) and the line-up condensed to an even four members: Mista Sinista, Roc Raida, Rob Swift, and Total Eclipse, all from New York City.

Their acclaimed debut *X-Pressions* was released in 1997 via San Francisco based indie label Asphodel, followed by *Built from Scratch* in 2002 and *Revolutions* in 2004, although by now Mista Sinista had left the group. In between group releases, Rob Swift put out several solo albums, including the highly acclaimed *Soulful*

Fruit in 1997 as one of the first significant releases on Stones Throw Records, and 1999's *The Ablist*.

Roc Raida also released several albums during this period, but died in 2009 as a result of a freak accident while training martial arts. DJ Total Eclipse has kept The X-Ecutioners name going with new members in recent years, but the group was never the same once Roc Raida had gone and Rob Swift had left.

SIR MENELIK

If Kool Keith is the master of rap alter egos and aliases, then his friend and frequent collaborator Phillip Collington is his apprentice. Collington has made records under many different guises, but he's best remembered for his work using the names Sir Menelik, Cyclops 4000, and Scaramanga. As Sir Menelik, he appeared on several tracks on Kool Keith's classic Dr. Octagon album, *Dr. Octagonecologyst,* in 1996, and on Keith's *Sex Style* a year later in 1997. The appearances were enough to get Collington noticed by Rawkus, who dropped several acclaimed 12"s by him as 'Sir Menelik AKA Cyclops 4000' (including "Space Cadillac" b/w "Nightwork" and "Physical Jewels" b/w "So Intelligent" in 1997). Two of those tracks also featured on *Soundbombing*, and the relationship with Rawkus extended when Sir Menelik and Kool Keith were invited to 'host' CD 2 of the *Lyricist Lounge, Volume One* compilation in 1998.

There was also a Sir Menelik track on *Soundbombing II* in 1999, but after that Collington began releasing records on his own label, Sun Large Music. The debut Scaramanga album, *Seven Eyes, Seven Horns*, came out in 1998, including collaborations with Godfather Don, followed by *Snake-Eyes* in 2005. It is unclear if the man of many names is still making music today.

INFAMOUS MOBB

It didn't take much to figure out that when Infamous Mobb were introduced in 1994, the group were piggybacking on the reputation of Mobb Deep. Infamous Mobb did have credible connections with the more famous duo, however, having made minor contributions to Mobb Deep's classic *The Infamous* album in 1994, and featuring more significantly on subsequent Mobb Deep albums *Hell On Earth* (1996), *Murda Muzik* (1999) and *Infamy* (2001). They also featured on the 1996 *Episodes of a Hustla* album by another Mobb Deep affiliate, Big Noyd.

Infamous Mobb was made up of four members, all from Queensbridge: Ty Nitty, Godfather Part III., and real life twin brothers Twin Gambino (now known as Big Twins) and Twin Scarface. Tragically, Twin Scarface was killed in 1996 before he had a chance to record much music with the group.

Infamous Mobb's debut *Special Edition* came out in 2002 on their own IM3 label, with both members of Mobb Deep (Havoc and the late Prodigy) making appearances. The album also featured heavy production from Alchemist, and he and Twin Gambino would work together several more times, including on the memorable "Different Worlds" 12" in 2001.

JEMINI THE GIFTED ONE

Jemini the Gifted One had to wait a while before he got his chance to shine. He recorded an EP named *Scars and Pain* in 1995 which attracted some attention, and had contributions from Organized Konfusion and Buckwild. It would be another eight years before Jemini the Gifted One got his breakout moment thanks to a collaboration with a producer on the cusp of bigger things.

Danger Mouse had been making remixes of other people's songs for several years when he signed to UK indie Lex Records. From 2004 onwards Danger Mouse caused a sensation with *The Grey Album*, his *The Mouse & The Mask* album with MF DOOM, the Gnarls Barkley project with Cee-Lo, production for Gorillaz, Beck and many more. Before any of that, he and Jemini the Gifted One made *Ghetto Pop Life*. Recognizing the quality of the record, and perhaps sensing that Danger Mouse was about to blow up, Lex Records went all in for *Ghetto Pop Life*, enhancing the release with three EPs of remixes, and a mix CD.

Many years later in 2023, Jemini the Gifted One and Danger Mouse released a second album, *Born Again*. If the new album sounded like the artists were starting right where they left off, it was because they were. The sessions for *Born Again* were from 2003-2004, recorded just after *Ghetto Pop Life* came out.

Ghetto Pop Life proved to be the pinnacle of Jemini the Gifted One's career, but *Scars and Pain* did at least get a reissue in 2023 via 90's Tapes/HHV.

———

The New York artists covered in this chapter were the main players in the underground from 1995-2005, but there was also a strong supporting cast of other artists from New York who dropped excellent music in the timeframe. It would be remiss not to include them, so here they are (listed alphabetically, as all are of equal importance), with one highlight from their discography: AK Skills ("East Ta West"), Black Attack ("My Crown"), Brainsick Enterprize/Brainsick Mob ("Playin' For Keeps"), Breeze Evahflowin ("Forsaken"), Dutchmin ("Surrounded"), Dysfunkshunal Famile (*Mixed Emotions*), East Flatbush Project ("Tried By 12"), Finsta Bundy ("Feel the High"),

G-Depp ("Head Over Wheels"), I.G. Off & Hazadous ("Hip-hop Till I Die"), L-Fudge ("What If?"), Lace Da Booms ("Cut That Weak Shit"), Missin' Linx ("M.I.A."), Neek The Exotic (*Exotic's Raw*), Rezidue ("Inner City Blues"), Shades of Brooklyn ("Change"), Street Smartz ("Metal Thangz"), Thirstin Howl III ("Brooklyn Hard Rock"), and Yak Ballz ("Home Piss").

Author's Note: Several of the key albums and 12"s discussed in the previous pages are looked at in more detail in the What's Golden chapter later.

4

CALI AGENTS

CALIFORNIA

I n 2024 a battle raged between officials in Oakland and San Francisco over the naming of an airport. After close to a century in operation, the owners of Metropolitan Oakland International Airport proposed a name change that would solve the problem of many international travelers never actually having heard of Oakland, or knowing where it is. After several rounds of consultation and fierce debate the owners got their way and the name of the airport was officially changed to San Francisco Bay Oakland International Airport. Fans of hip-hop have no trouble knowing about Oakland, thanks to decades worth of good rap music having been made there. Due to another local airport related incident, however, the direction of Oakland hip-hop history may have turned out differently, and one of the best live rap battles may never have happened.

The much bigger San Francisco International Airport – the one the newly-renamed San Francisco Bay Oakland International Airport is now trying to ride the tails of – was a point of call for many flights operated by Trans World Airlines in the 1990s, and on the evening of July 30, 1992, scheduled flight TWA 843 was due to arrive from JFK. Unfortunately, the flight barely left the tarmac in New York when the airplane – a Lockheed L-1011 Tristar, which had a solid safety record – crashed on the runway and burst into flames after an aborted take off went spectacularly wrong. There were no fatalities but several passengers sustained injuries, including Oakland local Reggie Gibson, who hurt his back during the emergency evacuation. The intensity of the fire destroyed the Lockheed, showing how deadly the accident could have been had passengers and crew not followed evacuation procedures.

If Reggie Gibson hadn't made it out of that plane alive, it would have cut short his promising career in the rap world, where he was better known as the emcee Saafir. By the time of the crash, Saafir had been steadily building his reputation, working with Digital Underground, hanging out with 2Pac, and forming his crew, Hobo Junction. And if TWA flight 843 had denied the world Hobo Junction, then their explosive battle with the rival Hieroglyphics crew, live on radio in 1994, would never have happened. It was a battle for the ages that featured several of the main protagonists in the deep and sprawling story of Californian underground rap. A story that began around the same time Reggie Gibson got on that plane.

FREESTYLE FELLOWSHIP AND PROJECT BLOWED

The west coast has been synonymous with gangster rap ever since a young Ice-T heard Philadelphia emcee Schoolly D's "P.S.K. What Does It Mean?" in 1985 and decided to import the sound to the streets of South Central Los Angeles. By 1994, thanks to the major success of Ice Cube, Dr. Dre and the rest of N.W.A., Snoop Doggy Dogg, Above the Law, Mack 10, WC, E40, Too Short, 2Pac, and more, the average hip-hop fan could have been forgiven for thinking that rappers from California solely made gangster rap and nothing else.

There was, in fact, a buzzing underground scene, largely centered around a health food cafe in the Leimert Park neighborhood of Los Angeles. The Good Life Cafe had been running an open mic night every week since the late 80s, a notoriously brutal training ground for budding rappers, who only had a short window in which to impress the crowd, or else succumb to vicious booing and heckling. Some of rap's biggest stars graced the stage of the Good Life Cafe early in their careers, including Snoop Dogg and will.i.am, but the venue was also renowned for being the home of the godfathers of L.A. independent hip-hop, Freestyle Fellowship.

Having met in the 80s, Aceyalone, Myka 9, P.E.A.C.E., and Self Jupiter honed their skills at the Good Life Cafe before releasing their classic 1991 debut, *To Whom It May Concern..*, on an independent label named Sun Music. The album was critically acclaimed, and by the time the group released their next album, 1993's *Innercity Griots*, Freestyle Fellowship had established themselves as the leaders of Los Angeles' *other* hip-hop scene, providing an alternative listening experience for those who wanted something deeper and more thought-provoking than the rampant violence and misogyny of gangster rap.

It wasn't that the members of Freestyle Fellowship had not had the same lived experiences as those making gangster rap. They had, but simply decided to express themselves and their surroundings in a different way, with eclectic lyrics and rhyme patterns, influenced by freeform jazz.

Outside of the group dynamic, each member of Freestyle Fellowship has released their own impressive solo albums, especially Aceyalone. His debut, *All Balls Don't Bounce*, came out in 1995, including contributions from Freestyle Fellowship and a range of producers associated with the Good Life Cafe. Like several other underground groups at the time, the moderate buzz of Freestyle Fellowship's music got the attention of the major labels, *All Balls Don't Bounce* subsequently coming out on Capitol. Amongst the list of collaborators on the album was acclaimed producer Mumbles, and he and Aceyalone went on to release the lauded *A Book of Human Language* album in 1998. If *A Book of Human Language* leaned towards a jazz-influenced sound, Aceyalone was back to a more straight up underground feel on 2001's *Accepted Electric* album, working with his Freestyle Fellowship brothers but also with Dilated People's Evidence, and producer Joey Chavez. This was followed a year later by another one-producer project, *Hip Hop and the World We Live In,* this time with Elusive, before Aceyalone returned again to more familiar territory with 2003's *Love & Hate.*

Myka 9 (sometimes alternatively spelled as Mikah Nine, Mikah 9 or Myka Nyne on early releases) was also busy during this time, starting with his debut in 1999, *It's All Love,* followed by *Timetable* in 2001, and *A Work In Progress* in 2003. *Timetable* is perhaps the most notable, not just because it is great, but also for the involvement of Los Angeles' most important independent artists, including the rest of Freestyle Fellowship, Jurassic 5 producer Cut Chemist, Daddy Kev, and turntablist D-Styles.

P.E.A.C.E. released his own debut in 1999, *Southern Fry'd Chicken*, and *Megabite* in 2004, the latter being released by another important indie hip-hop label of the era, Battle Axe Records. Self Jupiter's solo debut came in 2000 with *Hard Hat Area*, which highlighted his skill at spoken word poetry.

The group's influence, and the wealth of like minded talent coming through the doors of the Good Life Cafe, resulted in the creation of one of California's most creative rap collectives, Project Blowed, with Freestyle Fellowship considered the de facto leaders.

The sheer breadth of artists laying claim to membership of Project Blowed in the mid-90s makes it difficult to know who was an official member and who wasn't, but the tracklist of the *Project Blowed* compilation, produced in 1994, introduced most of the crew's brightest stars. Freestyle Fellowship members dominated the playlist, especially Aceyalone, but outside of the group, the other name that appears most is Abstract Rude. Although it would take until 2009 for Abstract Rude to release a solo album (*Rejuvenation*), he was key to the first few years of the Project Blowed movement, firstly as a member of the group Abstract Tribe Unique. Also featuring DJ Drez and Fat Jack, the group released five albums between 1996-2003, with 1997's *Mood Pieces* a particular highlight. DJ Drez and Fat Jack have mostly since faded from people's memories, but Abstract Rude's prolific run of albums, EPs and mixtapes form the backbone of Project Blowed's legacy.

In addition to Abstract Tribe Unique, Abstract Rude recorded collaborative projects with several other crew members, especially Aceyalone, with whom he formed the duo The A Team, releasing *Who Framed The A-Team?* in 1999, and *Lab Down Under* in 2003. He also branched out in 2001 to record an album with two members of Canadian underground group Swollen Members, Moka Only and Prevail, under the name *Code Name: Scorpion*.

In the same year that Abstract Rude and Aceyalone released the first The A Team album, they also formed another subgroup, this time joined by Myka 9. Named Haiku d'Etat, their self-titled 1999 album incorporated live instrumentation with contributions from several renowned session musicians, while their second and last album, *Coup de Theatre*, featured production by Abstract Rude's Abstract

Tribe Unique bandmates, Fat Jack and DJ Drez. The album is also notable for the track "Top Qualified", where the group is joined by members of another premiere west coast underground crew, Quannum Projects. Coup de Theatre also features early work from Kenny Segal, who today is one of the most respected producers in the latest generation of talent to originate from Project Blowed.

Another group skilled enough to stand out from the multiple artists emerging from the Project Blowed collective in the mid 90s was The Nonce (an unfortunate choice of name for rap heads from the UK, where that word means something very bad), made up of emcees Yusef Afloat and Nouka Basetype, both from Los Angeles. The group had some buzz with their 12" "Mix Tapes" in 1994, a quintessential underground hip-hop record that introduced them as ones to watch. When The Nonce were ready to release their full length album in 1995, *World Ultimate*, label backing came from an unlikely and fortuitous place. Producer Rick Rubin – who had already secured his place in the history of rap music thanks to co-founding Def Jam Recordings and his work with Run-DMC, LL Cool J, Public Enemy, Beastie Boys and countless others – had largely moved on to rock and heavy metal by 1995. His American Recordings label did, however, still have a hand in hip-hop, and it was their sub-label Wild West Records who released *World Ultimate*. The album is a masterclass of rhyming, further cementing the reputation of Project Blowed as being an incubator of raw talent.

World Ultimate is strictly focused on Yusef Afloat and Nouka Basetype, but has uncredited input from Aceyalone, and another act that is an important footnote in the history of the Good Life Cafe, the group Figures of Speech. Women emcees had been a fixture of the open mic nights at the cafe since inception, including Medusa, and both members of Figures of Speech; Eve and Jyant.

Figures of Speech's rap career was fleeting, but Eve would go on to become a successful filmmaker under her real name, Ava DuVernay. Her 2008 documentary *This is the Life* provides a rich history of the Good Life Cafe.

The Nonce additionally released an EP named *The Sight of Things* in 1998, and although it didn't surface until 2018, the duo's *1990* captures the rawness of their earliest recordings. The group came to a sad end in 2000 with the death of Yusef Afloat at just 28 years of age. Decades later, the mystery of how his lifeless body ended up next to a Los Angeles freeway has never been solved.

Other breakout artists from the ranks of Project Blowed included Busdriver, Pigeon John, and Nocando, all of whom released impressive albums and EPs during the period. In 2005, the history of the crew was celebrated with the release of another compilation, *Project Blowed: 10th Anniversary*. The stacked tracklist is a fitting tribute to how the collective began and how far it had come, featuring the latest generation of recruits alongside Freestyle Fellowship, Abstract Tribe Unique, and other founding members.

The legacy of Project Blowed still lives on today in the music of many different artists who had a connection to its various core members, including 2Mex of the group The Visionaries, Open Mike Eagle, and members of the Hellfyre Club. The spirit of the collective also lived on for years after the Good Life Cafe closed in 1999, in particular at the Low End Theory club night, where producers such as Dibia\$e, Daddy Kev and the late Ras G all cut their teeth, before that event also closed shop for good in 2018.

The long lasting impact of Freestyle Fellowship was bookended in 2023 when *To Whom It May Concern...* was nominated in the Best Historical Album category at the GRAMMY Awards. They ultimately lost out to Wilco's *Yankee Hotel Foxtrot*, but it was a nice bit of recognition from an organization with a patchy history when it comes to celebrating hip-hop. Photos from the night show how much the occasion meant to the group, each member enjoying their moment in the spotlight.

HIEROGLYPHICS

If California's underground hip-hop scene aspired to be the opposite of what gangster rap was about, the family tree of Teren Delvon Jones provided an unlikely bridge between these two different worlds. Jones, better known as Del The Funky Homosapien, was born and raised in Oakland but had family in Los Angeles, including a cousin named O'Shea Jackson, who the world knows better as Ice Cube. The artist Del would become – a unique, eclectic talent who helped create the image of what a smart, semi-nerdy underground rapper looks like – was about as far removed from the image of Ice Cube, the hard-edged pioneer of gangster rap, as you could get. Yet Del's skill as a writer saw Ice Cube assign him ghostwriter duties on songs by Cube's protégés, Da Lench Mob. Ice Cube was also an executive producer on Del's debut album in 1991, *I Wish My Brother George Was Here*.

Ice Cube was no longer part of Del's creative process by the release of his next album, 1993's *No Need For Alarm*, replaced instead with a new collective that Del founded when he was recording *I Wish My Brother George Was Here*, a crew that would become one of indie rap's most influential dynasties, Oakland's Hieroglyphics crew. The classic Hieroglyphics line-up – the one that still tours together today – is Del, Casual, Domino, Pep Love, and the four members of the group Souls of Mischief: A-Plus, Opio, Phesto and Tajai. The first song credited to the group was "Burnt", a b-side on the Billboard-charting single "Mistadobalina" from *I Wish My Brother George Was Here,* with A-Plus, Casual, Opio and Tajai all making an appearance on the track.

The crew had known each other for years before that, however, with some members having been friends since high school, and some even further than that, right back to kindergarten. The story goes that the original name for the crew was to be The Maad Circle (not to be confused with a different west coast rap group, WC and the Maad Circle), but the far cooler name of Hieroglyphics became available when one of their peers who was already using the name decided to quit rapping. In the early days of the crew there were also three additional members: Snupe, Mike G, and Jay-Biz. All three would eventually part ways with the crew, but not before making their mark. Snupe produced a track on *No Need For Alarm*, and he and Mike G also formed the sub-group Extra Prolific, releasing *Like It Should Be* in 1994. Jay-Biz also produced on *No Need For Alarm*, and years later in 2003 recorded *The Shamen* album with Pep Love.

No Need For Alarm also included tracks produced by Casual and Domino, who would become the driving musical forces of the Hieroglyphics, plus a track produced by A-Plus. His group, Souls of Mischief, released their classic album *93 'til Infinity* in 1993, bringing Hieroglyphics to wider attention and acclaim. Souls of Mischief had formed during high school, with Tajai and A-Plus having known each other the longest. Opio and Phesto joined later, and at some point the group decided to ditch their original name of The Syndicate in favor of Souls of Mischief.

Casual released his own acclaimed album in 1994, *Fear Itself,* with input from multiple crew members, followed a year later by Souls of Mischief's second album, *No Man's Land.*

Capitalizing on the growing popularity of various members, Hieroglyphics began releasing a series of crew compilation tapes in 1996, including *Hiero Oldies Vol. 1*, and *Hiero B Sides* and *Live.97* in 1997. Also in 1997 came the release of the second Casual album, *Meanwhile...*, and the *Future Development* album by Del The Funky Homosapien. *Future Development* was significant in the Hieroglyphics story because it was released on the crew's own indie label, Hieroglyphics Imperium Recordings, whereas Del's first two albums had been released by the much bigger Elektra. Souls of Mischief followed suit by releasing their third album, 1998's *Focus*, on Hieroglyphics Imperium Recordings (*93 'til Infinity* and *No Man's Land* had come out on the famed Jive Records).

In 1998 the crew dropped Vol. 2 of *Hiero Oldies*, and also finally released their first fully-fledged group album, *3rd Eye Vision*. The album was a critical and commercial success, at least by indie album standards, and included group tracks and solo songs that allowed individual members to shine.

The first year of the new millennium kicked off a very active decade for Hiero. Highlights included Souls of Mischief's fourth album, *Trilogy: Conflict, Climax, Resolution*, and the first of many solo albums by members of the four-man group. Tajai released two projects in 2000, *Projecto: 2501* and *Nuntype*, both of them collaborations with SupremeEx, the alter ego of producer Yameen Friedberg. That same year Del The Funky Homosapien released his fourth album. Although it featured heavy input from the rest of Hiero, Del also worked with both Prince Paul and El-P on *Both Sides of The Brain*. The relationship with El-P later led to Del's 2008 *Eleventh Hour* album coming out on Definitive Jux. The year 2000 was also when Del released his most ambitious album. He formed the group Deltron 3030 with San Francisco producer Dan the Automator and Canadian deejay Kid Koala, and they released their esoteric, other-worldly concept album *Deltron 3030* on 75 Ark.

Casual came out with his third album, *He Think He Raw*, in 2001. Pep Love, meanwhile, released his first album that same year, titled *Ascension*. Pep Love worked with original Hiero member Jay-Biz on two *Ascension* tracks, and the album also featured Evidence and The Grouch, therefore crossing paths with members from two of California's other leading underground rap collectives, the Likwit Crew and Living Legends, respectively.

Another retrospective Hiero compilation tape arrived in 2002, *Hiero Classix Vol. 1*, before the second full crew album, in 2003. *Full Circle* was another triumph, and proved Hiero had lost none of their collective power in the five years since their debut. Pep Love topped off the year with *The Shamen* album from him and Jay-Biz, plus his second solo album, *Ascension Side C*.

The next Souls of Mischief solo album arrived in 2004 with Opio's *Masterpiece Theatre*. The album included a crossover with another of Cali's premiere rap crews, this time members of Quannum Projects on the track "Extravaganza." Additional 2004 releases came in the shape of another Hiero compilation, *The Building*, and *Truck Driver*, Casual's fourth album. The production credits for *Truck Driver* include a track by the SD50's, aka the Stimulated Dummies. The three-man production crew included the late John Gamble and Geeby Dajani, and famed hip-hop A&R man, Dante Ross. They produced on both *Truck Driver* and *He Think He Raw*, their work with Casual providing a nice callback to the early Hiero days when the SD50's produced on Del The Funky Homosapien's *No Need For Alarm*.

2005 was another flagship year for the collective with another compilation, *The Corner*, and a live album, *Full Circle Tour*. Tajai

120

finally released his proper solo debut, *Power Movement*, followed shortly after by *Power Movement Remixes*. His Souls of Mischief cohort Opio released *Triangulation Station*, while Casual dropped *Smash Rockwell*, and Pep Love released *The Foundation*. *Smash Rockwell* is notable for featuring guest verses from some of the Bay Area's most famous rappers, including Too Short, E-40 and Richie Rich, alongside the obligatory Hiero contributions.

There have been countless other Hiero-related albums since 2005, and today the crew are still highly regarded as pioneers of California indie rap. The distinctive 'third-eye' logo is itself iconic, recognized all over the world..

SAAFIR AND HOBO JUNCTION

Having survived the earlier mentioned plane crash in 1992, Saafir focused on his rap career, and his affiliation with Oakland legends Digital Underground saw him feature heavily on their third album, 1993's *The Body-Hat Syndrome*. Being from Oakland meant that Saafir would inevitably be operating in the same circles as Hieroglyphics, and he duly appeared on the track "That Bullshit" from Casual's *Fear Itself*.

Saafir released his debut album with *Boxcar Sessions* in 1994, via Qwest Records, a label founded by Qunicy Jones with backing from Warner Bros. Records. *Boxcar Sessions* was also the platform through which to introduce Saafir's own collective, Hobo Junction. A sizable group of emcees and beatmakers, the crew released their *Limited Edition* album in 1995, a showcase for the various members. Several low key releases followed in subsequent years, including *The Black Label* in 1998 and *The Cleaners* in 1999.

What most people now remember Hobo Junction for, however,

is the epic rap battle they took part in 1994. Saafir might have been down with Hieroglyphics, but hip-hop is a competitive sport, where rappers battle to prove their skills. Tensions and rivalry had been bubbling between Saafir and Casual, and both emcees were invited to battle live on air as part of the influential *The Wake Up Show* hosted by deejays Sway and Tech on the radio station KMEL. Casual brought along members of Hiero, and Saafir came with Hobo Junction, and each crew went hard at the other with various verbal beatdowns and vicious bars. The jury is still out on the winner, with both sides faring better than the other at various points. Hip-hop was the real winner, being gifted one of the most thrilling live battles in its decades-long history. You can find a short documentary named *The Battle* from 2021 on YouTube, where director Shomari Smith breaks down the history of the event.

Saafir followed up *Boxcar Sessions* with *Trigonometry* in 1998 (released under the name Mr. No No instead of Saafir), and *The Hit List* a year later in 1999. Both albums featured collaborations with Digital Underground leader and rap icon Shock G, and he and Saafir appeared to have remained close until Shock G's death in 2021. Saafir himself had been suffering from his own health issues for decades, including paralysis that left him wheelchair bound. He died in late 2024, aged 54.

Mirroring how Del The Funky Homosapien got his start in the rap game via an unlikely route, there's a similar plot point in the story of Hobo Junction. In addition to being associated with the early days of the crew, and a family relative of Saafir, Hobo Junction member King Saan later formed the duo The WhoRidas with Mr. Taylor. Their 1997 debut album, *Whoridin'*, is a gangster rap record, and therefore at odds with the typical Hobo Junction sound.

LIKWIT CREW

King T was already a rap legend when he released his third album, *Tha Triflin' Album*, in January, 1993. Compton born and raised, King T had helped establish Los Angeles as the home of west coast gangster rap in the 1980s, alongside Ice-T, N.W.A. and Above The Law, taking the attention of listeners away from New York for the first time.

Tha Triflin' Album features contributions from fellow west coast icons Ice Cube, DJ Pooh and DJ Aladdin, but also allowed for King T to introduce a group of protégés named Tha Alkaholiks, who appear on two tracks. The trio, made up of Tash, J-Ro and E-Swift, would go on to release their debut album, *21 & Over*, later that same year, and the guest feature on King T's album was the promotional push they needed. When *21 & Over* dropped Tha Alkaholiks not only returned the favor to King T by featuring him on two tracks, they also showcased some new talent themselves on the track "Turn Tha Party Out", a young and fresh group known as Lootpack. The song, combined with Tha Alkaholiks' appearance on *Tha Triflin' Album,* were foundational moments not just in the career of one of the most respected producers in hip-hop, but also the creation of one of the genre's most creative collectives; a loosely affiliated cadre of rappers, producers and deejays known as the Likwit Crew.

Tha Alkaholiks would find a modicum of commercial success in the years after *21 & Over*, as would other members of the collective, including rapper Xzibit, who later found huge success working with Dr. Dre and presenting the TV show *Pimp My Ride*. Mostly, however, the Likwit Crew was firmly rooted in the underground.

While King T was from Compton and Tha Alkaholiks from Los Angeles, Lootpack were representing the city of Oxnard, hardly known for its hip-hop pedigree. Nonetheless, the three members of the group, Madlib, Wildchild and DJ Romes, were making a mark on the local music scene, and convinced Madlib's father to fund the release of their first 12" record in 1996. They also continued building their rep as part of the Likwik Crew, guesting on the track "WLIX", which Madlib also co-produced, from Tha Alkaholiks second album, 1995's *Coast II Coast*.

By 1999 Lootpack were ready to release their own debut album and by now had been courted by Stones Throw Records. The label – founded by producer Peanut Butter Wolf – would end the 2000s as the premier destination for quality underground hip-hop, but were still finding their feet in 1999. Lootpack's debut, *Soundpieces: Da Antidote!* breathed fresh energy into California's rap scene, with sharp, intelligent raps from Wildchild, and unique yet still quintessentially hip-hop production from Madlib. *Soundpieces: Da Antidote!* also introduced a supporting cast of other rappers from Oxnard, such as Medaphor (aka M.E.D.), Declaime, and Madlib's younger brother, Oh No.

Declaime – real name Dudley Perkins, who sometimes also records under this title – secured his Likwit Crew credentials when he appeared on the same track from Tha Alkaholik's *Coast II Coast* in 1995. In addition to his contribution to *Soundpieces: Da Antidote!,* he released his debut EP the same year, *Illmindmuzik*, fully produced by Madlib. They would go on to collaborate several more times in the following years, with highlights including 2001's *Andsoitisaid*, 2003's *A Lil' Light*, and *Conversations With Dudley* in 2004. M.E.D. joined Madlib at Stones Throw Records after making his debut on *Soundpieces: Da Antidote!* M.E.D.'s first two albums, 2005's *Push Comes To Shove* and 2011's *Classic*, featured several tracks produced by Madlib and Oh No, and he still works regularly with Madlib today.

Lootpack called it quits as a group after the release of *The Lost Tapes* in 2004, but Wildchild and Madlib continued working together before and after, with Madlib splitting production credits with Oh No on Wildchild's debut album in 2003, *Secondary Protocol*, released via Stones Throw. The album was another Likwit Crew affair, with contributions from M.E.D., Tha Alkaholiks, and newer member Phil Da Agony. DJ Romes has stayed mostly under the radar since the Lootpack days, but is still active today.

As for Madlib, his time with Lootpack and the rest of the Likwit Crew was a springboard to becoming one of the most critically acclaimed and much-loved producers in music. His discography as a producer for Stones Throw and artists on other indie labels between 1999 and 2005 features several important records in the underground movement, including work with MF DOOM, J Dilla, Oh No, Prince Po and Vast Aire.

During the same period, Madlib also found time to release several solo projects on Stones Throw, under different names and genres of music. His forays into jazz began in 2001 with the release of *Angles Without Edges* by Yesterdays New Quintet, ostensibly a band, but actually Madlib alone, playing all members and every instrument. This was followed by *Shades of Blue: Madlib Invades Blue Note* in 2003, where the producer put his own spin on music from the famed jazz label Blue Note Records; another Yesterdays New Quintet album in 2004, *Stevie*; *A Tribute to Brother Weldon* in 2004 under the name Monk Hughes & The Outer Real (again, really just Madlib playing every instrument); and an album under yet another imaginary jazz band, Sound Directions, for 2005's *The Funky Side of Life*. He also took the name DJ Rels and created a house album in 2004 named *Theme for a Broken Soul*.

When it comes to straight up hip-hop, however, among Madlib's greatest gifts to rap music are the albums he recorded as his alter-ego, Quasimoto. The origin is vague, but the accepted back-story of Quas, who manifests as a yellow, animated character that looks part-alien, part anteater, is that Madlib used to write raps but didn't like the sound of his own voice. One day, while high as a kite on mushrooms, Madlib experimented with taking some of his verses, recording them slowly, and then pitching them up. It gave the vocals a distinct tone, and once Stones Throw's Peanut Butter Wolf heard the tapes, he convinced Madlib to make more. After introducing Quas on *Soundpieces: Da Antidote!* and Peanut Butter Wolf's own album, *My Vinyl Weighs A Ton*, both in 1999, Madlib unleashed a full album as the character in 2000 with *The Unseen*, followed by *The Further Adventures of Lord Quas* in 2004.

With his older brother being Madlib, it has been tricky for Oh No, whose real name is literally Michael Jackson, to escape the shadow of his older sibling. He's done it though, thanks to several impressive albums, starting with *The Disrupt* in 2004; another Likwit-heavy album with production from Madlib, and guest features by Wildchild, M.E.D. and Dudley Perkins.

Before pivoting to a more commercial rap sound, Xzibit built on the momentum of his appearances on albums by crew members King T and Tha Alkaholiks with two acclaimed albums of his own, 1996's *At the Speed of Life* and 1998's *40 Dayz & 40 Nightz*, both released by Loud Records. Each album featured King T and Tha Alkaholiks, giving the Likwit Crew some of their widest ever exposure. Both albums also formed a connection between the Likwit Crew and two other Californian underground rap stalwarts, Ras Kass, and the aforementioned Saafir. In addition to appearing together on Xzibit's first two albums, the trio of emcees also featured on Ras Kass's *Rasassination* in 1998, and planned to release music as a supergroup named Golden State Project (originally set to be named the Golden State Warriors before the NBA team of the same name nixed that idea). Sadly, an album never materialized, although the group did feature on the soundtrack for the 2001 movie *Training Day*.

The extended Likwit Crew family tree also branches out to include another of the most influential Los Angeles based groups, Dilated Peoples, consisting of emcees Rakaa Iriscience and Evidence, and DJ Babu. Plans to release their 1995 debut *Imagery, Battle Hymns & Political Poetry* were shelved in favor of 12" singles on ABB Records, before they eventually released their proper debut, *The Platform*, in 2000, followed by *Expansion Team* in 2001, and *Neighborhood Watch* in 2004. Their place as Likwit Crew alumni was secured when Evidence and Rakaa featured on one of the standout cuts from Lootpack's *Soundpieces: Da Antidote!*, while Tha Alkaholiks also featured on *The Platform* and *Expansion Team*.

Although not strictly classed as a member of the Likwit Crew, producer Alchemist (real name Alan Maman) played a key role in the story of Dilated Peoples, and similar to Madlib, he has since gone on to become one of hip-hop's most revered producers. After a mostly forgettable start in the rap industry as one half of the short lived group The Whooliganz alongside future Hollywood star Scott Caan, who were given their shot by L.A. rap royalty Cypress Hill, Maman dropped his emcee name Mudfoot, and focused on perfecting his skills as a producer under the name Alchemist. Having known Evidence since childhood, he produced a large chunk of Dilated People's debut, and all of their subsequent albums.

Incidentally, the first two Dilated Peoples albums also featured production by Joey Chavez. In addition to releasing a couple of 12"s of his own via ABB Records, Chavez later joined with Bravo to form Sid Roams, who went on to produce for major label artists including Eminem and Drake.

Alchemist and Evidence were also heavily involved in producing the music of another member of the Likwit Crew, rapper Defari. His albums *Focused Daily* in 1998 and *Odds & Evens* from 2003 were full blown Likwit Crew projects featuring multiple members. Defari is also in a duo with DJ Babu, the appropriately-named Likwit Junkies. Their 2005 album *The L.J.'s* sees them collaborate with various members of the collective.

The final Likwit Crew branch that released music in this period is rapper Phil Da Agony and his group Strong Arm Steady. Their debut album, 2007's *Deep Hearted*, included contributions from Dilated Peoples, Xzibit and Tha Alkaholiks, and years later they would go on to work extensively with Madlib.

There have been plenty of projects released by members of the Likwit Crew post-2005, in particular from extended members like Madlib, Alchemist and Evidence, and group members still occasionally collaborate today, most notably Oh No and Alchemist, who record together as the group Gangrene. Collaborations between the original members of the collective have been less forthcoming, but King T still appeared on Tha Alkaholiks' later albums, and they all featured on "Louis XIII", a Dr. Dre produced cut from Xzibit's *Napalm* album in 2012.

The legacy remains strong regardless of whether or not the crew has fizzled out in recent years. King T helped draft a blueprint that opened doors for countless other artists from Los Angeles and beyond; Tha Alkaholiks are today considered legends of the game; and in Madlib and Alchemist, two of hip-hop's most iconic names, the roots of the Likwit Crew continue to spread.

SOLESIDES AND QUANNUM PROJECTS

At a distance of hundreds of miles north of Los Angeles, and with a demographic that skews overwhelmingly white, the city of Davis, California, is not the first place that springs to mind when thinking about breeding grounds of hip-hop. It is, nevertheless, home to University of California, Davis, and college campuses, where creativity is encouraged, and where people from different places come together, are where many of the best musical movements started.

In the case of the SoleSides crew, another of California's most important underground rap collectives, the group assembled after meeting at the college's radio station. Here, Joshua Davis, soon to be known as DJ Shadow – still in high school at the time and not even a Davis student – would find kindred spirits in a group of budding artists that included Lyrics Born, Chief Xcel, The 8th Wonder and Jazzbo. DJ Zen (aka Jeff Chang, now a celebrated journalist), who had a hip-hop show on the college radio station, was also a member of the circle, and soon after Lateef the Truthspeaker and Chief Xcel's high school friend Gift of Gab were also added to the mix. They named themselves SoleSides, and began putting music out via their own indie label.

The collective really started to hit their stride in 1994 with the release of the *Melodica* EP by Blackalicious, a group made up of Gift of Gab and Chief Xcel. DJ Shadow was then able to elevate the crew to a much higher level thanks to the critical acclaim he received for his debut album in 1996, *Entroducing......* A painstakingly crafted masterwork of sampling, the instrumental album is heralded as a classic of the genre, but it took some assistance from overseas to put the record out. British musician James Lavelle founded the independent Mo Wax label in the early 90s, and although it was focused towards trip-hop and other genres, it was releasing rap records by the middle of the decade. It was here that DJ Shadow found the right fit for *Entroducing.....,* and Mo Wax also later released albums from other Soldsides members. The instrumental nature of *Entroducing.....* meant there were no contributions from any of the collective's emcees, but some of them did still play a part: The iconic album cover shows two people digging for vinyl at Rare Records in Sacramento; Chief Xcel and Lyrics Born.

And then, with the crew still basking in the glory of DJ Shadow's critical acclaim, they decided to shut SoleSides down, later restarting it as Quannum Projects (although some releases were still labelled as SoleSides for a while after the transition). Similar to how Freestyle Fellowship and the wider Project Blowed collective fostered collaboration and the forming of sub-groups, so did the members of Quannum Projects. In 1997, Lyrics Born and Lateef The Truthspeaker formed the group Latyrx, releasing *The Album*, featuring production by Lyrics Born himself, plus DJ Shadow and Chief Xcel, and a guest spot from Chief's Blackalicious partner, Gift of Gab. Quannum Projects then regrouped to release a fully-fledged crew album in 1999, named *Spectrum*, with appearances by each member, alongside other indie rap royalty such as Jurassic 5, Souls of Mischief, and El-P.

Blackalicious' *Melodica* EP in 1994 was a solid introduction to the group, but 1999 would be the year they would break out for real thanks to the release of another EP and their debut album. First came *A2G*, an EP that singled out Gift of Gab as being one of the most skillful emcees in the business, thanks to the track "Alphabet Aerobics", where he runs through the alphabet with impeccable writing. The project also expanded Chief Xcel's repertoire as a producer, although ironically, "Alphabet Aerobics", still today the group's most well known song, was produced by Jurassic 5 member Cut Chemist.

Blackalicious followed *A2G* with their debut LP, *Nia*, first released by Mo Wax in Europe, and then in the US several months later. The album is nothing short of a masterwork, crossing over with critics and fans alike, giving SoleSides/Quannum Projects their second certified classic album in the space of just a few years. It was also another crew effort, with contributions from DJ Shadow, Lyrics Born and Lateef The Truthseeker.

The new millennium started with a walk down memory lane and the release of the collective's compilation album, *SoleSides Greatest Bumps*. As the name suggested, the album was a look at the pre-Quannum Projects days featuring several cuts recorded in the 1990s. *SoleSides Greatest Bumps* was released in collaboration with indie label Ninja Tune. Similar to Mo Wax, Ninja Tune was a UK label, created by production duo Coldcut. That the crew had to get an assist on several occasions from labels based on the other side of the Atlantic ocean could be considered as a fail on the part of the US indie hip-hop scene for taking so long to catch on to the talents of the crew, but also speaks to the global appeal and reach of underground hip-hop at the time.

After the critical success of *Nia*, expectations were high for the release of Blackalicious' next album, *Blazing Arrow*, which came out in 2002. There was to be no sophomore slump, however, as Black-alicious delivered another masterclass in emceeing and production, meaning the duo had pulled off the rare feat of producing back-to-back classics. The album also proved to be another celebration of not just Quannum Projects, but of California underground hip-hop in general, thanks to appearances from Jurassic 5 members Chali 2na and Cut Chemist, and Dilated Peoples. *Blazing Arrow* also includes input from Questlove of The Roots. Always a champion of independent hip-hop, but still selective about who he works with, Questlove's involvement was further validation that Blackalicious and the rest of the Quannum Projects collective were now well and truly on the radar of everyone that mattered.

Despite having been a founding member and involved with all of the most significant Soleside/Quannum Projects albums, it took until 2003 for Lyrics Born to finally release his debut album. *Later Than Day...* was another acclaimed work that boosted the profile of Lyrics Born as a skilled emcee, but also as a producer, handling virtually every track on the album. It's important to note that Lyrics Born was also breaking new ground for the Japanese-American diaspora, and today is an inspirational figurehead for the still underserved community.

Meanwhile, Lyrics Born's Latyrx partner, Lateef The Truthseeker, was busy forming another Quannum Projects sub-group, this time partnering with one half of Blackalicious, Chief Xcel. The duo named themselves Lateef & the Chief, and released their one and only album, *Maroons: Ambush*, in 2004. Lateef The Truthseeker would later go on to be part of a third Quannum Projects sub-group, The Mighty Underdogs, this time with the other half of Blackalicious, Gift of Gab, and Headnodic.

The following year, Blackalicious regrouped for the release of another hallmark album for the collective, 2005's *The Craft*. It was a lauded release, capping off a near-perfect three album run, which is practically unheard of in the world of independent, underground hip-hop, where many artists are lucky to make it even to one album, let alone three, and let alone three held in such high regard. *The Craft* also saw another change of record labels for Blackalicious. No longer affiliated with the British indie Mo Wax, and after having briefly dabbled with the larger label system with MCA for the release of *Blazing Arrows*, *The Craft* came out on the Anti label, which was relatively new at the time, and not necessarily known for hip-hop. Anti is, however, owned by Epitaph, one of the music industry's most respected indie labels. Epitaph's own relationship with Blackalicious started the previous year in 2004, when they released Gift of Gab's acclaimed solo debut *4th Dimensional Rocketships Going Up*, in partnership with Quannum Projects. In a departure from his work with Chief Xcel, the album is produced by Jake One and Vitamin D, with no input from core SoleSides/ Quannum Projects members. *The Craft* is also light on input from the rest of the Quannum Projects crew, although Lyrics Born and Lateef The Truthseeker do feature on one track each.

Tragedy struck the Soleside/Quannum Projects collective in 2021 when founding member Gift of Gab passed away at just 50 years of age. He had been stricken with kidney disease for a number of years, making live touring a painful operation, and limiting his energy for making new music. Blackalicious did manage to release a fourth album, *Imani Vol. 1* in 2015, and Gift of Gab continued to put out occasional solo projects, but the frequent and very grueling dialysis sessions took a major toll. A kidney transplant in the final months of Gift of Gab's life offered some hope, but the battle proved to be one he was unable to win. Time will tell where the death of Gift of Gab leaves the remaining crew members, but their legacy is already secured.

THE PHARCYDE

As impactful as collectives like Project Blowed, Hieroglyphics, Liktwit Crew and Quannum Projects were, they were not the only Californian artists dropping underground and independently-released hip-hop between 1995-2005. The group dynamic was especially strong in Los Angeles, where one group in particular proved to be most influential. By 1995 The Pharcyde – aka Bootie Brown, Fatlip, Imani, and Slimkid3 – were already west coast rap icons on the strength of their debut album, 1992's *Bizarre Ride II the Pharcyde*. The album's playful lyrics and soulful production, courtesy of J-Swift, aligned them with other groups like Souls of Mischief, helping to usher in a new style of rap music that was soaked in the feel good vibes of the California sunshine.

Their second album, *Labcabincalifornia*, took a darker tone, but is today recognized as another classic. The album is also notable for being one of the first times people began to notice the work of producer J Dilla (at the time going by the name Jay Dee), who produced several tracks, including acclaimed singles "Drop" and "Runnin". *Bizarre Ride II the Pharcyde* and *Labcabincalifornia* were both released on Delicious Vinyl, a groundbreaking independent label who scored some huge crossover rap hits in the late 80s and early 90s, and later partnered with majors such as Atlantic Records and Capitol Records.

Personal differences saw The Pharcyde fall apart in subsequent years, and few people remember, or are even aware, that the group released two further albums after *Labcabincalifornia; Plain Rap* in 2000 and *Humboldt Beginnings* in 2004, by which time only Bootie Brown and Imani were still in the group. The Pharcyde line-up has changed several times since the 1990s, with various members leaving and returning over the years. At time of writing, Fatlip, Imani and Slimkid3 appear to be back in the fold, with only Bootie Brown absent.

JURASSIC 5

Throughout The Pharcyde's 90s run, another Los Angeles group had started to emerge from the underground scene, from a familiar breeding ground. Though not part of the Project Blowed collective, the members of Jurassic 5 had come of age at the Good Life Cafe, but before they became a six-man group, they started life as two separate crews.

High school acquaintances Chali 2na, Cut Chemist and Marc 7 were in a group together named U.N.I.T.Y. Committee. Meanwhile, Akil, Soup and DJ Numark were in a group called Rebels of Rhythm. Mutual respect brought them together, and they released their first record as a unified crew in 1997, the EP *Jurassic 5*. This was then expanded and re-released the following year as a full album. With Akil, Chali 2na, Marc 7 and Soup on the microphone, and Cut Chemist and DJ Numark producing, the group developed a fun, infectious style that provided some relief from the more harder edged music that was being made across the country in New York's underground scene, influenced by Freestyle Fellowship and Souls of Mischief for sure, but also a throwback to a much earlier time in the history of hip-hop, where ensemble crews would pass the mic around and perform routines on stage.

Jurassic 5's sophomore album, *Quality Control*, arrived in 2000, followed by *Power In Numbers* in 2002. The group disbanded in subsequent years, and hasn't released an album since 2006's *Feedback*.

LIVING LEGENDS

Like Jurassic 5, L.A.'s Living Legends crew is born from a bunch of earlier rap groups. PSC and BFAP formed the duo Mystik Journeymen in 1994, later changing their artist names to Luckyiam and Sunspot Jonz. Mystik Journeymen released various albums and EPs starting with *Walkman Invaders* in 1995. Meanwhile, Scarub, Eligh and Murs, highschool friends at Alexander Hamilton High School, were busy forming the group 3 Melancholy Gypsys.

Elsewhere still, The Grouch was building a solo career. Like Sunspot Jonz, The Grouch was actually from Oakland, but soon became a fixture of L.A.'s indie rap circuit. They would each release projects as solo artists or as members of sub-groups like Log Cabin and The Righteous Brothers, but eventually came together as one unit, the Living Legends. Later joined by Bicasso and Asop, their crew debut came in 2001 with the *Almost Famous* album, followed by *Creative Differences* in 2004 and *Classic* in 2005. The discographies of each group member run very deep, but highlights include 1999's *Project* by The Righteous Brothers, the 2000 *G&E Music Vol. 1 & 2* album by The Grouch and Eligh, and *Grand Caravan to the Rim of the World* by 3 Melancholy Gypsys, released in 2005.

Each member has managed to carve out a level of success with their solo endeavors, but Murs has had the widest impact. He released his debut, *F'Real*, in 1997, but really came into his own with his fourth album, 2003's *The End of the Beginning*. Although it was still rooted in California – with input from various Living Legends members, and even an appearance by west coast rap royalty Shock G of Digital Underground – Murs also looked towards New York, drafting in Aesop Rock and El-P among others. The El-P connection was also on account of *The End of the Beginning* being released by Definitive Jux.

Another of the producers on *The End of the Beginning* was Ant of the group Atmosphere. The previous year, in 2002, Murs released the first of several albums under the name Felt, a duo he formed with the other half of Atmosphere, Slug. That first album, *Felt: A Tribute to Christina Ricci*, was produced by The Grouch, while Ant produced the next Felt record in 2005, *Felt 2: A Tribute to Lisa Bonet*. In 2004, Murs also collaborated with producer 9th Wonder for *Murs 3:16: The 9th Edition* via Definitive Jux, the first of several projects they'd go on to create together.

PEOPLE UNDER THE STAIRS

Among the peers of the 3 Melancholy Gypsys and Log Cabin members at Alexander Hamilton High School was another aspiring rapper, Double K. He would sometimes collaborate with Log Cabin, but by 1996 had formed his own group alongside Thes One, known as People Under The Stairs. Their 1998 debut, *The Next Step*, was the first of many outstanding albums the duo released between then and 2019, each one mellow and laid back for the most part, occasionally venturing into more serious themes. The four albums they released from 1996-2003 – *The Next Step*, *Question In The Form Of An Answer* in 2000, *O.S.T.* in 2002, and *...Or Stay Tuned* in 2003 – were all released by San Francisco based independent label Om Records. Similar to the aforementioned Mo Wax, who released various albums by the Solesides crew, the label was home to many different genres, but found a comfortable niche in hip-hop, mostly from the west coast.

The People Under The Stairs story came to a sad end when Double K died in 2021 at the age of just 43. In the world of hip-hop, where way too many artists die young, Double K is not even the only former student of Alexander Hamilton High School who became a rapper and died in their prime; the school was also attended by Nipsey Hussle, murdered in 2019 aged 33.

VISIONARIES

Elsewhere in Los Angeles in 1995, another collective of rappers and producers had formed, this one fully representing the diverse, multi-ethnicity of the city, with members of Japanese, Filipino and Mexican descent, among others. The full line-up of the Visionaries – Dannu, DJ Rhettmatic, KeyKool, LMNO, Lord Zen, and 2Mex –

dropped their debut, *Galleries*, in 1998, but the first record of note in their discography was the *Kozmonautz* album by DJ Rhettmatic and KeyKool, in 1995. Two more crew albums followed in 2000 and 2004 respectively, *Sophomore Jinx* and *Pangaea*, each released on an independent label named Up Above Records, co-founded by members of the group.

There's been a huge amount of solo material from various members of the Visionaries, especially 2Mex and LMNO. 2Mex's first albums were collaborations with artists outside of the Visionaries, working with Xololanxinxo under the name Of Mexican Descent for *Exitos y Mas Exitos* in 1998, and with producer Mum's The Word as the group The Mind Clouders for 1999's *Fake It Until You Make It*. His first proper solo album came in 2000 with *Words Knot Music*, followed by several others, including an album in 2005 released under the name SonGodSuns (*Over The Counter Culture*). LMNO had a prolific run of albums and EPs between 2000 and 2005, the highlight being his debut, *Leave My Name Out*. Meanwhile, Dannu and Lord Zen joined forces as the duo Writer's Block, recording *En Route* in 2001, and *Next Stop* in 2005.

BEAT JUNKIES AND INVISIBL SKRATCH PIKLZ

In addition to being a member of the Visionaries, DJ Rhettmatic is also part of the Beat Junkies collective, one of two renowned turntablist crews from California. After being founded in the early 90s by J Rocc, Melo-D and DJ Rhettmatic himself, the crew swelled to include other members, such as D-Styles, DJ Shortkut, and Dilated Peoples' DJ Babu. Various members released important mixes between 1995-2005, including DJ Rhettmatic and DJ Babu's *Wild Stylus* in 1997, volumes 1-3 of *The World Famous Beat Junkies*, and several volumes of DJ Babu's *Super Duck Breaks* and *Duck Season* series. J Rocc and DJ Babu also mixed and hosted one of the most important underground hip-hop albums of all time, 1999's *Soundbombing II*.

D-Styles and DJ Shortkut are also members of California's other notable turntablist crew, San Francisco's the Invisibl Skratch Piklz. A revolving door approach has seen several deejays join and leave the line-up since the crew was founded in the late 80s, but the core line-up includes founding members DJ Q-bert and Mix Master Mike, and D-Styles and DJ Shortkut. They released a number of routines and tapes from 1997-2000, including various editions of *The Shiggar Fraggar Show* series. D-Styles is additionally a member of the group Third Sight, who released their *Golden Shower Hour* album in 1998.

UGLY DUCKLING

In Long Beach circa 1993, while homegrown hero Snoop Doggy Dogg was emerging as the next big rap star, three other men from the same city were forming a group and working on their first demos. Those men were Andy Cooper, Dizzy Dustin, and Young Einstein, and they called themselves Ugly Duckling. Similar in spirit to People Under The Stairs and Jurassic 5, there's a throwback, old school feel to Ugly Duckling's music, evidenced on their debut EP in 1999, *Fresh Mode*, and their first album, *Journey to Anywhere*, in 2001. Continuing the previously discussed trend of US underground hip-hop being championed by UK indie labels, Fresh Mode first came out on DJ Dan Greenpeace's Bad Magic imprint, before Ugly Duckling later signed to 1500 Records, backed by the much larger A&M Records.

The group followed up with several further projects, many with food-themed titles, including *Taste The Secret* and *The Leftovers EP*, both released in 2003. The feel good, upbeat nature of their music has allowed Ugly Duckling to capitalize on lucrative licensing deals for use of their music across several different media. The group seems to be on hiatus today, but Andy Cooper still occasionally releases music.

ZION I

Although Hieroglyphics dominated the indie rap scene in Oakland during the 90s and aughts, several other acts emerged from the Bay Area city. Baba Zumbi started the group Zion I in 1996 with K-Genius and Amp Live, who was originally from Texas. Their impressive debut, *Mind Over Matter*, came out in 2000, followed by *Deep Water Slang V2* in 2003, and *True & Livin'* in 2005. These, and the group's subsequent albums, came out on several, long since forgotten indie labels, including Ground Control Records, Raptivism, and Live Up Records.

Amp Live's range as a producer saw Zion I experiment with different sounds across their discography, but they remained hip-hop to the core, and collaborated frequently with the cream of the California underground, including members of Hieroglyphics, Freestyle Fellowship and Living Legends, and even connecting with Aesop Rock, Talib Kweli and others from the east coast. Zion I later became a solo act after Amp Live and K-Genius left, leaving just Baba Zumbi. In 2021 Zumbi died aged 49 under a cloud of mystery. He was in hospital at the time, suffering from Covid 19, but also to assess what was said to be deteriorating mental health. A psychotic incident led to him being restrained, during which it was determined he was choked to death. It was a tragic end to the story of a talented artist, and another rapper dead too soon.

———

There were several more rappers and groups from north of Los Angeles who shone bright for a while between 1995-2005 that were not connected to the various aforementioned collectives and groups.

The group The B.U.M.S. were making waves in Oakland at the same time as Zion I. The name stood for Brothas Unda Madness, and the duo consisted of E-Vocalist and D-Wyze. Their 1995 *Lyfe 'N' Tyme* album was relatively obscure on release, but has found a wider following in recent years thanks to the work of reissue labels such as 90's Tapes/HHV.

Oakland was also the base for factions of the Anticon collective, including co-founder Jel. He released his debut, *10 Seconds*, in 2002, and the albums *Them* and *The No Music* in 2000 and 2002 respectively, with Doseone as the group Themselves. Passage is also from Oakland, and released *Moods & Symptoms* with San Francisco producer Bomarr in 2002; his solo debut *The Forcefield Kids* in 2004; and several projects with Bomarr and Oakland producer Telephone Jim Jesus as the group Restiform Bodies.

In San Francisco, Dan the Automator had been making music since way before he formed Deltron 3030 or his work on *Dr. Octagonecologyst*. He released an EP named *A Better Tomorrow* in 1996, which was expanded upon in 2000 as *A Much Better Tomorrow*, featuring heavy input from Kool Keith. He also partnered with another icon of New York hip-hop, DJ Prince Paul, to form the duo Handsome Boy Modelling School. Their 1999 *So... How's Your Girl?* album was another pivotal moment in the history of underground rap, followed in 2004 by *White People*.

In San Jose, Peanut Butter Wolf and Charizma had been friends since 1989. By 1993 they were ready to release their debut album, *Big Shots*, but it wasn't to be. In December 1993 Charizma was murdered aged 20 by a car jacker. Peanut Butter Wolf started his Stones Throw Records label in order to put out his and Charisma's music, and the label's first ever release was a 12" single from *Big Shots*, "My World Premier." In 2003, by which time Stones Throw was now the most influential indie rap label, the *Big Shots* album was finally released in full, followed a year later by *Big Shots Bonus EP*. Peanut Butter Wolf's own solo album, *My Vinyl Weighs A Ton*, came out in 1999 with contributions from many renowned rappers and turntablists.

An hour's drive away in Santa Cruz, KutMasta Kurt was building a solid reputation as a go-to producer for indie rap acts. Although he is primarily remembered for his work with east coast artist Kool Keith, he also produced for Dilated Peoples and Lootpack among others. Motion Man – KutMasta Kurt and Kool Keith's fellow group member in Masters of Illusion – released the *Clearing The Field* album in 2002, via KutMasta Kurt's own label, Threshold Recordings.

The city of Fresno is another outlier not often associated with hip-hop, but here is where Planet Asia was born and raised. By the late 90s he had decamped to the Bay Area and was working with Madlib and Evidence, releasing records on two of the most influential indie rap labels of the era, Stones Throw and ABB Records. Planet Asia has released scores of albums since, and today is an elder statesman to the current crop of underground rappers. In 2000 he formed the duo Cali Agents with Rasco. They released the acclaimed *How the West Was One* that year, followed by *Head of the State* in 2004. Although Rasco isn't from California – he was born two thousand miles away in Ohio – he is an adopted son of the Golden

State's underground scene. His own debut album came out in 1998 via Stones Throw, *Time Waits For No Man*. The album sees Rasco collaborate with some of the west's most respected underground artists, including Peanut Butter Wolf, Dilated Peoples, Defari, and Rasco's Cali Agents partner, Planet Asia.

Rasco's later albums were released via indie label Copasetik Recordings, and via his own short lived label, Pockets Linted Entertainment. *Time Waits For No Man* is also notable for production by DJ Paul Nice. A native New Yorker, Paul Nice worked with several west coast artists and also released a series of influential break records. He died in 2024 at fifty six years of age.

———

There are a few other artists that also deserve an honorable mention. Some got their start during the period but only went on to greater things later, others dropped one album and then mostly disappeared, while others ended up moving away from hip-hop. The group Styles of Beyond – featuring DJ Cheapshot, Ryu, Tak, and Vin Skully – veered towards a more rock sound on their later albums, frequently working with Linkin Park's Mike Shinoda. Their debut, however, 1998's *2000 Fold*, was a straight up hip-hop album.

Originally forming in 1994 under the name Numbskulls and briefly getting signed to Loud Records, Chace Infinite and DJ Khalil changed their name to Self Scientific and released the acclaimed *The Self Science* album in 2001. It was their only release of note, but DJ Khalil has found major success as a producer, most notably for Dr. Dre's Aftermath Entertainment, where he has worked on records for Eminem, 50 Cent, Kendrick Lamar and various other stars.

Aloe Blacc scored several global hits as a soul singer in the 2010s, but years before that rapped as one half of the group

Emanon, with producer Exile. They released various records from 1996 onwards, including 2005's *Waiting Room*. Two years prior to that, Blu recorded his first album, *California Soul*. He and Exile later joined together to record the highly regarded *Below The Heavens* album in 2007, and between them have made some of California's best hip-hop since.

Author's Note: Several of the key albums and 12"s discussed in the previous pages are looked at in more detail in the What's Golden chapter later.

5

UNIVERSAL MAGNETIC

N ew York and California were the dominant states from where underground hip-hop was coming from during the period, but there were also regional scenes brewing everywhere across the US and Canada.

NEW JERSEY

The commercial and critical success of New Jersey acts like Naughty By Nature, Queen Latifah, Redman and Lords of the Underground influenced the next wave of independent artists to emerge from the state. Some stayed within the lanes of traditional, hard-edged boom bap, but there was also space for something a little different, like MC Paul Barman, a polarizing figure in the rap scene. Though New Jersey is a comparatively small state, and despite only being around thirty minutes drive from Newark, the suburb of Ridgewood is definitely not a place where you'll find mean streets. It was this affluent background from where MC Paul Barman came, later developing a taste for hip-hop at college. He self-released a record named "Postgraduate" in 1998, which somehow made it into the hands of DJ Prince Paul. Having the ear of one of hip-hop's most accomplished producers put MC Paul Barman in a fortunate position, which only got better when DJ Prince Paul produced Barman's first EP, 2000's *It's Very Stimulating*.

His full debut came in 2002 with *Paullelujah!*, with more production from DJ Prince Paul, and also MF DOOM. While some find Barman's unique, nerdy and wordy vocal tone, flow and rhyme schemes unbearable, he is highly regarded by other artists. Working with DJ Prince Paul and MF DOOM is more than enough validation of his skills, but Barman has additionally collaborated with Deltron 3030, Masta Ace, DJ Yoda and countless other leading lights in underground rap.

Scienz of Life were on more familiar, New York influenced territory, and in fact group members and real life brothers Lil Sci and ID 4 Windz were born in the Bronx and raised in Queens, before decamping to New Jersey. They put out the "Powers of Nine Ether (Distorted Views of Life)" and "Scienze of Life (Metaphysic)" 12"s between 1996-1997 on Fondle 'Em Records, and then signed to Sub Verse Music, a label co-founded by Bigg Jus from Company Flow.

There they released two acclaimed albums, 2000's *Coming Forth by Day: The Book of the Dead*, and *Project Overground: The Scienz Experiment* in 2002. The latter included a guest feature by MF DOOM, who Scienz of Life formed a strong bond with. After meeting briefly in New York around the time they were all on Fondle 'Em, the group and Dumile connected on a deeper level in Atlanta, during the period when Dumile was living there. Scienz of Life also later moved to Atlanta to be closer to label head Bigg Jus, who had migrated there, post-Company Flow. The move allowed Scienz of Life to focus on their music in fresh surroundings, while also learning how to promote and distribute it in the burgeoning world of e-commerce. It also brought them closer to Dumile, eventually leading to collaborating on *Project Overground: The Scienz Experiment* with the song "Yikes!!!".

Lil Sci, who now goes by his real name John Robinson, has stated in interviews that Dumile liked hanging with Scienz of Life because the group having Lil Sci and his brother ID 4 Windz reminded him of the dynamic he had with his brother in the group KMD, the late DJ Subroc. Robinson even claims there were briefly plans for Dumile to resurrect Zev Love X as part of a new incarnation of KMD with Scienz of Life. That never manifested, but John Robinson and MF DOOM did later put out the joint album *Who is this Man?* in 2008. Some of the beats on the album also appeared on volumes of MF DOOM's *Special Herbs* series, but different to other projects that used beats from those albums, John Robinson says that he had many of the beats from Dumile before they were put on *Special Herbs*, but release schedules meant his album came out after. He also recorded his vocals over the beats with Dumile in the room, another personal touch that not many who collaborated with Dumile can claim. Scienz of Life also showed how much Dumile meant to them on the tribute track "Dear Zev (Never Give Up)" from *The Blaxploitation Sessions*, released in 2006. According to Robinson, Dumile appreciated the gesture, but the song now hits on a deeper level in light of Dumile's death in 2020.

John Robinson is still active today, but the third member of Scienz of Life, Inspector Willabee, sadly died in 2019.

After releasing their debut in 1994, *Between a Rock and a Hard Place*, the Artifacts found a degree of commercial success with the follow up, 1997's *That's Them*, bolstered by heavy radio play on the east coast of the single "The Ultimate". This was to be their only dalliance with the mainstream, however, and by 1998 they had firmly integrated with the budding underground scene, especially as the

147

12" they recorded under the name Brick City Kids was released on Rawkus, and featured on *Soundbombing*.

Members El Da Sensei and Tame One both released solo albums in 2003, *Relax, Relate, Release* and *When Rappers Attack*, respectively. Tame One also released *Leeked to the Public* and *O.G. Bobby Johnson* in 2005, as well as his earlier-discussed work with Cage as the duo Leak Brothers, and as a member of The Weathermen.

We never did get a third proper album from the Artifacts, and their run was bookended by the death of their deejay, DJ Kaos, in 2019, and Tame One's death in 2022, but a collection of unreleased and new songs materialized in the same year Tame One died. *No Expiration Date* is fully produced by Buckwild, a full circle moment considering he also produced on their debut back in 1994.

Born in the Bronx but raised in New Jersey, rapper Chino XL was primed for a successful career when he signed to Rick Rubin's American Recordings. Despite the powerful backing, the sound on his 1996 debut *Here to Save You All* was underground through and through. The deal with American ended soon after, and all of Chino XL's subsequent albums were released independently. As one of hip-hop's most well-loved artists, there was an outpouring of grief from across the industry when Chino XL took his life in 2024 aged 50.

Although not strictly independent – their 1996 album, *The Turnaround: The Long Awaited Drama*, came out on Big Beat via Atlantic Records – New Jersey group Real Live had all the hallmarks on an underground rap group. Made up of emcee Larry-O and K-Def – a man described earlier in this book as one of hip-hop's most underrated producers – the duo dropped solid 12"s in 1995 in the run up to their album release, helping to bring K-Def into the indie space, where most were already familiar with his production work earlier in the decade for Lords of the Underground.

MASSACHUSETTS

Boston, Massachusetts, is often made to look like a second-tier city for good hip-hop, when in fact it has a long history in the genre, back to the early 1980s when producer Arthur Baker and the Jonzun Crew worked on records for Tommy Boy.

The profile of the city's rap scene was boosted significantly in the late 80s and early 90s due to the success of groups like The Almighty RSO, Gang Starr and Edo.G & The Bulldogs, and the cultural impact of influential magazine The Source, which has its roots in Boston college radio.

Reflecting what was happening across the country, there was a nascent underground scene by the mid-90s in Boston and the surrounding area. The group Concrete Click – made up of Killa Tactics, Dagger & DJ Sugar Child – released *Lyrical Terrorism* in 1995, which was reissued by a small German label in 2018. That same year, the group Street Poets (Punch, Polecat and Dif Productions) dropped their self-titled debut, reissued in 2023 by the 90's Tapes/HHV imprint.

In 1996, rapper M-Slash emerged on the scene, eventually releasing the *Look* album in 2000. In 1997, Laster released the "Off Balance" 12" featuring Edo.G, and L Da Headtoucha released "Too Complex". Both records got significant exposure when they were featured on the influential DJ Premier mixtape, *New York Reality Check 101*. Twenty years later, an indie label from Belgium released a collection of Laster's tracks in 2017, *Liberal Art – 90's Unreleased*. L Da Headtoucha debuted with *Destined for Greatness* in 2003, but years later boutique reissue label Chopped Herring Records released two volumes of unearthed tracks by the emcee (*The 1997-1998 Demos EP* in 2013 and *1997-1999 Demos EP Vol. 2* in 2019). Left-field rapper Mike Ladd also debuted in 1997 with the *Easy Listening 4 Armageddon* album.

The final year of the 1990s saw the debut of the group Kreators, consisting of Big Juan, G-Squared, Jaysaun and XL. They released *No Contest* in 1999 and *Live Coverage* in 2004. Jaysaun also later formed the group Special Teamz with Edo.G and Slaine. The latter emcee has released music since, both as a solo artist and as a member of the supergroup La Coka Nostra. Kreators member Big Juan passed away in 2016.

The most prolific indie label out of Boston in this period was Brick Records (see later chapter for more on the label's history), and the artists featured on their 1997 compilation *Rebel Alliance* would define the sound of Boston's underground for the new millennium. Two artists in particular would have a major impact, rapper Mr. Lif, and the duo 7L & Esoteric.

After releasing records with Brick, and even briefly via the Beastie Boys' Grand Royal label, Mr. Lif was welcomed into the fold of El-P's Definitive Jux label. First came the release of two EPs, *Enters the Colossus* in 2000, and *Emergency Rations* in 2002, followed the same year by Mr. Lif's full album debut, the highly regarded *I Phantom*.

Definitive Jux also released the debut album by Mr. Lif's group with two other important Boston artists, Akrobatik and DJ Fakts One. As The Perceptionists they released *Black Dialogue* in 2005, with features that connected the group with prominent underground artists from outside of Massachusetts, namely Phonte from Little Brother, and Camu Tao. Akrobatik released his own acclaimed

150

debut in 2003 with *Balance*, while DJ Fakts One worked on mixes for labels such as Brick and Detonator Records.

7L & Esoteric started out as a three-man group under the name God Complex, with rapper Karma as the third member. They were a duo by the time of their debut EP in 1999, *Speaking Real Words*, which was followed by three albums between 2001-2004.

Edan is not from Boston, he is from Maryland. His most creative years were in Boston, however, where he collaborated with many of the names listed here, and released two landmark albums. It would be remiss therefore to not include him here. After self-releasing his earliest material on CDr, Edan's full introduction was via the *Primitive Plus* album in 2002, followed by *Beauty and the Beat* in 2005.

Among the more familiar names making guest appearances on *Beauty and the Beat* are two additional Boston underground mainstays, Dagha and Insight. Dagha began releasing albums in 2005 with *Object in Motion*, and Insight released several instrumental and vocal projects from 2001 onwards, with highlights that include 2004's *The Blast Radius*. He is still very active today and his recent work includes collaborations with Count Bass D, Damu the Fudgemunk, and Edo.G.

Throughout all of the above, arguably Boston's two most iconic hip-hop figures continued to release their own music, embracing the indie scene they helped inspire. Edo.G released *The Truth Hurts* in 2000 and *Wishful Thinking* in 2002, and earned praise for his collaboration album with Pete Rock, 2004's *My Own Worst Enemy*.

Guru released two installments of the *Jazzmatazz* series (*Guru's Jazzmatazz, Vol. 2: The New Reality* (1995) and *Guru's Jazzmatazz, Vol. 3: Streetsoul* (2000)), and solo albums in 2001 (*Baldhead Slick & da Click*) and 2005 (*Version 7:0: The Street Scriptures*). He and DJ Premier also reunited as Gang Starr in 2003 for *The Ownerz*.

Guru also maintained his support for Boston artists, old and new. He and Premier were heavily involved in 2005's *Who's Hard?* by original Gang Starr member, Big Shug, and Guru was a mentor to rapper Krumb Snatcha, who released his debut, *Respect All Fear None* in 2002. When Guru succumbed to cancer in 2010 at 48, he was mourned by hip-hop fans around the globe, but it hit the hardest in Boston.

There is an active underground scene in Boston today, and three of its current leading names started out in the early aughts. REKS released several albums and EPs between 2001-2005, including his debut, *Along Came the Chosen*, and Termanology also released his first album in 2005. Producer Statik Selektah is today based in New York, but he's from the Boston area. Before working his way up to becoming one of rap's premier beatmakers, his first credits came at the start of the millennium, producing tracks for REKS and Krumb Snatcha among others.

PENNSYLVANIA

Like Boston, Philadelphia, Pennsylvania, has also sometimes been overlooked in its contributions to hip-hop, despite being the home-town of heavyweight hit makers like Jazzy Jeff & The Fresh Prince; one of the greatest rappers of all time in Black Thought (backed by Questlove and the rest of The Roots); successful street rappers like Beanie Sigel; and influential artists like Schoolly D, Lady B, Steady B & Cool C, and Three Times Dope.

The underground sound in Philly gathered steam from 1993 onwards, buoyed by the minor-level success of groups like Illegal and Da Yungstaz, who each dabbled with major label contracts. Key indie artists from Philly between 1992-1994 included Lord Aaqil, 2

Kannon (K-Swyft, 2Fresh and Groove-Da-Moast), Sons of Sam (The Xav and Samson), and Ruggedness & Maddrama.

In 1995, there were 12"s by Tasc 4orce (Sonni Blak, Eyse Da Superstar, Russ Cool and DJ Kid Kaos); Pauly Yams & DJ Jazz; Prophets of the Ghetto (Meat Matter, Big Bob da Norfstar, D.B.L., Phat-Nice, Benellis, Gamez, DJ Ken-Cut and DJ Dyce); Tainted Mindz (Dame Dollaz); Ram Squad (Boy Backs, Six Nine, Suave and John Wilson); and Jamal from Illegal; followed by records in 1996 and 1997 by Da Fat Cat Clique (brothers Al and Darren Robinson, brothers Larry and Aaron Anderson, Carl Madison, and Craig Collier); Da Minds of Sol (Da Organizer, Da Unforgiven, and Ill Produc'); and D.O.D. (Mally The Kid, Onassis, Don and Sojourner).

Bahamadia got her breakout moment in 1995 with "Ukno-whowwedu", which led to the release of her debut album in 1996, *Kollage*, championed by high-profile collaborators like Gang Starr, Da Beatminerz, and her fellow Philladelphians, The Roots.

Mr. Eon and DJ Mighty Mi made their debut as The High & Mighty in 1999 with *Home Field Advantage* as a joint venture between Rawkus Records and their own Eastern Conference label, followed by the *Porn Again* album in 2001 as the group Smut Peddlers with Cage, and three further The High & Mighty albums (*Air Force 1* in 2002, *The Highlite Zone* in 2003, and *The 12th Man* in 2005). Also debuting in 1999 were the Mountain Brothers (CHOPS, Peril-L & Styles) with *Self: Volume 1*, which they followed up with *Triple Crown* in 2003.

By the year 2000, a second wave of underground artists from Philadelphia emerged. It was a breakout year for The Last Emperor, who released his official debut album in 2003, *Music, Magic, Myth*, and later had 12"s out on Rawkus Records. Grand Agent released several albums in the period, including 2001's *By Design* and 2003's *Fish Outta Water*, as did Maylay Sparks, including his debut in

2003, *Legend In My Own Mind*. And although he is not originally from Philly, Phill Most Chill has been based there for years, and released *The Lo-Fi Theory E.P* in 2005.

The biggest impact during 2000-2005 was by the group Jedi Mind Tricks. Made up of emcee Vinnie Paz and producer Stoupe the Enemy of Mankind, and on-and-off member Jus Allah, the group debuted in 1997 with *The Psycho-Social, Chemical, Biological & Electro-Magnetic Manipulation of Human Consciousness*, the start of a long line of hard hitting albums that continues today, including *Violent by Design* (2000), *Visions of Gandhi* (2003), and *Legacy of Blood* (2004).

Vinnie Paz also co-founded the loose collective of artists known as Army of the Pharaohs. Membership extended beyond the borders of Philadelphia, but current and past members from the city include Reef The Lost Cauze and Chief Kamanchi (both also members of the JuJu Mob), the duo OuterSpace (Planetary and Crypt the Warchild), King Syze, and Bahamdia. The first of several Army of the Pharaohs albums didn't arrive until 2006, but each of the artists listed released impressive albums during the period.

CONNECTICUT

Same as how not all members of the Army of the Pharaohs are from Philadelphia, not all members of the Demigodz are from Connecticut, but that's where the collective was founded in the early 90s by local emcees Reflex and Open Mic (not to be confused with Chicago rapper Open Mike Eagle) under the name The Nobility. Apathy later joined the crew, and over the following years the lineup was something of a revolving door, with past and current members including Esoteric, Eternia, Ryu from the group Styles of

Beyond, Louis Logic and L-Fudge, with several also doubling up as members of Army of the Pharaohs.

The group's most consistent members, however, have been Apathy and Celph Titled, who were the driving force behind their most remembered release, 2002's *The Godz Must Be Crazy* EP. Although Apathy didn't release his debut until 2006, his first mixtape came out in 2003.

RHODE ISLAND

Coming from the smallest state in the country, Sage Francis was always going to have his work cut out trying to put Rhode Island on the hip-hop map. He essentially *is* the entire history of the scene, thanks to his own releases and those on his label, Strange Famous Records. A seasoned battle rapper, he released his first solo album in 2002, *Personal Journals*, and then *A Healthy Distrust* in 2005.

He was also in the duo Non-Prophets with producer Joe Beats, who released *Hope* in 2003. Other artists from Rhode Island signed to Strange Famous include Prolyphic, who released *An Alarm Clock Set for 9:01* in 2003. Sage Francis was also a mentor for the group Clokworx (Arms Uno, DJ Orator and Phes) from the Rhode Island city of Woonsocket. They released the "Mental Flux" 12" circa 1998, and became a fixture of Boston's underground scene.

MAINE

Two of the other founders of the Anticon collective represented one of the least hip-hop places in the country, the northern state of Maine. Sole and Alias, from Providence and Hollis respectively, had been rapping together since their teens, way before the Anticon years. The first releases from Sole were with producer Moodswing, calling themselves Northern Exposure, and then the Live Poets. His official solo debut, *Bottle of Humans*, came out in 2000, followed a year later by *Paint by Number Songs* with Alias and DJ Mayonnaise as the group So-Called Artists. He has built a sizable discography of solo projects and collaborations since.

Alias' debut came with *The Other Side of the Looking Glass* in 2002, and he similarly amassed a huge number of projects, until his death at just 41 after suffering a heart attack. Alias and Sole were also members of Deep Puddle Dynamic – see the section on Doseone for more on that project.

WASHINGTON D.C.

It's not hyperbolic to say that almost the entire early 2000s underground rap scene in Washington D.C. sprung from the Low Budget Crew. Membership of the collective fluctuated, but the primary players were Kev Brown, Kenn Starr, Cy Young, Oddisee, Kaimbr, and the duo Critically Acclaimed. After a couple of 12"s by Kenn Starr and Critically Acclaimed, the crew caught the attention of DJ Jazzy Jeff, calling on Oddisee and Kev Brown to produce tracks for Jazz's solo debut, 2002's *The Magnificent*. Oddisee and Cy Young also contributed guest vocals. Kev Brown's acclaimed debut, *I Do What I Do*, arrived in 2005. Oddisee released his first mixtape that same year, and has since become one of indie's rap's most consistently brilliant artists.

Producer K-Murdock also hails from D.C., and released *Thinking Back, Looking Forward* in 2004 as one half of the duo Panacea, with Philly emcee Raw Poetic. They later signed with Rawkus Records during the label's short lived reemergence in 2006.

Asheru, from neighboring Maryland, also released much material between 1997-2005, including his 2002 debut album, *Soon Come...*, with Blue Back, calling themselves The Unspoken Heard.

VIRGINIA

Conversations about Virginia hip-hop tend to be dominated by The Neptunes and Timbaland coming from there. There's also Nottz, however, a producer more associated with indie rap. He produced on *Lyricist Lounge, Volume One* and 2, and even as his stock was rising on the commercial side, he still produced for Black Moon, Krumb Snatcha, Pitch Black and other indie artists in the first half of the aughts.

Another Virginia artist, Skillz, released his renowned *From Where???* album in 1996, and although it was on a major, it was rooted in the 90s boom bap sound that was now influencing the underground. He was soon fully embraced by the burgeoning scene, going on to release music on Rawkus Records and Eastern Conference.

Elsewhere from the state, the group Ill Biskits (Kleph Dollaz and Deeda) released the *Chronicle Of Two Losers: First Edition* album in 1995, including production by Buckwild and Lord Finesse. Their planned major label deal with Atlantic Records never happened, and Kleph Dollaz died in 2012.

NORTH CAROLINA

North Carolina has a rich heritage of jazz, blues and gospel musicians, but wasn't known widely for hip-hop until the beginning of the new millennium.

Raleigh-Durham group Yaggfu Front had earlier helped put

North Carolina hip-hop on the map in 1994. For the uninitiated, the 'Yaggfu' part was short for 'you are gonna get fucked up', but this was more like a reference to partying and having fun than a violent threat, and the group took an off-beat, positive approach to hip-hop, influenced by De La Soul and others of that ilk. Group members D'Ranged, Damaged, Jingle Bel and Spin 4 were briefly signed to a major, delivering the *Action Packed Adventure!* album in 1994. They mostly disappeared not long after, but are today remembered as pioneers of the North Carolina underground.

It was also around this time that rapper Omniscence was making moves, even once making it into The Source magazine's fabled 'Hip-Hop Quotable' column in 1995. Like Yaggfu Front before him, Omniscence's debut, *The Raw Factor*, was set to come out on a big label, in this instance Elektra. This never happened, and Omniscence dropped off the radar for many years after. *The Raw Factor* finally got a release in 2024, courtesy of Dutch indie label Below System Records, who packaged it with bonus tracks.

By the early aughts there was a vibrant underground scene across North Carolina. Influential releases included *Food, Clothing & Sheltuh* by the group Bomm Sheltuh (Nervous Reck and Filthe Ritch), and *Spirit of 94* by emcee Haze.

Many of the scene's budding artists tended to first get exposure via members of the World Famous Butta Team, a collective of radio deejays and tastemakers who hosted emcee battles and promoted local artists across college radio. The college connection was crucial, as the biggest underground hip-hop movement to come out of the state has its roots in the dorms of North Carolina Central University and North Carolina State University.

These two seats of learning were home to a blossoming group of like-minded emcees, deejays and producers who came together to form the Justus League collective in 1999. The line-up of members included Rapper Big Pooh, Phonte, Cesar Comanche, Chaundon, Edgar Allen Floe, L.E.G.A.C.Y. and Sean Boog on the emcee side, and 9th Wonder, Khrysis, and Big Dho on production. The joining of Rapper Big Pooh, Phonte and 9th Wonder as a group was the turning point for the Justus League, giving the crew national attention, and in Little Brother, a hugely respected and influential act.

A product of the message board era, where artists shared their music direct with fans on forums like Okayplayer, Little Brother earned instant acclaim with the release of *The Listening* in 2003, hailed as a continuation of the legacy of groups like A Tribe Called Quest, and a more sophisticated alternative to other 'southern rap'. There was similar high regard for the following album, 2005's *The Minstrel Show*, and mixtapes Little Brother dropped between albums, including *Chittlin Circuit* and *Chittlin Circuit 1.5*. Later albums had little to no input from 9th Wonder, who officially left the group in 2007.

By 2010, Rapper Big Pooh and Phonte had called time on what was left of Little Brother. Pooh released his first solo album in 2005, *Sleepers*. Phonte would also later release solo material, but first formed the duo The Foreign Exchange with producer Nicolay, releasing their debut in 2004 with *Connected*.

The success of Little Brother propelled 9th Wonder to become one of hip-hop's most sought after producers, later leading to work with Jay-Z, Beyonce, Kendrick Lamar, Anderson .Paak and Erykah Badu, among others. He released many impressive projects during the period, including *God's Stepson* and *Black is Back!* In 2003 and 2004 respectively, on which he remixed Nas's *God's Son* and Jay-Z's *The Black Album*, and *Murs 3:16: The 9th Edition*, the first of what would become a long-running series of collaborations with rapper Murs. In 2005, 9th Wonder released his official debut, *Dream Merchant Vol. 1*, *Spirit of '94: Version 9.0* with fellow North Carolina artist Kaze, and *Chemistry*, which was the first of three albums where he collaborated with Black Moon emcee Buckshot.

There were also several other projects from Justus League members, with highlights including the debut album by Cesar Comanche in 2000, *Wooden Nickels*; *Legsclusives* by L.E.G.A.C.Y. in 2003; *True Links* by Edgar Allen Floe; and *National Anthem* by The Away Team (Sean Boog and Khrysis), both in 2005.

After several years of acrimony, Little Brother performed as a group for the first time in more than a decade for a one-off show in 2018. Inspired by the death of A Tribe Called Quest's Phife Dawg, and how he and Q-Tip had resolved their differences before his passing, Phonte and Rapper Big Pooh had slowly been rebuilding their relationship since before 2018, and their reconciliation led to the release of a new album in 2019, *May The Lord Watch*. The group still remains as a duo, with 9th Wonder opting not to reunite, despite his appearance at the live show in 2018, and early plans for him to be involved in *May The Lord Watch*. The return of the group was a triumph of love and friendship, captured in the 2023 documentary film, *May the Lord Watch: The Little Brother Story*.

Another impressive artist to have emerged from North Carolina in recent years is Greenville emcee Supastition. Although his most acclaimed work came post-2005, his debut *7 Years of Bad Luck* came out in 2002, followed by *Chain Letter* in 2005, which included guest vocals by Little Brother, and production from Phonte's The Foreign Exchange partner Nicolay.

Today, North Carolina can claim one of rap music's biggest stars as their own, J Cole, who himself crossed paths with many of the state's renowned indie artists in the early years of his career, back when he was known by the name Therapist. J Cole's contemporary Drake, meanwhile, has spoken about how Phonte is one of his biggest musical inspirations.

GEORGIA

The commercial dominance of Outkast and the Dungeon Family, Lil Jon, T.I. and Future means that Atlanta, Georgia, is not a city that easily comes to mind when discussing underground hip-hop. Dungeon Family alumni Killer Mike having a relationship with El-P as the duo Run The Jewels does at least provide a tenuous link between the city's music scene and the dusty days of vinyl releases by Rawkus and Definitive Jux, but Atlanta also had its own budding underground circuit.

Starting out as members of an Indianapolis based group named deadpoetsociety, Manchild and DJ Dust maintained the group, morphing into a duo when other members left the music scene, and changing the name to Mars III. They released *Raw Material* in 2000, but their momentum was damaged thanks to sample clearance issues that derailed the release of their *ProPain* album by several years.

The group Mass Influence consisted of Tone, Cognito, H20 and Spearhead X, and debuted in 1998 with a project named *Live From Mitchell Street*. They reached wider attention beyond the Atlanta region when they released *The Underground Science* in 1999, backed by distribution via Fat Beats, who at the time was experimenting with a spin off named Fat Beats Atlanta, mirroring was was happening in the mainstream, where major labels were cashing in on local rap scenes via regional sub-labels like Def Jam

South. It also helped that Fat Beats had opened a physical store in Atlanta.

Also making records around the same time as Mass Influence was the group Prophetix, made up of emcees Eddie Meeks and Mello, and producer Jon Doe. The peak of their career came in 2002 with *High Risk*. Similar to Scienz of Life, Prophetix were able to benefit from the time Daniel Dumile spent living in Atlanta, bagging a feature from him for *High Risk* track "Sumpthin's Gotta Give". *High Risk* also features another Atlanta based artist, Empress Stahhr, who released a 12" on Sub Verse Music in 2002, and formed her own working relationship with MF DOOM that led to her being featured on *MM..Food*, *Take Me to Your Leader*, and *Born Like This* (2009), sometimes credited as Empress Stahhr, sometimes as Angelika (a reference to Angelica Jones, the government name of *Spider-Man & His Amazing Friends* character Firestar). In recent years, Stahhr has been very vocal and passionate on social media about protecting MF DOOM's legacy, especially since Dumile's death, calling out those who try to exploit his name, and campaigning to make sure his estate sanctions, and benefits from all subsequent music releases and merchandise.

Producer Guillermo Scott Herren also grew up in Atlanta, and released the first of several albums under the Prefuse 73 persona in 2001 with *Vocal Studies + Uprock Narratives*, which includes features by Aesop Rock, MF DOOM and Myka 9.

OHIO

Most of the underground scene in Ohio from 1995-2005 came from the state's biggest city, Columbus. The MHz collective was founded circa 1997 by rappers Copywrite and Camu Tao, with RJD2, Tage

Future and Jakki Da Motamouth also later joining. Some members were previously in a different collective, Opium Prodigy, which also included the rapper Illogic.

As with so many others, MHz got their first significant exposure when Bobbito Garcia heard their demo and released the "World Premiere" 12" on Fondle 'Em Records in 1998, and "Rocket Science" a year later. A collection of old and unreleased tracks came out in 2001 named *Table Scraps*, but the one and only full group album came out years later in 2012, credited as MHz Legacy, four years after Camu Tao's death. Copywrite has stated that the album was originally planned to be named *Tero Smith* (Camu Tao's real name), but the surviving members didn't want to appear as though they were cashing in on the loss of their group mate.

Copywrite worked on solo music with both Rawkus Records and Eastern Conference, including for the release of his debut album in 2002, *The High Exhaulted*. Jakki Da Motamouth released a 12" on Fondle 'Em Records in 2000, and released albums in 2003 and 2005 (*Built to Last* and *God Vs. Satan*).

The most accomplished MHz member is RJD2, who has been very active since releasing a number of acclaimed projects on Definitive Jux: his debut *Deadringer* in 2002, *The Horror* in 2003, and *Since We Last Spoke* in 2004. RJD2 also formed the duo Soul Position with fellow Columbus artist Blueprint, releasing *Unlimited EP* in 2002, and *8 Million Stories* in 2003, both via Rhymesayers Entertainment.

When Camu Tao died of lung cancer in May 2008 at just 30, it left a huge hole in the MHz, the Definitive Jux family, and the entire indie rap scene. He never got to release a full solo album during his lifetime (there were a few low-tech CDr releases, however), but he crafted an important body of music outside of his membership in MHz. There were 12"s in 2001, and in 2002 he joined with Cage to form Nighthawks, releasing an album of the same name (see Cage section for more on this).

The following year came another collaborative project, this time with Metro as the duo S.A. Smash. Their *Smashy Trashy* album came out in 2003 on Definitive Jux, where Camu Tao formed a very close friendship with El-P. Both were also members of The Weathermen, and their "WMR (Weathermen Radio)" track appeared on the *Definitive Jux Presents III* compilation in 2004. Camu and El-P later dropped a full album together under the name Central Services (2010's *Forever Frozen in Television Time*).

Camu Tao also appeared on several other key Definitive Jux albums, namely El-P's *Fantastic Damage*, Aesop Rock's *Fast Cars, Danger, Fire and Knives*, and The Perceptionists' *Black Dialogue*. The posthumous *King of Hearts* album came out in 2010, providing closure on the career of a unique talent gone way too soon.

Emcee and producer Blueprint co-founded the group Greenhouse Effect in the late 90s alongside Inkwell and Manifest. They released the *Up to Speed* EP in 1991, their debut album *Life Sentences* in 2003, and *Columbus or Bust* in 2005. Inkwell and Manifest left the group in later years, replaced by Illogic, with he and Blueprint since going by the shortened name of Greenhouse. Blueprint has enjoyed an acclaimed solo career, starting with *The Weightroom* album in 2003, before receiving high praise for *1988* in 2005 (released by Rhymesayers Entertainment). Illogic has achieved similar critical success since his debut, *Unforeseen Shadows*, in 2000, and in particular for *Celestial Clockwork* in 2004. Several Blueprint and Illogic releases have come out on Blueprint's own indie label, Weightless Recordings.

Columbus is also the hometown of producer J. Rawls. In addition to his work producing for groups like Black Star, he released several works between 2001-2005, including his debut *The Essence of J. Rawls* in 2001, and two albums with Fat Jon as the duo 3582. He later formed the group Jay Are with John Robinson, and True Ohio Playas with Count Bass D.

J. Rawls is also one half of the Lone Catalysts with Pittsburgh rapper J. Sands, and together they released *Hip Hop* in 2000, and *Good Music* in 2005.

Although he was born in New York, Count Bass D himself was based in Ohio for several years. He released a number of acclaimed works, including 1995's *Pre-Life Crisis*, and 2002's *Dwight Spitz*, where he collaborated with both Edan and MF DOOM.

Ohio's third largest city, Cincinnati, nurtured its own share of indie rap talent during the era. Prominent producer Hi-Tek and the group Mood (made up of Donte, Main Flow and Jahson) started their careers together, with Hi-Tek producing the weight of Mood's thrilling 1997 debut, *Doom*.

With a very different vibe and aesthetic, the city is also home to three members of the multi-artist Anticon collective: Doseone, Odd Nosdam, and Why?. Doseone released his debut in 1998 with *Hemispheres*, and collaborated with Why? in the groups Greenthink, Object Beings (also with Pedestrian), and Blud N Gutz (with Jel). Odd Nosdam began releasing music in 1998, and he and Why? released *In The Shadow of the Living Room* in 2002 under the name Reaching Quiet. In addition to the collaborations mentioned above, Why? also released several solo projects from 1999 onwards, and he, Doseone and Odd Nosdam recorded as the group cLOUDDEAD, dropping their self-titled debut in 2001.

Doseone was also a member of the supergroup Deep Puddle Dynamics with fellow Anticon founders Alias and Sole, and Slug from the group Atmosphere. Their only full-length album was 1999's *The Taste of Rain... Why Kneel*, although there was also an EP named *We Ain't Fessin' (Double Quotes)* in 2002.

Cincinnati producer and deejay Mr. Dibbs released a vast collection of mixtape projects between 1998 and 2005. He also co-founded the celebrated Scribble Jam hip-hop festival, hosted in the city every year for more than a decade.

ILLINOIS

In the years before Kanye West exploded into the mainstream after producing hits for the biggest names in rap and with his 2004 debut *College Dropout* – later going on to undo all the goodwill he had from the underground by making a lot of terrible hip-hop and proving himself to be an all round horrible human being – there was a bubbling underground scene in West's native Chicago, Illinois, inspired by hometown rap heroes like Common and his producer No I.D.

One such group was All Natural, who were originally meant to have an album come out in the dying days of the once legendary hip-hop label Wild Pitch. After the label collapsed, the duo made up of emcee Capital D and producer Tone b. Nimble went the independent route, dropping 12"s on their own All Natural Inc label, and the album *No Additives, No Preservatives* in 1998. The *Second Nature* album followed in 2001, and Capital D also released solo albums, the highlight being 2002's *Writer's Block (The Movie)*, a collaboration with production crew Molemen.

The Molemen are from Chicago themselves, and although there are many listed members, the core of the crew is made up of Memo, Panik, and PNS. They released *The Soundtrack To The*

Underground Instrumentals in 1999, and worked with several emcees from Chicago and beyond on 2000's *Below The Ground Buried Alive* and 2001's *Ritual Of The…*. The latter includes the track "Put Your Quarter Up", an epic posse cut featuring vocals by Aesop Rock, Slug and MF DOOM. The group also operated the Molemen Records label, which put out records by several Chicago artists, among them Vakill, who released his debut *The Darkest Cloud* in 2003. Molemen also collaborated with other Chicago artists, including a pre-fame Rhymefast, and the group Rubberoom (emcees Lumba Blackwood and Meta-Mo, and producers Isle of Weight and Mr. Echoes), although their *Architechnology* album from 1999 came out on 3-2-1 Records.

The multi-hyphenate Psalm One was championed in the early days of her rap career by two of the underground's most important figures. First she was discovered by Hieroglyphics legend Casual, and then she signed to Rhymesayers Entertainment after the label had been wisened to her talents by Eyedea. This eventually led to the release of *The Death of Frequent Flyer* in 2006, but previous to that, Psalm One dropped *Bio: Chemistry* in 2002 – aptly named since she worked on the album while completing a chemistry major at the University of Illinois – and a sequel in 2004 (*Bio: Chemistry: Esters and Essays*). Although Rhymesayers Entertainment was her label for many years, she later called for a boycott of the label when allegations of sexual misconduct by certain artists on the roster began to surface. As the first woman signed to the label, and their only artist who is openly queer, Psalm One understandably felt compelled to make a stand, and her actions helped prompt a response from Rhymesayers, who claimed to have ended contracts with the accused, and reevaluated their business practices.

Other underground artists from Chicago who released records

during the period include the group Rec Center. Following the tradition of over-subscribed rap groups, Rec Center had nine members, but still managed to drop a cohesive album with *Lonely People* in 1999. Around the same time, rapper Serengeti was perfecting his skills at college, bonding with a like-minded artist who is today one of the leading lights in the new world of indie rap, Open Mike Eagle. Although most of Serengeti's music and acclaim came post-2005, he released *Dirty Flamingo* in 2003, giving everyone a taste of what was to come.

MICHIGAN

The history of underground hip-hop in Detroit, Michigan is a tale of two separate family trees: artists that came up with Eminem, and those that came up with J Dilla. Though these may at first glance feel like two very different strains of hip-hop, they connected and intertwined at many points, reflecting the deep sense of collaboration that runs through the Detroit scene, with seemingly everyone having worked with everyone at some point.

Eminem is one of the biggest-selling artists in any genre of music, but his roots in the Detroit underground scene run deep. Way back in 1988 the young Marshall Mathers started out rapping under the name MC Double M as part of the groups New Jack and Soul Intent, whose members also included Proof (one of several groups Proof was part of, another being 5 Elementz). He was going as Eminem by the independent release of his debut in 1996, *Infinite*, and although that album is now largely forgotten, his next was a mega hit, and everyone knows the story from there on out. In between *Infinite* and *The Slim Shady LP*, Eminem featured on tracks with several key figures of the new burgeoning underground, including Thirstin

Howl III, Shabaam Sahdeeq, and The High & Mighty.

Crucially, Eminem brought his various contemporaries from Detroit with him into the big time. Obie Trice, Proof (who was tragically murdered in 2006), Denaun Porter, and the rest of the D-12 collective all benefited from his success, either by releasing music on Eminem's label, or by having their independently-released music boosted by association.

Another Detroit artist who has benefited exponentially by having a connection with Eminem is Royce da 5'9". He and Eminem recorded as the duo Bad Meets Evil, and Eminem also features on Royce's official debut album, 2002's *Rock City*. In addition to the Eminem connection, Rock City was also boosted by the inclusion of the single "Boom", which had actually come out three years previous in 1993. The song is an underground classic, mainly because it boasts one of DJ Premier's most raucous beats. Royce da 5'9" has experienced an unfair share of record label drama since, dabbling with the majors, while also releasing several later albums on indie labels.

While Eminem was working hard to make it, in another part of Detroit, Conant Gardens to be exact, the city's other strain of hip-hop was starting to take shape. The story of how James Yancey became J Dilla starts with another Detroit producer who is also now departed, Amp Fiddler. It was the acclaimed musician who first allowed Yancey, who was going by the name Jay Dee at this stage, into his basement studio in 1992 to produce beats for a group of local rappers, teaching him how to use the tool that Dilla would make his own, the Akia MPC60 sampler.

Prior to that, Jay Dee had joined forces with emcees T3 and Baatin, who had known each other since high school, and rapper Que D as a peripheral member, to form the group Ssenepod (read it backwards if you haven't figured it out yet). T3 and Baatin had been introduced to Jay Dee by another famed producer from Detroit, Waajeed, who had been hearing good things about the Yancey kid. When they also found out Jay Dee could rap, his place in the group made even more sense.

Ssenepod went nowhere, but the group refined their sound, and scaled down to just three members. T3, Baatin and Jay Dee renamed themselves Slum Village, and eventually recorded their first songs as a group in 1996.

Meanwhile, in 1994, Amp Fiddler had been on tour with A Tribe Called Quest and played Q-Tip some of Jay Dee's beats, who then played them for Trugoy from De La Soul. Everyone else Q-Tip played the tapes for was suitably impressed, and by the end of the 90s Jay Dee had become hip-hop's hottest producer. He provided beats for A Tribe Called Quest, De La Soul, Busta Rhymes, Mad Skillz, The Pharcyde, and many more, both on his own and as part of The Ummah with Q-Tip and Ali Shaheed Muhammad.

Jay Dee still continued to work with Detroit artists, like Phat Kat (with whom Jay Dee formed the duo 1st Down), and several rappers in Eminem's orbit, briefly bringing together the two dynasties of Detroit hip-hop, including Proof (both as a solo artist and as part of the group 5 Elementz), and the rest of D-12.

All of this was happening while Slum Village had yet to release any music, and so, sensing that Jay Dee was about to have way less time on his hands, the group hit the studio for a week and created their debut album, *Fan-Tas-Tic (Vol. 1)*, selling it by hand to hungry local listeners. Though Slum Village released records on indie label Barak (founded by RJ Rice, whose son Young RJ years later would become a member of Slum Village), by their second album they were signed to A&M. *Fantastic, Vol. 2* was completed by 1998, but issues with A&M meant the album didn't actually come out until 2000. That same year also saw the release of the *Best Kept Secret* EP (under the name J-88), which included remixes by Madlib, marking the first time the two future legends crossed paths.

Jay Dee left Slum Village shortly afterwards, and T3 and Baatin added a new member, Elzhi, who debuted on their third album, 2002's *Trinity (Past, Present and Future)*. Baatin's struggles with poor mental health saw him leave the group for Slum Village's fourth and fifth albums, *Detroit Deli* (2004) and *Slum Village* (2005). He returned to the fray for sixth album *Villa Manifesto*, released in 2010, but died the following year after an accidental drug overdose. He was 35.

Despite having left the group in 2001, Jay Dee continued to contribute production and vocals to many of the Slum Village albums listed above. No longer being an active member allowed him to continue his career as a producer, and focus on his solo album. Here is where he began to call himself J Dilla, but his planned debut, where J Dilla was to focus fully on rapping with other producers providing the beats, never materialized. Instead, he connected with the BBE label to release *Welcome 2 Detroit* as part of their *Beat Generation* series.

Next came the *Ruff Draft* EP in 2003 (years later expanded and reissued by Stones Throw Records in 2007), and in the same year, *Champion Sound*, where J Dilla collaborated with Madlib as the duo Jaylib, cementing their creative partnership. And then came *Donuts* in 2006, a masterpiece of production that came out three days before J Dilla died, aged 32. He left a comprehensive catalog of production for artists across the spectrum of rap music and soul, and multiple posthumous projects have been released in his name since his death.

Welcome 2 Detroit featured guest vocals from a selection of other Detroit artists who would go on to have respected careers in their own right: Phat Kat, Frank N Dank, and Elzhi. After his time with J Dilla in the duo 1st Down, Phat Kat released his solo debut *The Undeniable LP* in 2004, featuring contributions from J Dilla, Slum Village, and Obie Trice among others. *The Carte Blance* album followed in 2007.

Frank N Dank, aka Frank Nitt and Dankery Harv, had their 2003 album *48 Hours* aborted due to label disagreements, but the J Dilla produced album still came out unofficially. This was followed in 2004 by their second album, *Xtended Play*. Years later, Frank Nitt released an album with J Dilla's younger brother, Illa J, under the name Yancey Boys. Most of Elzhi's acclaimed post-Slum Village music would come post-2005 (see later chapter), but he released several EPs and mixtapes from 1998 onwards.

Several other Detroit artists also got their start during the period, though they would only earn major acclaim post-2005, including Guilty Simpson (who was a member of the Almighty Dreadnaughtz collective), Black Milk and Danny Brown (see later chapter for more on these artists).

Almost completely outside of the Eminem and J Dilla circles, the group Binary Star were from another city in Michigan, Pontiac. The duo of OneManArmy and Senim Silla released the *Waterworld* EP in 1999, and then released an expanded version in 2000, the acclaimed *Masters of the Universe*.

MINNESOTA

For all intents and purposes, Rhymesayers Entertainment *is* the hip-hop scene in Minneapolis, Minnesota, because essentially everyone who has released music from the state has an association with the label started in 1995 by Slug and Ant of the group

Atmosphere, and Musab and Siddiq. Atmosphere and Musab were each members of the Headshots collective, and the latter released his debut album in 1996, *Comparison*, under the name Beyond, and various other projects as Musab. Atmosphere came out with *Overcast!* (at which point the group also included rapper Spawn) as their first album in 1997, starting an epic streak of releases that is still in full swing today. Highlights from the period include 2002's *God Loves Ugly;* 2003's *Seven's Travels*; and *You Can't Imagine How Much Fun We're Having* and *Headshots: Se7en* in 2005. Ant also released solo mix projects in 2001 and 2005 (*Melodies and Memories* and *Melodies and Memories 85–89*), and another acclaimed release came in 1998 with *The Dynospectrum*, a group made up of several Minneapolis artists who each took on an alias: Slug as Sep Sev Sev Two; Musab as General Woundwar; I Self Devine as Pat Juba; Swift as Mr. Gene Poole, and Ant on production as Solomon Grundy.

Born in Los Angeles but raised in Minnesota, I Self Devine had been involved in hip-hop since the early 90s as a member of Micranots, alongside DJ Kool Akiem, and Truth Maze, who left the group in 1994. They debuted with *Return of the Travellahs* in 1996, but got traction with their second album, 2000's *Obelisk Movements*, released on Bigg Jus' Sub Verse Music. Micranots then signed with Rhymesayers Entertainment for their third, and so far final album, *The Emperor & the Assassin*. I Self Devine's solo debut also came out on Rhymesayers Entertainment, 2005's *Self Destruction*.

Another Minneapolis artist who has released many records via Rhymesayers Entertainment is Brother Ali, originally born in Wisconsin but based in Minnesota since the beginning of the 90s. After releasing *Rites of Passage* in 2002, Ali gained wider exposure with his next projects, 2003's *Shadow's on the Sun* and

2004's *Champion EP*, both produced by Ant. Much of Brother Ali's music is political, bringing back some of the activism hip-hop had lost since Public Enemy's heyday, and in fact Chuck D is known to be a huge fan of his music.

Over in the city of Saint Paul, the 'twin' city of Minneapolis, rapper Eyedea had been turning heads with his savage battle rap performances. He connected with producer DJ Abilities, and the duo released *First Born* in 2001 via Rhymesayers Entertainment. The *E&A* album followed in 2004, while Eyedea also released a solo album in 2002 under the name Oliver Hart, *The Many Faces of Oliver Hart*, and DJ Abilities dropped mixtapes in 1997 and 2000, all on Rhymesayers Entertainment.

The Rhymesayers Entertainment family and the underground at large were left devastated when Eyedea was found dead in October 2020 at 28. Many tribute songs have been released over the ensuing years, and the man affectionately known as 'Mikey' by those that knew him is still missed today.

Other indie artists from Minnesota who got their start during the period include P.O.S., who released his solo debut *Ipecac Neat* in 2004, and would later release music as part of the group Doomtree; and Muja Messiah, starting with the *Wutz Going Down?* EP in 2001.

WASHINGTON

Seattle, Washington's biggest claim to rap music fame is being the place where Sir Mix-a-Lot made his name. His 1992 pop-rap smash "Baby Got Back" is about as far away as you can get from underground hip-hop, but Seattle is also the hometown of emcee and producer Vitamin D, who released *Tables Manners 2* in 1998, and *No Good* in 2003 via Rhymesayers Entertainment.

Producer Jake One is also from the city, and before he began producing for some of rap's biggest stars, he provided beats for MF DOOM, I Self Divine, Rasco, Vast Aire, and Gift of Gab, among others. Seattle was also home to DJ Sureshot and Mr. Supreme's Conception Records.

OREGON

Nestled between California to the south and Washington state to the north, Oregon feels just about close enough to the indie scenes in Oakland and Los Angeles, but still way too far to be considered a key player. The group Lifesavas (Vursatyl, Jumbo and Rev Shines) was, however, given an assist by their southerly neighbors when Blackalicious invited them into Quannum Projects for the release of their debut in 2003, *Spirit in Stone*.

TEXAS

Texas has birthed some of rap's most creative artists, but is not exactly known for having much of an underground scene. None of this mattered to the members of K-Otix, made up of rappers Micah and Damian, and producer The Are. They released the *Universal* album in 2001, and *The Black Album* in 2003. That same year, The Are came out with his own debut, *Hustlers Theme*.

KENTUCKY

A hip-hop group coming out of the Bluegrass stronghold of Lexington, Kentucky, must have felt like a longshot for Deacon the Villain and Kno when they founded CunninLynguists in 1999. They debuted in 2001 with *Will Rap for Food*, and added a new member, Mr. SOS, for their second album, 2003's *SouthernUnderground*. In later years the group added Natti to the line-up, and earned plaudits for *A Piece of Strange* in 2006.

———

If one was to say that the Canadian hip-hop scene is just an annexed version of what happens across the border in the US, one would be correct to a degree. Hip-hop transcends cultures, race and borders, after all, and Canada's biggest rap act, Drake, is looked upon as being a 'rap star', not a 'Canadian rap star'.

That being said, the rap community across the provinces of one of the world's largest countries has its own personality and nuance, and lots of local pride. It is also a story of hard work and resilience, where artists have to fight to be recognised and taken seriously by the wider Canadian music business.

ONTARIO

Among the most important artists to help and inspire the nation's underground scene are Maestro Fresh Wes, and Kardinal Offishal. Canadian Music Hall of Fame inductee Maestro Fresh Wes, from Toronto, Ontario, released the successful *Symphony in Effect* in 1989, boosting the national rap scene exponentially. He continued to release albums for years after, and by 1998's *Built to Last* was collaborating with key names from the bubbling Canadian underground.

Kardinal Offishal, also representing Toronto, began his career in the early 90s as KoolAid, but had settled on the more familiar name by the release of his debut album in 1997, *Eye & I*. He has achieved various levels of commercial success since, working with some of the world's biggest artists, but remains an iconic figure to the underground heads.

Toronto based crew The Circle was also co-founded by Kardinal Offishal. Other members of the collective included Jully Black and Solitair, but the two most impactful members were Saukrates and Choclair. After getting some traction with singles he released in 1994, and a short spell being signed to a major, Saukrates endeared himself to the underground community with the release of the *Brick House* EP in 1997, put out on his own label, Capital Hill Music (which also released Kardinal Offishal's *Eye & I*). *Brick House* has appearances from Masta Ace and O.C. and a remix to the track "Play Dis" by No I.D., and this heavyweight backup helped the EP to reach far beyond the local Toronto circuit. The momentum was sustained for the release of Saukrates' full debut in 1999, *The Underground Tapes*. The mostly self-produced album secured Saukrates' place as a leading light in Canadian indie hip-hop, and further strengthened his reach in the US thanks to contributions by Common, Heltah Skeltah, Pharoahe Monch and Xzibit.

Choclair landed on listeners' radar in 1995 with the single "Twenty One Years" (released as the b-side to the "Father Time" single by Saukrates), another of the many songs that gained a following in the US thanks to it being included on the DJ Premier hosted *New York Reality Check 101* compilation in 1997 (listed on the tracklist under the different spelling "21 Years"). The emcee launched his own indie label, Knee Deep Records, on which came the 1997 *What It Takes* EP. By 1999, Choclair was signed to a major (Virgin), and released his debut album *Ice Cold* in 1999, produced by Saukrates, Kardinal Offishal and Solitair, among others.

Another important faction of the Toronto underground was the group Da Grassroots, made up of Mr. Attic, Mr. Murray, and Swift.

They produced for various acts from 1993 onwards, including Ghetto Concept (Kwajo Cinqo and Dolo, who later released their self-titled debut in 1998), and pioneering Canadian group the Dream Warriors, before releasing their acclaimed debut album, 1999's *Passage Through Time*. Mr. Attic has also provided beats for artists as a solo producer, but Swift died in 2018 after a battle with cancer.

Other essential records from Toronto during the period included the 1999 *Deliverance* album by the group Citizen Kane (Aje, Rob Blye and Spade); 12"s by the groups Point Blank (Jackal, Kidd, Pikihed, RPD, Stump and Trouble) and Redlife (Remy Res and Cryp2Nite), and emcee Frankenstein; the 1996 *Past, Present, Future* (1996) album by rapper Thrust; several albums, EPs and mixtapes by Dan-e-o and the collective he co-founded, Monolith; and the 2005 *No Division* album by Mathematik.

Producer Marco Polo is most associated with the New York underground scene, but is actually from Toronto. His first production credit of note was on Masta Ace's 2004 album *A Long Hot Summer*, and the two have worked and toured frequently together since. Marco Polo's debut, *Port Authority*, was released via Rawkus Records in 2007, followed by numerous other solo albums and collaborations.

Elsewhere in Ontario, there were releases from Ottawa group Flight Distance, consisting of Bender, Calkuta, and Patience. Bender released *The Squidmilker Instrumentals* as his solo debut in 2004, but died aged only 37 in 2018. Rapper Eternia is also from Ottawa, and released her first album in 2005, *It's Called Life*.

Anyone who wants to know what life looks like when rappers mature, get older and have normal responsibilities need look no further than Eternia's Instagram feed, where photos promoting her rap career are interspersed with images of domestic bliss at the home she shares with husband Mr. Lif, and their children.

QUEBEC

In Montreal, Quebec, years before he became known primarily as a house music producer and touring deejay, A-Trak was deeply entrenched in the local and national hip-hop scene. He won the DMC World DJ Championships at just 15, and picked up other titles in subsequent years. He co-founded the group Obscure Disorder in 1995 with his brother Dave One, and Eclipse, Logik and Troy Dunnit. They released a string of 12"s between 1997-2002, but never managed a full album. A-Trak and Dave One also ran the short-lived Audio Research Records label, but A-Trak has fared better since he co-founded Fool's Gold Records in 2007, releasing music by hip-hop acts including Run The Jewels, Mayhem Lauren, and Danny Brown.

NOVA SCOTIA

In Nova Scotia, a small but steady indie rap scene has been ticking along since the mid 1990s. The group Hip Club Groove, which consisted of Cheklove Shakil, DJ Moves and MC, made some noise with the *Cool Beans* EP in 1993 and each of their albums that followed. Occasional Hip Club Groove member Sixtoo also kicked off his solo rap career around the same time, going on to release a huge number of projects before moving on to other types of music.

Sixtoo's partner in the duo Sebutones is arguably Nova Scotia's most successful underground artist, rapper Buck 65. Today he operates in genres away from hip-hop, but released a ton of rap projects during the era. His most fertile period was during his time on the Anticon label, earning praise for 2001's *Man Overboard*.

Classified, from the Enfield area of Nova Scotia, has had success and stints on major labels over his long career, but has also collaborated with many of Canada's underground artists since 1995. Deejay and producer Skratch Bastid also hails from Nova Scotia, and although most of his success has come in recent years, his first mixtape came out in 2003, and in 2005 he released *Taking Care of Business* with fellow Canadian artists Pip Skid and John Smith.

BRITISH COLUMBIA

On the other side of this vast country, in Vancouver, British Columbia, the success of the pioneering group Rascalz started a local scene that is still buzzing today. Group members DJ Kemo, Misfit and Red 1 formed in 1991, releasing their debut *Really Livin* in 1992, which was then re-released on a major in 1993. They followed with three additional albums: *Cash Crop* in 1997, *Global Warming* in 1999, and *Reloaded* in 2002. *Cash Crop* attracted the most attention, for two main reasons. First was the track "Northern Touch", which is remembered as one of the most important songs in the history of Canadian hip-hop. The track became an anthemic rallying cry for the rest of the underground scene, and also crossed over with some mainstream success. "Northern Touch" features contributions from Canadian hip-hop pillars Kardinal Offishal and Choclair, plus Checkmate and Thrust. The second reason why *Cash Crop* is still renowned is down to what happened at the 1998 Juno Awards. When *Cash Crop* won Best Rap Recording, the Rascalz rejected the award in protest of how the category was not deemed important enough to be in the televised portion of the ceremony. It was a valid point, and the statement endeared Rascalz to the independent artists watching.

Vancouver group Swollen Members have also been influential, and one member in particular has gone on to have the most prolific career in hip-hop, releasing well over 100 different albums. The group was founded circa 1995 by three original members, Madchild, Moka Only, and Prevail. Their peak came with their first album *Balance*, released in 1999 and recorded in Los Angeles. This location, miles away from their hometown north of the border, explains why the list of contributors is heavy on rappers from California's underground scene, including Aceyalone, Del the Funky Homosapian, Dilated Peoples and Saafir, plus early 90s stalwarts Everlast and Son Doobie. Second album *Bad Dreams* (2001) was another California-centric affair, yet by third album *Monsters in the Closet* in 2002, the group was focused on collaborating with homegrown talent, even working with Nelly Furtado. Several more albums followed, some with involvement from Moka Only, some without much at all, and some with Rob the Viking added as a member.

The group also spawned side projects, including Madchild and Moka Only as the duo Perfect Strangers, and the *Code Name: Scorpion* album Moka Only and Prevail recorded in 2001 with Abstract Rude. All of these, and every single Swollen Members album, were released on Madchild's own indie label, Battle Axe Records.

The artist with the 100+ albums is Moka Only, who is still dropping new projects on a regular basis today, and shows no sign of stopping. Many of Moka Only's albums have been on Urbnet, an indie label founded in 1999 that has supported and promoted the work of scores of Canadian artists.

6

THE ANTIPOP CONSORTIUMS

On the anonymous internet, where you can run an entire business from your phone, operating a record label can mean whatever you want it to mean. Anyone can upload music to a streaming site with just a few clicks, and the barrier for entry into the DIY world of self-releasing music is therefore lower than ever. Spotify, for example, is estimated to have around two million songs uploaded to their platform every month, which by any metric is a fuck-tonne of music.

It was very different in the pre-streaming days of the 90s, when running a label was a physical business, with people and overheads to pay, and the physical, cumbersome process of getting music manufactured onto CDs and wax. This set the quality bar a lot higher, because nobody would choose to spend the amount of time, effort and money needed to run a label unless they really wanted to make it work.

For the labels of different sizes putting out underground hip-hop during the era, the goal was to bring dope rap music to new ears, and preferably make some money.

What follows is a look at the most impactful and memorable labels from 1995-2005, in alphabetical order, and what happened to them.

ABB RECORDS

ABB Records was started in 1997 in Oakland by Ben Nickleberry Jr., aka Beni B, with the 'ABB' standing for Always Bigger and Better. It was an ambitious and lofty phrase to name a company after, but for a few years ABB did prove to be a premier label for Californian underground rap. The first artist to release music on the label was Defari, and the partnership would go on to produce a deep collection of 12"s and albums, including some that Defari released under the name L.A.'s Own Billy The Kidd. In 1998, ABB signed Dilated Peoples, again forging a lasting alliance that also included solo records from group members Evidence and DJ Babu (as the Likwit Junkies with Defari). Joey Chavez also signed the same year. In 1999 Planet Asia joined the label, and in 2006 ABB showed some love to their native Oakland by releasing music from Saafir.

Other artists from California who released records on ABB include production duo Sound Providers (Jay Skillz and Soulo) from San Diego, who released *An Evening with The Sound Providers* in 2004, Superstar Quamallah, including the "Just Rap" 12", and the San Jose based group Foreign Legion (Prozack, Marc Stretch, and DJ Design).

ABB then branched out wider than California when North Carolina's Little Brother joined the roster and released several 12"s and their first two albums, *The Listening* and *The Minstrel Show* (vinyl version only), in 2003 and 2004 respectively. The records with Little Brother also lead to ABB releasing a 12" by the Hall of Justus (aka Justus League) collective, of which Phonte and Rapper Big Pooh were both members, and 12"s by another Justus League member, Cesar Comanche.

The label's reach also extended to Detroit, with 12"s released by Jay Dee (aka J Dilla), Frank-n-Dank, and Big Tone. ABB additionally put out records by Washington D.C.'s Kev Brown, the Springfield, Massachusetts group Maspyke (DJ Roddy Rod, Tableek, and Hanif Jamiyl), and one record by New York freestyle legend Supernatural.

In recent years it has come to light that Beni B, allegedly, didn't always do right by his artists. Little Brother in particular have been vocal about money owed to them by ABB for *The Listening* and *The Minstrel Show*, and when ABB reissued *The Minstrel Show* in 2021, Phonte and Rapper Big Pooh urged fans not to buy copies of the reissued vinyl, or listen to any of the tracks on streaming services, seeing as they would receive no revenue from any of it. In an interview at the time, Phonte pointed out the irony that despite indie labels seemingly treating their artists well, the only label they never had any issues with is the one major they were signed to, Atlantic Records. It's a depressing bookend to the story of a record label that introduced the world to so much good hip-hop.

ANTICON RECORDS

There were mixed feelings in 1997 when the newly-formed Anticon Records announced their mission statement of wanting to release "music for the advancement of hip-hop". Some were excited for what it meant, while others were left scratching their heads. The sentiment also created some tension, especially in New York, where anything seen as being too far outside the parallels of traditional hip-hop could be considered an affront to everything the culture stood for. Although it was almost certainly blown out of proportion, there were rumors at the time that the bubbling animosity between Anticon's approach and the rest of the underground was a catalyst for a short beef between Sole and El-P.

Anticon was founded as a collective by eight different owners:

artists Why? (later known as Yoni Wolf), Doseone, Sole, Jel, Odd Nosdam, Alias, and Pedestrian, and Baillie Parker on the business side. The various members came from different states, including Maine, Ohio and California, but the day to day operations of the label were run from Oakland. As a city with an established pedigree for straight up hip-hop, the type of sound Anticon championed was far at the fringes of the local scene, and a million miles away from the Oakland gangster rap sound.

The label set out their intentions with the *Music For the Advancement of Hip-hop* EP in 1998, featuring various members, plus Slug and Eyedea. Anticon followed with numerous releases, including Sole's debut album (*Bottle of Humans*), the first (and only) full album from Deep Puddle Dynamics (Sole, Slug, Alias and Doseone), and records by Alias, Buck 65, and 1200 Hobos among others.

The release schedule ramped up significantly between 2003-2005 as Anticon brought out music by Sole, Sage Francis, Odd Nosdam, Why?, Dosh, Alias, Themselves (Doseone and Jel), Passage, Pedestrian, Bomarr and Telephone Jim Jesus, a lot of which veered away from traditional hip-hop into other genres.

Since the death of Alias in 2018, the collective has called time on the label. It leaves behind a varied body of work that took hip-hop in several different directions.

DEFINITIVE JUX

El-P is less angry today about what went down with Rawkus Records, but was big mad about it at the start of the millennium. Company Flow's second album – *Little Johnny from the Hospitul: Breaks & Instrumentals Vol.1*, recorded without Bigg Jus – had come out in the middle of Rawkus' epic 1999, but the relationship between the group and label was by now a flaming dumpster fire. By the end of 2000, Company Flow had departed.

The decline of Rawkus and the pain of getting fucked over by a label who once shared his view was the impetus El-P needed to finally build his own thing, and so Definitive Jux was born, co-founded with El-P's longtime business partner and manager, Amaechi Uzoigwe.

In truth, having his own label was always El-P's plan. Rawkus may have started out in support of independence, but by being on a label, Company Flow was not fully independent. From as far back as the days of Company Flow's own Official Recordings label, it was El-P's hope to one day put out his music by himself. First, however, there was a legal wrinkle to iron out. The label was originally named Def Jux, but El-P's new company was hit with litigation threats by Def Jam, due to the similarities. The case was ironic, in that on one hand, being sued by a corporate entity could be seen as a badge of honor to the fiercely anti-corporate El-P. On the other hand, Def Jam was responsible for some of the classic era albums El-P was most inspired by. Either way, an out of court settlement was reached, and the name was changed to Definitive Jux.

For a label so deeply rooted in New York City, surprisingly the first release on Definitive Jux was by Boston emcee Mr. Lif', who dropped the *Enters the Colossus* EP in late 2000. If 1997-1999 were Rawkus' breakout years, then 2001-2005 were Definitive Jux's, in which time the label released landmark albums and EPs by Cannibal Ox (*The Cold Vein*); Aesop Rock (*Labor Days, Daylight, Bazooka Tooth, Fast Cars, Danger, Fire and Knives*); Mr. Lif (*Emergency Rations, I Phantom*); RJD2 (*Deadringer, The Horror, Since We Last Spoke*); Murs (*The End of the Beginning, Murs 3:16: The 9th Edition* with 9th Wonder); S.A. Smash (*Smashy Trashy*); Party Fun

Action Committee (*Let's Get Serious*); C-Rayz Walz (*Ravipops: The Substance, Year of the Beast*); Hangar 18 (*The Multi-Platinum Debut Album*); Rob Sonic (*Telicatessen*), The Perceptionists (*Black Dialogue*); and Cage (*Hell's Winter*). That time span also included three editions of the *Definitive Jux Presents* series, and the release of El-P's own solo debut, *Fantastic Damage*.

It was a mesmerizing discography of releases that breathed new life into the underground scene, and by branching out to include artists from Columbus, Boston, and Los Angeles, El-P was able to show that the indie rap wave was no longer just New York or California centric.

The Definitive Jux launch had also coincided with the end of another indie rap label, run by someone close to El-P's heart. Like almost everyone who dropped indie 12"s in the mid 90s, Company Flow's profile had been boosted by airplay from Stretch Armstrong and Bobbito on their legendary radio show. In 2001, when Bobbito called time on Fondle 'Em Records, he considered Definitive Jux to be the natural successor to keep the spirit alive of what he set out to achieve, and so in 2001 Bob and El-P put out a tribute record to celebrate what had made Fondle 'Em so great. First came the "Fondle 'Em Fossils" 12" with vocals by the dream line-up of MF DOOM, Godfather Don, Q-Unique, Breeze Brewin and J-Treds, followed by the *Farewell Fondle 'Em* album that also featured Arsonists, Kool Keith, Cage, MHz, Yak Ballz and MF Grimm.

Additional music came out in subsequent years, including more from El-P, Mr. Lif, Aesop Rock, Rob Sonic, Cage and Hangar 18, plus releases from new signings such as the group Sonic Sum (Fred Ones, Rob Sonic, Preservation and Eric M.O.) and Cool Calm Pete, and albums from west coast indie rap royalty Del the Funky Homosapien, and Gift of Gab, Lateef and Headnodic as the group The Mighty Underdogs.

Then, in 2010, El-P pulled the plug, making an announcement that Definitive Jux was to be no more. There are several reasons why the label ended, and there are many different theories floating about online, but the most accepted are that El-P had become dissatisfied with the direction the label had taken, and how it was pigeon-holded as a label seemingly only for white backpackers. He also wanted to get back to solely making music and not having the stress of running a business, especially in a climate where illegal downloading was very quickly killing off small indie labels across the board.

Similar to the aforementioned death of Camu Tao having been a key reason why The Weathermen supergroup had ended, Tao's death was also a big factor in El-P losing his enthusiasm for Definitive Jux. As a close friend it hit him hard, but it was a suitable tribute to both the artist and label that Definitive Jux's final release was the posthumous Camu Tao album, *King of Hearts* (released in partnership with Fat Possum Records, who two years later released El-P's third album, *Cancer 4 Cure*, which he dedicated to Tao).

El-P's Company Flow partners also briefly had their own post-Rawkus labels. Bigg Jus launched Sub Verse Music in 1998 which put out music by Scienz of Life, Micranots and more, and played a part in the history of MF DOOM by releasing KMD's *Black Bastards* and a reissue of *Operation: Doomsday*. Mr. Len created Smacks Records (sometimes credited as Dummy Smacks Records) to release his own music, side projects Roosevelt Franklin and The Dix, and others.

Rapper and producer Uncommon Nasa also credits Definitive Jux for inspiring him to start his own label, Uncommon Records, with Nasa learning how to run a music business during his years as Definite Jux's in-house mix engineer.

DUCK DOWN MUSIC

"Duck Down" is a brash and fierce song by KRS-One and his Boogie Down Productions posse, from their 1992 *Sex and Violence* album. It also inspired the name of one of hip-hop's longest running labels, known for making music as hard hitting as BDP.

After Dru-Ha and Buckshot moved their artists Black Moon and Smif-N-Wessun with them from Wreck/Nervous (see later section) to their newly-founded Duck Down Music, they began signing other artists to the label. Similar to the model RZA had created with the Wu-Tang Clan, the original plan was to introduce the Boot Camp Clik, with each artist and group then spinning off with their own albums.

By 1996 the label was ready to drop its first proper releases, a double-whammy of albums destined for classic status, kicking off an aggressive schedule of releases over the next few years. First came *Nocturnal* by Heltah Skeltah, followed months later by O.G.C.s *Da Storm*. Like *Enta Da Stage* and *Dah Shinin'* before them, these first Duck Down releases were powered by Da Beatminerz, who became a huge part of the label's history, and continue to be today.

The first Boot Camp Clik album came out in 1997 (*For The People*), followed by sophomore albums by Smif-N-Wessun (*The Rude Awakening*, under the name Cocoa Brovaz); Heltah Skeltah (*Magnum Force*); Black Moon (*War Zone*); O.G.C. (*The M-Pire Shrikez Back*); a compilation (*Duck Down Presents: The Album*); a solo album by Buckshot (*The BDI Thug*); and the debut album by Representativz (Supreme The Eloheem and Lidu Rock), all released between 1997-99.

The reach and exposure of these albums was helped by Duck Down having signed a label distribution deal with Priority Records, at a time when Priority's parent company, EMI, was investing heavily in rap music.

From 2000-2004, after the deal with Priority had ended, the label went on another relentless run, including a greatest hit compilation from Boot Camp Clik (a mere three years after their debut album!); a second Boot Camp Clik album (*The Chosen Few*); and a third Black Moon album (*Total Eclipse*). Sean Price's *Monkey Bars* came in 2005, as did a new Smif-N-Wessun album (*Smif 'n' Wessun: Reloaded*, actually just credited to Tek and Steele on the artwork); and *Chemistry*, the first of an eventual three albums by Buckshot and producer 9th Wonder.

There is, however, a sad footnote in the Duck Down story. A few months before he died, 2Pac was working on a project named *One Nation*, aimed at easing the east v west tension. Boot Camp Clik was one of the groups he reached out to, because, according to those in Pac's inner circle, Duck Down's independence meant there wouldn't be any industry pushback about working with an artist at war with New York. Sessions were recorded, but 2Pac's death put an end to the album.

Post-2005, Duck Down began working with artists outside of the Boot Camp Clik, and today is still releasing good hip-hop decades into their reign.

EASTERN CONFERENCE

Mr. Eon and DJ Mighty Mi of The High & Mighty set up Eastern Conference Records in 1996, basing it in New York, a couple of hours drive from where they grew up in Philadelphia.

The business model for how Eastern Conference released their records aligned with the approach Rawkus was using around the same time, and what Definitive Jux would also later do: drop lots of 12"s, full albums for the artists with enough quality material, and occasional compilations bringing the roster together. The label also borrowed from the Fondle 'Em playbook by being vinyl only, although unlike Bobbito's label, Eastern Conference later embraced CDs for several of their albums.

The first releases under the Eastern Conference name were two The High & Mighty 12"s in 1997, and the *Eastern Conference All Stars* compilation in 1998. Eastern Conference then entered a deal with Rawkus, where Rawkus would be the distributor, similar to how they had partnered with Ghetto Gold Recordings and Official Recordings in their early days. As a result, several key releases in the Eastern Conference catalog have both their logo and the famous Rawkus razor blade, including The High & Mighty's *Home Field Advantage*, and *Porn Again* by the Smut Peddlers. Both of these albums did relatively well, benefitting from coming out during the period when Rawkus had a distribution deal with Priority.

In an interview with writer Robbie Ettelson for his Unkut site, DJ Mighty Mi stated how the deal with Rawkus was originally for three albums, with the third likely to have been by Cage. This never happened, because despite selling a lot of copies, *Home Field Advantage* and *Porn Again* were not as successful as Rawkus would have liked.

When the distribution deal with Rawkus ended, Mr. Eon and DJ Mighty Mi struck out on their own. In that same Unkut interview, Mighty Mi tells a funny story about meetings with Rawkus where he and Mr. Eon pretended to be mad about their partnership going sideways, because history dictates that a label splitting up with their artist has to be contentious. In reality they were ok with how the situation was going down, and took Eastern Conference into the new millennium with several important albums and EPs. Highlights over the next few years included new music by The

191

High & Mighty, Cage, Tame One, Nighthawks (Cage and Camu Tao), Leak Bros (Cage and Tame One), Copywrite, Yak Ballz, Vast Aire, and The Weathermen.

Outside of the many releases from mostly New York and New Jersey based artists, Eastern Conference also supported talent from Mr. Eon and DJ Mighty Mi's hometown of Philadelphia, including the *Feast or Famine* album by Reef The Lost Cauze, and *Black Candles* by the group JuJu Mob (of which Reef was a member).

The label also released four editions of *The High & Mighty Presents Eastern Conference All Stars* compilations, which are almost on a par with the *Soundbombing* series in how influential they were.

Mirroring the demise of Rawkus, the end for Eastern Conference came amid rumors of bad blood, including claims of mismanagement and a frustrating lack of available budgets for new projects. Cage was particularly vocal about these issues when he left the label. The drama was perhaps overblown or misunderstood, because Cage later rejoined in its final years.

The label had effectively ended by 2007, but six years later, when Cage released his *Kill The Architect* album, it was on Eastern Conference. *Kill The Architect* turned out to be the final release on the label, bringing Mr. Eon, DJ Mighty Mi and Cage full circle. Although The High & Mighty haven't put out an album since 2005, they did release some new singles in 2024. There, on the digital artwork and in the credits on streaming platforms, was the Eastern Conference logo and name, back from the dead. In another full circle moment, one of the new singles featured Breeze Brewin, back working with Eastern Conference more than two decades on from the release of The Weathermen's *The Conspiracy* mixtape. A 25th anniversary edition of *Home Field Advantage* was also released in

2024, again with the Eastern Conference label on it. If Mr. Eon and DJ Mighty Mi resurrect it in full, we may yet see more chapters in the rollercoaster history of the label. It has already outlived Fondle 'Em, Rawkus, Definitive Jux and all their other competitors.

FAT BEATS RECORDS

If you own any amount of underground hip-hop 12"s released between 1995-2005 it's almost certain most of them will have the words Fat Beats printed somewhere on the label or sleeve. The company was a distributor for many individual artists and small indie labels throughout the era, getting wax onto the shelves of their own stores, other people's shops around the world, and into a nascent infrastructure of online stores gaining traction at the time.

Fat Beats made the shrewd business decision to start a label in 1996, Fat Beats Records, giving them control of both the release and distribution of records, and therefore expanding the services they could offer an artist. It took some time to convince new and hungry rappers hell bent on getting a major record deal that going the indie route would be beneficial – and likely make them more money up front – but eventually many artists came to see that putting a record out on Fat Beats was a good proposition.

Fat Beats was started by Joseph Abajian, aka DJ Jab, who opened the first physical Fat Beats store in a small basement location in Manhattan's Lower East Side in July 1994 after spotting a gap in the market. Frustrated that the home of hip-hop had no record stores dedicated to rap music – and how he and other rap heads would have to go to multiple different stores to find the records they were hearing on Stretch Armstrong and Bobitto's radio show – Abajian grinded hard to establish the store through word of mouth. It worked, with initial stock selling out in the first few days of opening, and just two years later Fat Beats moved to a larger (but cheaper to rent) location in the west village.

The store became the home of underground hip-hop, where you could find all of the latest releases, budding rappers and producers working behind the counter (DJ Eclipse, Ill Bill, Breeze Brewin, J57 and Q-Unique are among the names who worked at the store), upcoming and established rappers hanging out, in-store sessions from the hottest acts (including some who today are megastars), and ciphers taking place outside. There would later be branches of the shop in Los Angeles and Atlanta, and overseas in the Netherlands and Japan.

The first official releases to bear the 'FB' catalog number were Rob Swift and Cracker Jax's "Sly Rhymes" b/w "Nickel And Dime" and Non Phixion's "Legacy" b/w "No Tomorrow". Multiple records came after that with basically everyone who was anyone in indie rap having released a record on Fat Beats Records at some point.

The store in New York has been closed since 2010, but Fat Beats is still alive as a web store and distributor. The offering has widened to a selection of other genres, but the brand is still focused on releasing the latest independent hip-hop.

FONDLE 'EM RECORDS

If you've ever heard an episode of *The Stretch Armstrong and Bobbito Show*, or watched the 2015 *Stretch and Bobbito: Radio That Changed Lives* documentary, you'll know that Bobbito Garcia is a funny guy who likes to laugh. This is further evidenced by the fact he sometimes went by the name DJ Cucumber Slice, and how he named his record label Fondle 'Em, complete with claims that the label was a division of 'Tickle 'Em Label Group', itself a subsidiary of 'Squeeze 'Em Entertainment', and how the whole concept of the record label was thought up on a whim. You'd be naive to assume this meant Bob didn't take developing artists and putting out their music seriously, however, and he'd been doing it for years.

In addition to the artists managed and developed by Bobbito and Pete Nice in the early 90s via their Hit-U-Off Management – many of which are included in this book – they also owned a small label named Hoppoh Recordings, distributed by Columbia, and opened in 1993 after Bob left his job working for Def Jam. Hoppah was short-lived with only two releases, although both were strong: Kurious' 1994 album *A Constipated Monkey*, and *Pre-Life Crisis* by Count Bass D in 1995.

That same year, Bob regrouped and founded Fondle 'Em as a vinyl-only label, after being convinced by an associate from a distribution company that people would be interested in buying the kind of gritty hip-hop records he and Stretch played on their show. The radio program provided a rich stream of unsigned and hungry artists shopping their demos, and the ones he dug the most stood a good chance of getting their music put out on Fondle 'Em. There would be no formal contracts between the label and artist, no budget for promotion of any kind, and all profits made would be shared equally.

Bob decided that Fondle 'Em would be dedicated to only putting out the rawest underground records, starting off with Kool Keith and Godfather Don's *The Cenobites* EP. By the year 2000 Fondle 'Em had racked up releases by a line-up of artists that are today considered to be amongst the best of the underground era, including 12"s by Scienz of Life, Arsonists, MF DOOM, MHz, MF Grimm, J Treds, KMD, Cage and Yak Ballz; EPs by Siah and Yeshua DapoED and The Boulevard Connection; and albums by The Cenobites, MF DOOM and the Juggaknots, including the revered *Operation: Doomsday* and *Clear Blue Skies.*

There was also a 12" by Bob's radio co host Lord Sear as his Stak Chedda character, plus records by some lesser remembered artists such as Mr. Live, Da Nuthouse, Rok One, Monsta Island Czars member Megalon (aka Tommy Gun), and South African group Cashless Society. Additionally, in 1999 a label known as Guntez Records licensed Fondle 'Em releases and put out a Japan-only compilation named *World of Fondle 'Em.*

True to Bob's vision of Fondle 'Em being wax only, virtually the entire discography was only ever pressed to vinyl, except for *Operation: Doomsday* and the extended version of the Cenobites project.

In 2001 Bobbito decided to shut the label down, happy to pass the torch to the various other labels he had inspired. He later founded two other indie labels: firstly Fruitmeat Records, with an eclectic mix of artists including some hip-hop, and then a 7"-only label named Alala.

It should be noted that Bobbito wasn't just an innovator for having written the blueprint for how to run an underground record label. He also helped pioneer the idea of a hip-hop record store being a hub for artists and fans to hang out and share music. Fat Beats is rightly remembered as the place to be in New York, but for a time Bobbito also had his own shop, named Bobbito's Footwork, with branches in New York and Philadelphia, selling vinyl, apparel, and the source of another of Bob's passions, sneakers.

Fondle 'Em is looked back upon today as being the gold standard for underground hip-hop from New York, and almost the entire catalog is now highly coveted and on sale for premium prices on sites like Discogs, especially as most of the records were only ever pressed in small amounts. The legacy of the label is another of the many reasons why Bobbito Garcia is one of the most important people in the history of the movement, if not *the* most important.

GUESSWHYLD

If you were starting a new record label, you needed to come out swinging, and that's precisely what Guesswhyld did when they released "Cut That Weak Shit " b/w "Ain't No Secret" by Brooklyn emcee Lace Da Booms, complete with a remix by Diggin' In The Crates (DITC) producer Buckwild.

Guesswhyld was the creation of New York producer and deejay Matthew 'Matt Fingaz' Schilt, established in 1996. Fingaz got his start on college radio and learned what he needed to know about running a record label while interning at different companies, including Relativity Records, where he got to work on campaigns for some of the most popular rappers at the time, and play a part in launching the careers of Just Blaze and Sha Money XL (when he was known as Sha Self).

By the metrics of what success looks like for a small, newly launched indie hip-hop label, "Cut That Weak Shit " b/w "Ain't No Secret" was a big success, shipping thousands of copies, mostly distributed by hand from the back of Fingaz's mom's ride.

The next artist to join the label was Mike Zoot, introduced in 1997 with the *Guesswhyld Presents Mike Zoot* EP. Another success, releases from Mike Zoot would dominate the Guesswhyld release slate for the next couple of years, driven by the popularity of the "High Drama, Pt. 3: The Search For 2" 12" with Mos Def, Consequence and Talib Kweli.

In 1999 Guesswhyld released a 12" by Artifacts emcee El Da Sensei, "Frontline" b/w "All Rise", featuring Mike Zoot and Organised Konfusion (El is incorrectly listed on the artwork as 'El The Sensei' instead of El Da Sensei.)

The previous year, El Da Sensei and Mike Zoot had both featured on a record by Norway's Tommy Tee ("International Connects" b/w "Blood Rush" released on Up Above Records), which Matt Fingaz executive produced. Tommy Tee then signed to Guesswhyld and released 12"s including "World Renown" b/w "No Holds Barred". The final Guesswhyld 12" of note was released as a double-header named *Bottom Line: The Soundtrack*, with a track by Street Smartz and Large Professor ("Yo, Yo") and a b-side from Mike Zoot ("Chessbumpin').

Matt Fingaz would later wind the label down after becoming disillusioned with the process of running a business, and the irre-coverable damage that illegal downloads did to the music industry in general.

A compilation named *Out The Vault* came out in 2009 featuring all of the highlights from the Guesswhyld catalog, including some of Matt Fingaz' own songs. Fingaz is still involved in the music business today, consulting on A&R and brand marketing for labels and artists.

HYDRA ENTERTAINMENT

During Mike 'Heron' Herard's time as one half of the production duo the Ghetto Professionals (with The Mighty V.I.C.), he provided beats for legendary artists like Kool G Rap, KRS-One, Mobb Deep and Parrish Smith, and indie rap mainstays such as Black Attack and Cage.

He was also the co-founder of Hydra Entertainment – with Jerry Famolari (who also owned the house music label Sneak Tip Records, and who had a working relationship with The Mighty V.I.C. since as far back as the late 80s through to his time as a member of The Beatnuts) – a label that provided an outlet for some of underground hip-hop's most unique talents.

Although Heron has stated 1997 as the year the label started, there were 12" releases bearing the Hydra name in 1995 and 1996, including records by the group Powerule (Prince Power, E Vill, and DJ Ax-Mill).

By 1998, Hydra had an impressive list of releases. Godfather Don earned critical acclaim for 12"s like "Styles By The Gram" b/w "World Premiere" & "Properties Of Steel", and Screwball released the "Screwed Up" b/w "They Wanna Know Why" 12", followed by the rowdy, popular "F.A.Y.B.A.N." b/w "Seen It All". In addition to more records by Godfather Don and Screwball, Hydra also released music by the groups Triflicts (Gab Gotcha, Creature and Buc Live) and Kamakazee (KL and Solo's first group before they joined Screwball); and solo emcees Lakey The Kid (best remembered for getting a shoutout by Nas on *Illmatic*) and Joell Ortiz. There were also releases by established artists Prince Po ("Where Ya Shoes At?" b/w "Shine"), The High & Mighty ("Sun, Moon, & Stars" b/w "The Conflict"), Royal Flush ("Its Royal Flush"), and Mobb Deep ("The Get Back" b/w "On The Real").

Hydra's biggest achievement, however, was how it highlighted the work of producers via the influential instrumental series, *Hydra Beats*. Fourteen volumes were released in total, featuring entries from Godfather Don, The Beatnuts, A Kid Called Roots, Nick Wiz, and Heron's own group, the Ghetto Professionals. Since the demise of Hydra, Heron has achieved big things in the music business, consulting for Rawkus Records and Tommy Boy, and later holding senior positions in A&R at Eminem's hugely successful Shady Records.

RAWKUS RECORDS

When TV show *Succession* emerged in 2018 and became a phenomenon, it didn't take a degree in Media Studies to work out that the plot was a not-so-thinly-veiled take on Rupert Murdoch's family and media empire. Power, corruption and lack of a moral compass are good descriptions of the Roy family, but they also accurately describe the music business, and in a quirk of history, there's an intersection between the real Roy family and underground hip-hop.

Rawkus Records was created in 1995 by Brian Brater and Jarret Myer who met at Brown University, an institution with some hip-hop pedigree, listing MC Paul Barman, and a brief stint by Chubb Rock as alumni. A shared love for rap music and entrepreneurism saw the partners create their own label, but they needed money if they were going to do it right. And here's where the Murdoch family connection comes into play. Brater and Myer were friends with James Murdoch, who at the time appeared to be going through a phase of trying to be cool, perhaps rebelling against the infamous and very corporate image of his media tyrant father. James clearly therefore had the money, and what better way to score cool points than being the owner of a hip-hop record label?

There are several obvious ironies about James Murdoch being involved in Rawkus. Although El-P of Company Flow has stated that Brater and Myer genuinely believed in the "independent as fuck" mantra and everything it stood for, there was nothing independent about a company being funded by a huge corporation worth billions of dollars, or the office in Manhattan and marketing budget that it paid for. By 1996, Robert Murdoch's News Corporation owned the majority of shares in Rawkus, again ironic considering the contempt and disdain News Corporation's Fox News has had for hip-hop culture over the decades.

The money was coming from a corporate place, but Brater and Myer branded Rawkus with an image that fully represented the organic, rugged and raw aesthetic of the underground, down to the Wu-Tang Clan-inspired name (Brater was apparently a big fan of "Bring da Ruckus"), the razor blade logo, the initial run of white label 12"s, and the music itself. Those signing to the label were also attracted to the model Brater and Myer were offering, giving artists 50/50 deals and an agreement to keep their masters, conditions they'd never have gotten on a major label.

The first credited Rawkus releases were not even by hip-hop artists, instead skewing towards rock and electronic. The full pivot towards hip-hop came in 1997 with exquisite 12"s by R.A. The Rugged Man, Reflection Eternal, Sir Menelik, Black Star, L-Fudge, Mos Def, B1, Indelible MCs, Medina Green, Common, Pharoahe Monch, Mr. Complex, The High & Mighty, Skillz, Black Attack and Brick City Kids (an alias of Artifacts). Some of these were released in partnership with smaller labels, with Rawkus essentially being the distributor (the Black Attack and Brick City Kids records were released with Ghetto Gold Recordings, while the Indelible MCs 12" was presented by Company Flow's own Official Recordings label), but most appeared as full Rawkus products, with yellow center stickers that soon became a familiar stamp of quality for diggers to look out for. Some of these 12"s even had full artwork, underlining Rawkus' seriousness in wanting to put out quality products. It was a wide and varied roster of artists, giving Rawkus the range of smoother, soulful emcees like Black Star on one side of the scale, the hardcore, dusty raps of Company Flow at the other, and all manner of different artists in between.

1997 was also the year Rawkus released its first album, *Funcrusher Plus* by Company Flow. It was followed by important titles from Black Star (*Mos Def and Talib Kweli are Black Star*); The High & Mighty (*Home Field Advantage*); Mos Def (*Black on Both Sides*); Pharoahe Monch (*Internal Affairs*); DJ Spinna (*Heavy Beats Volume 1*); Big L (*The Big Picture*), Reflection Eternal (*Train of Thought*); Smut Peddlers (*Porn Again*); Hi-Tek (*Hi-Teknology*); Da Beatminerz (*Brace 4 Impak*); Talib Kweli (*Quality*) and Kool G Rap (*The Giancana Story*), plus the compilations *Lyricist Lounge* (volumes 1 and 2) and *Soundbombing* (parts I, II and III).

Unlike the other indie rap labels operating at the same time, Rawkus had the financial backing to fully promote their releases across print media and radio, and on the streets. The net result helped Rawkus to become the only label of its kind to have genuine hit singles, posting numbers most indie outfits could only dream about.

The legacy of Rawkus Records today is lots of good music but bad business. El-P, Da Beatminerz, Sir Menelik and Kool G Rap are among the list of former artists to have criticized the way the label was run, how they were owed royalties, and how the owners seemed to care more about playing music moguls than actually looking after their artists, which sadly are charges all too common and accepted in the music biz. The negativity has mellowed in recent years. El-P – who lest we forget once dropped anti-Rawkus lyrics about how he'd prefer to be fellated by Nazis than still be signed to Rawkus – has discussed in interviews many of the positives of working with the label, including in a lengthy chat on a podcast presented by another former Rawkus artist who had his fair share of battles with Brater and Myer, Talib Kweli, hosted by the media brand Uproxx, which happens to have been founded by Brater and Myer.

Rawkus Records is no longer an active label, despite changing ownership several times. It became part of MCA records in 2002 before later being sold to Geffen. There was then a relaunch in

2006 with distribution via the Sony Music-owned RED. This deal ended in 2007 and Rawkus has been dormant since. That Rawkus was passed from one corporate entity to another shows there was at least some belief within the industry that indie hip-hop could be monetised at scale, and El-P has commended the label for having created a middle ground between the underground and the mainstream. Myer has done well out of Uproxx, running it as a group that now also owns news site Hip Hop DX. Brater is involved in a tech data company.

RHYMESAYERS ENTERTAINMENT

It is not an overstatement to say that Rhymesayers Entertainment single-handedly put Twin Cities hip-hop on the map. The label, founded by Slug, Ant, Musab and Brent 'Siddiq' Sayers, has championed artists from Minnesota and St. Paul since its inception, plus others from further afield. The label officially launched in 1995, but the group of artists had been using the name 'Rhymesayers' since the early 90s. Siddiq learned about the retail side of the music business working at Best Buy, while Slug spread the word about his crew during his time working at records stores, where he'd often slip customers tapes from him and his friends, convincing them to buy these instead of what they came in for. All of this was good experience not just for running a label, but also for when Rhymesayers opened their own store in Minneapolis in 1999, named Fifth Element.

The label's earliest releases were mixtapes and compilations of tracks by the Headshots crew, a collective of artists that included Slug, Ant and Musab among its many members, and the first Musab album, *Comparison*, under the name Beyond. In 1997, Rhymesayers released the first album by the group they would find the most consistent success with, Atmosphere's *Overcast!*. The following year came *The Dynospectrum* album, and the first releases from Ant and DJ Abilities. With the turn of the new millennium, the label signed Brother Ali, releasing his debut *Rites of Passage*, and the first project from Eydea & Abilities.

A ton of releases from Atmosphere followed, alongside records from Blueprint; Soul Position (Blueprint and RJD2); Mr. Dibbs; I Self Devine; UK duo The Planets (Ayman Raze and Nomadic); Grayskul (Onry Ozzborn and Ninjaface); Boom Bap Project (Karim, Destro and DJ Scene); Felt (Slug and Murs); Micranots (I Self Devine and Kool Akiem Allah); Vitamin D, and Semi.Official (I Self Devine and Abilities).

In 2004 Rhymesayers Entertainment went outside of the local scene with the release of another classic album by the iconic MF DOOM, *Mm..Food*. Having an MF DOOM album in their discography was a boon for the label, and resissues and DOOM-related merchandise continue to provide a reliable revenue stream. Since Dumile's death, Rhymesayers has partnered with the late rapper's estate, ensuring money earned from sales go to his surviving family.

Rhymesayers has also since expanded their repertoire way beyond Minnesota, and today is among hip-hop's most beloved independent labels, with a roster that now also includes Aesop Rock, Evidence, Lice (Aesop Rock and Homeboy Sandman), Sa-Roc, and more. The Fifth Element store closed for good in 2020.

SOLESIDES/QUANNUM PROJECTS

Similar to several of the other labels described here, SoleSides was created by a group of artists who had become frustrated by the music industry, wanting instead to put the power in their own hands.

The solution was to make SoleSides a crew *and* a record label.

The first SoulSides release was credited to DJ Shadow and the Groove Robbers, which came out in 1993. After that, the collective took a methodical approach to how the label released music, introducing acts one at a time. Blackalicious (Gift of Gab and Chief Xcel) had their turn in 1994 and 1995 with several releases including the *Melodica* EP, while 1996 was the year for Lateef and Lyrics Born to come out with their initial releases as solo artists, and then together as Latyrx in 1997 and 1998.

It was a gut-punch to fans when the label closed, but no sooner had it ended it opened again, now operating as Quannum Projects. Like SoleSides before it, Quannum Projects would be both the name of the crew and the label, with the artists themselves usually billed as the Quannum MCs. The name was different but the principal characters were still the same, and the new lease of life sparked a busy period of releases over the next few years. From 1999-2005 there were marquee albums and EPs by Blackalicious, Gift of Gab as a solo artist, Maroons (Lateef and Chief Xcel), Lateef and Lyrics Born, plus many other 12"s and records by artists outside of the core SoleSides/Quaanum MCs circle, and by artists adjacent to or outside of hip-hop (the label even put out a Fela Kuti compilation, *The Underground Spiritual Game,* mixed by Chief Xcel).

After guesting on Blackalicious' *The Craft,* Project Blowed member Pigeon John was brought into the Quannum Projects family, giving him the distinction of having been in two legendary Californian rap crews. He released his *And the Summertime Pool Party* album on the label in 2006. The lineup of talent featured on *The Craft* also included another group who had recently been welcomed into the Quannum Projects fold, one that extended the geographical boundaries of the crew beyond California. Lifesavas, whose members included Vursatyl, Jumbo and Rev Shines, were from Portland, way up in the northwest of Oregon and almost a thousand miles from Los Angeles. Their debut album, *Spirit in Stone*, was released under Quannum Projects in 2003, after having impressed Blackalicious' Chief Xcel, who had heard one of their tracks while record shopping in Portland.

There were also additional influential releases from the collective during this time period. The first was a throw back to the original SoleSides days, the *Quannum Presents SoleSides Greatest Bumps* compilation, while the other, *Spectrum*, was a crew album that showed how they had evolved since.

It's unclear today if the Quannum Projects label exists in any form, and for several years the only products bearing the name have been reissues of records from the crew's heyday.

STONES THROW RECORDS

The circumstances under which Peanut Butter Wolf founded Stones Throw Records – as a way to release his music with the slain Charizma – were unfortunate, but the success and longevity the label has earned is a tribute to his lost friend. Stones Throw is today known for having a varied selection of artists working across different genres, but hip-hop is where they started, and where they've experienced the biggest success.

Peanut Butter Wolf had dreams of starting a label from as far back as the mid-80s in his teenage years, dreaming of emulating the rap labels he admired, like Tuff City, Wild Pitch and Cold Chillin. While Stones Throw was a way to give a platform for him and Charizma, Peanut Butter Wolf also had other reasons for starting a label. He wanted to expose good local artists to a wider audience; he wanted to create a place where artists would be treated better than how he and Charizma were when briefly signed to the Disney-funded Hollywood Basic; he wanted the focus to be on vinyl albums; and most of all, he wanted to put out music that he personally liked, not just because he thought it would sell. As for the name 'Stones Throw', this was based on an in-joke between him and Charizma, about how success always felt just a stone's throw away (figuratively, due to the small progress the duo had made before Charizma's death, and physically, coming as they did from San Jose, 340 miles from Los Angeles). Peanut Butter Wolf ran the operation at first from his bedroom in a house outside of San Francisco, and later moved to the city itself. He would eventually move the business to Los Angeles, in part to be closer to the artist who was the backbone of the label's success in hip-hop, Madlib.

Being a deejay and producer, it was no surprise that the first selection of releases on Stones Throw, outside of music from him and Charisma, were by artists of a similar ilk. There were records by DJ Babu (under the name The Turntablist), producer Fanatik, and the *Soulful Fruit* album by Rob Swift. There were also vocal records from emcees including Rasco, Encore, and the group Homeliss Derelix. Things started to really get exciting in 1998 with the first 12"s by Lootpack, and the first of many highly-regarded albums from the label, including Rasco's *Time Waits For No Man*, followed in 1999 by Peanut Butter Wolf's own *My Vinyl Weighs a Ton*, Madlib's first singles as Quasimoto, and the *Soundpieces: Da Antidote!* album by his group Lootpack. Quasimoto's *The Unseen* kicked off the new century, and in the same year Madlib also produced a single by Kazi. They had actually recorded a full album together in 1996 named *Blackmarket Seminar* that was never released at the time, and only surfaced as an unearthed gem many years later.

The next half-decade of Stones Throw releases were dominated by Madlib and those in his circle, solidifying his reputation as a masterful producer. In only a few years he managed to deliver his first album as Yesterday's New Quintet (*Angles Without Edges*); the *Champion Sounds* album as Jaylib with J Dilla; *Madvillainy* with MF DOOM as Madvillain; a house album under the name DJ Rels; more albums by Yesterday's New Quintet (*Stevie*) and Quasimoto (*The Further Adventures of Lord Quas*); a jazz album using the Sound Directions alias; and the first entries of his *Beat Konducta* series. He also collaborated with Cut Chemist during this time, and produced on his brother Oh No's *The Disrupt* album, M.E.D.'s *Push Comes To Shove*, Dudley Perkin's *A Lil Light*, and Wildchild's *Secondary Protocol*.

Away from Madlib, Stones Throw additionally released the *Big Shots* album by Charizma and Peanut Butter Wolf, a compilation of hip-hop from Connecticut, and 12"s by Lootpack member DJ Romes, Dooley O, and 80s rapper Stezo. Post 2005, Stones Throw would put out several more significant hip-hop albums – most with input from Madlib, who effectively assumed the role of in-house producer – including titles by Guilty Simpson, Strong Arm Steady, and Percee P (2007's *Perseverance*). The Stones Throw rap album most people remember, alongside *Madvillainy*, is *Donuts* from 2006. By Peanut Butter Wolf's own admission, J Dilla's death just three days after *Donuts* came out had a profound effect on the label's relationship with hip-hop, and left he and Madlib unsure of where to go next.

Peanut Butter Wolf's commitment to quality vinyl releases extended to artwork. The credit for this goes to Stones Throw's in-house designer, Jeff Jank, whose covers for *Madvillainy*, *The Unseen*, *Donuts* and other albums are almost as important as the music.

The Stones Throw Records roster of today is light on hip-hop, the label mostly having pivoted to other genres. Peanut Butter Wolf has, however, stuck to his guns by still only putting out music he likes. He's stated in interviews that over the years he has had chances to sign artists who later became very successful, and he knew at the time that they would, but he passed because he simply didn't like their music. It may not sound like a logical business plan, but it has served him and the label well, and his integrity is admirable.

A few controversies have emerged over time, with accusations of unpaid royalties, and a legal wrangle between the estate of MF DOOM and the former Stones Throw General Manager about the ownership of DOOM's creative assets, but on the whole Stones Throw's reputation as the standard bearer of good indie rap remains intact.

WRECK RECORDS

Wreck Records was launched as a subsidiary of Nervous Records ('nervous wreck', get it?), which has a rich history in the music business. Nervous was started in 1991 by Mike Weiss, who spent most of his childhood living in the Bronx. Mike's father Sam Weiss was the founder of the disco label Sam Records, and Mike's uncle, Hy Weiss, worked at Stax Records. Both men served as inspiration for Mike to start Nervous.

Weiss quickly diversified into different genres via sub-labels of varied success. The company's entry into the hip-hop market with Wreck Records was both a commercial and critical hit.

The first hip-hop releases by the company came out on Nervous between 1991-93, including 12"s by Underground Mafia (Bodie and Bam, later known as Way 2 Real), Ganjah Posse (Manuel Napuri and The Undercover Brother), Groove Asylum (Frankie Feliciano),

Jazzie Joint (another alias of Feliciano), Mad Lion, and the group most associated with the label, Black Moon.

The Wreck Records name started appearing on releases in 1994, a year dominated by 12"s from Black Moon with tracks from their 1993 *Enta da Stage* album, and by Smif-N-Wessun, including songs that would later appear on their 1995 album, *Dah Shinin'*. There were also 12"s in 1994 from Redrum (Tone Rock and William Rosario), Rek Shit Rebelz (yet another Feliciano alias), and Brooklyn Slumlordz (DJ Eclipse, DJ Riz, and DJ Skribble). Between 1996-97 Wreck dropped music from Broadway, Kaotic Stylin (Beat Scott and Big Grand), Funkmaster Flex & The Ghetto Celebs, and Breeze Evahflowin', and the first installments of the *Nervous Breakbeats* series.

In 1998 the label introduced another series, *Hip Hop Independents Day*, and the follow up, *Hip Hop Independents Day: The Sequel*. Both series were influential, putting some of the finest underground artists on the radar. That year also saw releases by Wisdom Life and Network Reps. The final few active years of Wreck generated music from the Polyrhythm Addicts, and Clinton Sparks. Although there has been no new music from the label in years, the Wreck Records name can still be seen on various reissues of Black Moon and Smif-N-Wessun's catalog.

The larger Nervous Records is still going strong, fully focused on house. After many decades in the business, their catalog now has over five thousand releases. During the early days of Wreck Records and Nervous in 1992, Black Moon's Buckshot and his business partner Drew 'Dru-Ha' Friedman had started a management company named Duck Down. They had Black Moon and Smif-N-Wessun on their books, and so when Wreck Records stopped releasing music, the artists made the transition to Buckshot and Dru-Ha's new venture, Duck Down Music.

In addition to the well-remembered labels listed in the previous pages, there were many other, smaller indie labels that came and went during the period, while a few still exist today.

AUDIO RESEARCH RECORDS

Audio Research Records was started in Montreal, Canada, by A-Trak, his brother Dave One, and Willo Peron. The label released different tracks, mixes and breaks series by A-Trak and other deejays including D-Styles, DJ Serious and DJ Craze, and music by A-Trak and Dave One's Obscure Disorder group.

BAD MAGIC

UK deejay and journalist Dan Greenpeace set up Bad Magic in 1999, backed by the larger indie label Wall of Sound. Similar to Wordplay Records, Bad Magic licensed US hip-hop for UK release, but also put out its own material. Highlights include music by Blak Twang, Jerry Beeks, Cage, Ugly Duckling, Vinyl Dialect, The Creators, and Skitzofreniks.

BATTLE AXE RECORDS

Battle Axe Records began in 1996 when the group Swollen Members needed a way to get their music out. Ultimately, as the rest of the group decided to stay focused on the creative side, Madchild took on the running of the label, backed by a sizable cash injection loaned from family. Although the label sometimes released records by outside artists, most of Battle Axe's records were by Swollen Members as a group, and as solo artists.

BBE

Barely Breaking Even, aka BBE, is an accurate name for an indie label, although this particular company appears to have buckled the trend considering they still exist today (besides, the name was inspired by the 1982 The Universal Robot Band song). BBE started in 1996 in London, headed by Peter Adarkwah and Ben Jolly.

The label operates across multiple genres, but is renowned in hip-hop for the *Beat Generation* releases, a series of albums highlighting the work of esteemed producers. Between 2001 and 2003 there were editions from J. Dilla (*Welcome 2 Detroit*), Pete Rock (*Petestrumentals*), will.i.am (*Lost Change*), Marley Marl (*Re-Entry*), DJ Jazzy Jeff (*The Magnificent*) and DJ Spinna (*Here To There*), and later from Madlib (*WLIB AM: King of the Wigflip*).

BEYOND REAL

DJ Spinna put his Beyond Real label to good use by releasing his own music, both under his own name and as a member of the Jigmastas and Dome Crackers (with Grap Luva and Joc Max). Other releases were from artists he produced tracks for, including Basement Khemists (J Lee, Taha Khaliq and Joc Max), Old World Disorder (Shadowman and Skam2?), Channel Live, and I.G. Off & Hazadous. Beyond Real also put out compilations and mixes including two editions of *Beyond Real Experience*.

BI-COASTAL RECORDINGS

Bi-Coastal Recordings was very short lived but still deserves to be mentioned thanks to the release of a memorable 12". "The Big Daddy

Anthem" was a posse cut that came out in 1998 featuring vocals by L-Fudge, Mr. Eon, Shabazz The Disciple, Natruel, and Wicked Will.

BIG DADA

Journalist and author Will Ashon introduced the Big Dada label to the world in 1997, run as a sub-label of Ninja Tune. Over the following years the label released music by UK artists Roots Manuva, New Flesh For Old and TY, and Abstract Rude, Mike Ladd, Bigg Jus, Busdriver and cLOUDDEAD from the US. The label also had a relationship with Damiel Dumile, releasing the King Geedorah album *Take Me to Your Leader* in 2003. Big Dada still exists today, although Ashon is no longer involved.

BLUNT RECORDINGS

Blunt Recordings was based in New York and was part of the wider TVT Records group. The label lasted just a few years but in that time had some milestones releases, including Mic Geronimo's *The Natural*, Royal Flush's *Ghetto Millionaire*, and the *Doom* album by Mood, among others.

BOMB HIP-HOP RECORDS

DJ David Paul started publishing Bomb magazine in the Bay Area in 1991, and it eventually expanded into being a record label, known for the *Return of The DJ* releases, and records by the Kreators, Paul Nice and Blade, among others.

BOULEVARD CONNECTION

After dropping the *Sut Min Pik EP* on Fondle 'Em Records, Copenhagen, Denmark group Boulevard Connection (Sek, Marak, and DJ Typhoon) started a label of the same name, with a roster that included their own group, fellow Danish artist Creative, and US groups Aphillyation – from Philadelphia (whose members included Dice Raw) – and Mass Influence from Atlanta, releasing their *The Underground Science* album.

BRICK RECORDS

No record label has done more to boost the hip-hop scene in Boston than Brick Records, started in 1996 by Papa D. The label released the *Rebel Alliance LP* in 1997, featuring many Boston artists of note, including Mr. Lif and 7L & Esoteric, and also dropped records from Insight and Reks. In later years, the label would help launch the careers of Termanology, Statik Selektah, and Stu Bangas.

BRONX SCIENCE RECORDINGS

Bronx Science Recordings was the creation of David Walis and Lyvio G who founded the label in 1998 as a subsidiary of the New York based BUDS Distribution. The label is most remembered for dropping releases by the group K-Otix, but also had records by lesser known artists like K-Skills and Hycin Jo & Illin P, plus a who's who of acclaimed acts including Apani. B Fly, L-Fudge, Apathy, Celph Titled, Louis Logic and Nik Wiz.

CONCEPTION RECORDS

Conception Records operated out of Seattle and was started by Mr. Supreme and DJ Sureshot in 1992. The label was home to Canada's Da Grassroots, releasing their *Passage Through Time* album in 1999. The label also put out records by home-grown artists from Seattle, most notably Kutfather, and the group Diamond Mercenaries.

COPASETIK RECORDINGS

Although it was focused on releasing records by US artists, Copa-setik Recordings was a British label started by Jon Sexton. They released and licensed music by Rasco, Peanut Butter Wolf and Kool Keith (as Dr. Dooom), delivering Keith's *First Come, First Served* album in conjunction with Funky Ass Records. Incidentally, Sexton also ran another label named All Good Vinyl, and despite being known primarily for drum & bass, that label also released some of Peanut Butter Wolf's earliest work.

CORRECT RECORDS

Little seems to be known about Correct Records, but the short-lived label managed to release an impressive number of records considering it only operated for two years. Highlights included the *Audio Sedative* album by Los Angeles group Mannish (Jekill and Jive), and the *God Connections* album by former Beatnuts member Fashion, who by now was going by the name Al' Tariq.

D&D RECORDS

Of the many recording studios in New York where timeless hip-hop has been created, the most celebrated are Calliope, Chung King, Bassline, Battery, and D&D. The latter – located in Manhattan and home of DJ Premier and other boom bap legends – was opened by Douglas Grama and David Lotwin (hence the D&D). From the late 90s to the early 00s D&D also became a label that released compilations and 12"s by Afu-Ra, Craig G, Krumb Snatcha and QNC (Q Ball and Curt Cazal), plus a bunch of rap legends recording tracks under the name D&D All-Stars, including KRS-One, Jeru The Damaja, Fat Joe, Smif-N-Wessun and more. The label petered out by 2004, and D&D Studios closed in 2015.

D.I.T.C. RECORDS

With eight members in the collective, it was hard to tell who was driving the business decision to use the D.I.T.C. brand for releasing records, but Showbiz and Lord Finesse were definitely involved. The D.I.T.C. Records label released 12"s and promos credited to the crew and its members, distributed by Fat Beats. Some of the songs also appear on the 2000 album via Tommy Boy, *D.I.T.C.* There were additional releases by affiliated artists like Freddie Foxxx and M.O.P. Interestingly, Lord Finesse has stated in interviews how the crew made more money independently than when on larger labels.

DOLO RECORDS

When you have indie rap credentials that run as deep as Stretch Armstrong's, it probably makes sense to try your hand at running a label, so that's what Stretch did with the launch of Dolo Records in 1995 in partnership with industry insider Nicholas Eisenman. The release slate started modestly with compilations and 12"s by Akinyele and MF Grimm, followed by several of New York's most beloved 12"s. The "Up On Prospect" b/w "Boom!" record by Brooklyn's Hillfiguz (Dangga and Dogface) dropped in 1996, and then in 1997 came "Get Your Swerve On" b/w "Surrounded" from the group Dutchmin (L. Blades, True Tha Good and Tony Ruffin) and "Well Connected" b/w "Bright Lights, Big City" by Powerule. Both "Surrounded" and "Bright Lights, Big City" were included in PF Cuttin's portion of the seminal 5 Deadly Venoms of Brooklyn mixtape, giving them a decent boost.

There were also releases by Natural Elements and The Korp, and two installments of Stretch Armstrong's Lesson mixtapes, before Dolo disappeared from the radar by the end of 1998.

FORTRESS ENTERTAINMENT

Charlemagne's Fortress Entertainment label facilitated the release of several 12"s produced by the man himself from 1994 onwards, including records by Natural Elements and group members L-Swift and Mr. Voodoo, Nightbreed (Ka and Kev), K-Bomb, and the Raidermen.

FUNKY ASS RECORDS

The aforementioned Funky Ass Records had involvement from KutMasta Kurt, Kool Keith, Keith's fellow Ultramagnetic MCs member TR Love, and Peanut Butter Wolf. The label exclusively released records by Keith and Kurt, including the 1996 Big Time album by Keith and Tim Dog, under the name Ultra.

GAME RECORDINGS

Game Recordings promoted their records with a very blatant USP. Founded by Jonathan 'Shecky Green' Shecter – who was also co-founder of the iconic rap magazine The Source – Game eschewed the standard approach of putting images of the artist on record covers, substituting them instead with photos of their Hip-hop Honeys (who also starred in their own Game-branded soft-porn DVD).

The label released music by Royce da 5'9" – including his group Bad Meets Evil with Eminem – Agallah, Thirstin Howl III, Blahzay Blahzay (P.F. Cuttin and Outloud) and more, before Shecky Green called it a day in 2005.

GOOD VIBE RECORDINGS

Good Vibe Recordings was based in Beverly Hills and opened in 1996. They licensed music by Slum Village and Declaime, but also had their own signed artists, including producer CHOPS (of the Mountain Brothers), Da Nuthouse (Dave Ghetto, Fel Sweetenberg and Nex Millen), and Phil Da Agony. Good Vibe also released the second album by Bahamadia, 2000's *BB Queen*.

HEAD BOP RECORDS

While "The Head Bop" 12" came out on Raw Shack Productions, Yesh used it as the name of a label he was involved in running, Head Bop Records. It was the label that released records by Yesh's Wee Bee Foolish group, but also had material come out by Sub-Conscious from the group Sight Beyond Light, and Jedi Son of Spock. Head Bop was also responsible for the expanded *The Visualz Anthology* by Siah and Yeshua DapoED, released in 2008.

HIEROGLYPHICS IMPERIUM RECORDS

Various members of the Hieroglyphics had experienced the highs and lows of being signed to a major label by the mid-90s, including Del the Funky Homosapian with Elektra, and Souls of Mischief and Casual with Jive. When each one of these deals fizzled out, the collective decided to create their own thing, founding Hieroglyphics Imperium Records in 1997. Quickly realising the value of doing things outside of the major labels, Hieroglyphics Imperium Records would soon become the de facto platform for releases from the crew as a whole and for their solo endeavors, and would also occasionally collaborate with artists from the outside.

The label was also an early adopter of the internet, figuring out during the early years that it was the ideal place to create a community of fans, build hype and distribute and sell music directly to the consumer, thus helping to write the blueprint that everyone follows today.

Although Hieroglyphics is still active as a collective of artists who continue touring together and release music, Hieroglyphics Imperium Recordings now appears to be a legacy part of their brand, with the focus today seemingly on being a platform for merch. Since 2012 the crew has been running the annual Hiero Day festival, usually timed around September 3 as a tribute to Souls of Mischief's *93 'til Infinity* (as in the 3rd day of the ninth month).

ILL BOOGIE RECORDS

Ill Boogie Records started under the name Blackberry Records and was founded by Matt 'M-Boogie' Theriault. As Blackberry, the label released product by Mykill Miers, plus a host of deejays including Melo-D and DJ Revolution. Once transitioned to the Ill Boogie name, the label also worked with Styles of Beyond, Lexicon (Big Oak and his brother Nick Fury), Born Allah, and more. They also released the *Earplug Series* which had albums by Mars III (Greg Owens and Dust), The Demigodz, Yesh, and Emanom.

JAZZ FUDGE

DJ Vadim founded Jazz Fudge to release his more experimental music, parallel to also being signed to Ninja Tune. His own music was the focus, but the label also released music by some of the UK's most respected hip-hop artists, including Phi-Life Cypher, Killa Kela, Mr. Thing, and Mark B & Blade.

KNEE DEEP RECORDS

Knee Deep Records operated out of Toronto after being started by Choclair and Lee 'Day' Fredericks in 1995 in order to release music by Choclair himself, plus records by two other stalwarts of Canadian hip-hop, Saukrates, and Kardinal Offishal. The roster also included members of Toronto's The Circle collective.

LEWIS RECORDINGS

Mike Lewis spent years as a contributor to Hip-Hop Connection magazine in the UK before starting the Lewis Recordings imprint in 2001. The label is notable for being home to one of hip-hop's most enigmatic artists, Edan, releasing both *Primitive Plus* in 2002 and *Beauty and the Beat* in 2005.

Other Lewis artists during the period were Dooley O, who released the *I Gotcha* album in 2005, Boston emcee Mighty Casey, who released 2004's *Original Rudebwoy*, and another Boston artist, Dagha.

Mike Lewis has been trying to get another solo album out of Edan for decades, but this has yet to materialize.

LEX RECORDS

As the head of Lex Records, Tom Brown is one of only a handful of people to build a strong working relationship with the elusive MF DOOM, releasing *The Mouse and The Mask* and several other DOOM projects between 2005-2014. Most of Lex's other success has come from Danger Mouse's non-hip-hop projects, but the label also released a number of rap records during the indie era.

Aside from Jemini the Gifted One and Danger Mouse's *Ghetto Pop Life*, Organized Konfusion's Prince Po released his solo debut on Lex in 2004, *The Slickness*, as did the Non-Prophets (Sage Francis and Joe Beats) with their *Hope* album in 2003. Brown started Lex in 2001 as a subsidiary of Warp Records, where he previously worked, before later taking full ownership.

MO' WAX

Mo' Wax was started in 1992 by U.N.K.L.E. member James Lavelle, and while they specialized in trip hop and electronic, the label also put out several hip-hop records in its decade-long existence. The roster included DJ Shadow, who released his *Entroducing.....* album on Mo' Wax in 1996, plus Latyrx, Blackalicious, and DJ Krush. In 2016 a documentary named *The Man From Mo' Wax* came out, charting Lavelle's time running the label.

OLD MAID ENTERTAINMENT

In addition to being the platform for his own releases as J-Zone, Jay Mumford used his Old Maid Entertainment label for records by his frequent collaborators Huggy Bear and Al-Shid. Although today he has all but killed off the J-Zone character, Old Maid is now the outlet for Mumford's Du-Rites group.

PAYDAY RECORDS

Payday Records is mostly associated with the early-mid 90s boom bap era, putting out classic albums by Showbiz & A.G., Jeru the Damaja, Group Home and O.C, and they continued to release 12"s by these artists and more throughout the indie era. The label was founded in 1992 by Patrick Moxey, who has also been involved with other labels over the last four decades.

RAW SHACK PRODUCTIONS

Industry veteran George Sulmers had stints working for Def Jam and Epic Records before creating the Raw Shack Productions label in 1995. The first release was "Longevity" b/w "Braggin' Writes" by J-Live, a classic 12" that set the tone for the rest of the label's output. After more J-Live releases, Raw Shack dropped the "Visualise" b/w "Why Don't Cha" record by Mr. Complex, and "Directions" b/w "The Head Bop" by Yeshua DapoED, both in 1998. Sulmers was also a friend of the late Prince Be of the group P. M. Dawn, and Raw Shack released a few records by the group Mood Swingaz, which Prince Be produced under the name All Those Mutha Fuckin' Reasons.

SEVEN HEADS

The label Seven Heads was founded by seven friends who met at the University of Virginia. Though all seven remained involved in the business, Wes Jackson ran the label, which first released music by the group The Unspoken Heard, made up of Asheru and Blue Black. The label also put out records by Mr. Complex, the UK's Richie Rich and more, and the debut album by El Da Sensei in 2003, *Relax Relate Release*.

ST. NICK ENTERTAINMENT

St. Nick Entertainment is another little-remembered rap label, but released several 12"s by Inl emcee Rob-O, including "World Premier". It was founded in 1996 by A&R man and occasional artist Nicholas Taylor, and the label's other minor claim to fame is for releasing *The Outsider* album by CL Smooth (in partnership with another forgotten label, Blackheart Entertainment).

STRANGE FAMOUS RECORDS

Rhode Island emcee Sage Francis went the indie label route when he founded Strange Famous Records in 1996, a guerrilla-style DIY outfit where he used his time working at a radio station to burn CDs and photocopy artwork. For the first almost-decade of existence the label solely released Sage Francis' own material, including as one half of Non-Prophets. The only other artist to have a release was producer Joe Beats. From 2005 onwards, Strange Famous widened their offering with music from other artists.

SUPERRAPPIN

As a subsidiary of the much larger label and distributor, Groove Attack, German label Superrappin was able to bring the cream of the US underground to the attention of heads in Europe via editions of their *Supperappin* compilations, and the release of many 12"s of tracks from them. The label additionally released albums by Grand Agent and J. Rawls, and the debut solo album by A Tribe Called Quest's Phife Dawg, 2000's *Ventilation: Da LP.*

TAPE KINGZ

The Brooklyn based Tape Kingz label became synonymous with mixtapes, releasing projects by the most respected deejays, including DJ Premier, Mister Cee, Tony Touch, Doo Wop, Ron G and more. But they also released several important 12"s, including tracks by Finsta Bundy, Shades of Brooklyn and Group Home.

THRESHOLD RECORDINGS

There's a lot of crossover between Funky Ass Records and another label founded by KutMasta Kurt; Threshold Recordings. Kurt used this label as a channel not just for his music with Kool Keith but also other artists he worked with, including Motion Man. An unexpected high point in the label's history happened when the Threshold name appeared in the credits of a record by one of the most successful rap acts of all time: The UK release of the Beastie Boys' "Body Movin" single from their multi-platinum *Hello Nasty* (1998) album included a KutMasta Kurt remix.

TRU CRIMINAL RECORDS

There are only a few records bearing the Tru Criminal Records logo, a label started in 1996 by Alex Groothius and Lee Resnick, but they include some much loved 12"s, including "Problemz" b/w "Metal Thangz" by Street Smartz and "One Life Ta Live" b/w "East Ta West" by AK Skills. Other releases included singles by LS of the group Rumpletilskinz, God Sunz, Tonedeff, and F.T. of Street Smartz. Several Tru Criminal Records releases were produced by Eddie Smith, who went on to create music for various TV shows.

UP ABOVE RECORDS

Long Beach's Up Above Records was set up by two members of The Visionaries, DJ Rhettmatic and KeyKool, and Doug Kato. The label's catalog includes music by The Visionaries as a group, and by members LMNO and 2-Mex, and they also licensed releases by Jurassic 5, Living Legends, Chino XL, Prince Po, Kev Brown, and many more.

UNCLE HOWIE RECORDS

Ill Bill named his Uncle Howie Records imprint after his real uncle, Howard Tenenbaum, who died in 2010. Although it was the main outlet for releases by Non Phixion and Ill Bill himself, the label also put out records by Q-Unique, Block McCloud and E-Dot. Necro also founded a label, Psycho+Logical-Records in 1999, putting out his own music, plus records by Ill Bill and fellow Non Phixion members Sabac Red and Goretex.

WORDPLAY RECORDS

Wordplay Records was launched as a subsidiary of the French label Source, founded in 1995 by former Polydor and Virgin A&R man Philippe Ascoli. Mostly focused on releasing records by the French group Saïan Supa Crew, and UK artists such as Mark B & Blade (including their acclaimed 2000 album *The Unknown)* and the London Posse, Wordplay was also the license holder for Slum Village's music in the UK market, releasing *Fantastic, Vol. 2* and its singles, including J Dilla favorites "Climax" and "Raise It Up".

YEAR ROUND

DJ Premier – one of the most pivotal figures in rap history, and arguably its greatest producer – founded his own label in the early aughts, Year Round. The label put out mix CDs by Premier himself, and by original Gang Starr member Big Shug. Year Round also released records by Screwball emcee Blaq Poet, and the group NYG'z (Shabeeno and Panchino, who previously went by the name Operation Ratification and were signed to Ill Kid Records, owned by DJ Premier's Gang Starr partner, Guru).

25 TO LIFE ENTERTAINMENT

Another hip-hop veteran who tried their hand at running a label was Tragedy, who founded 25 To Life Entertainment. Primarily used to release his own 12"s and mix cds, Tragedy's role in developing Capone N Noreaga meant that 25 To Life Entertainment is also credited as one of the companies involved in the release of their classic *The War Report* album, along with Penalty and Tommy Boy.

———

In addition to the many indie labels listed above, there were also a number of companies who operated as both labels and distributors, releasing music from their own artists while also working with other labels to get their product into stores. Two companies in particular were significant for hip-hop: Landspeed Records, owned by A&R man Bob Perry from Boston, and Nu Gruv Alliance (sometimes credited as Nu Groove Alliance), out of San Francisco. Between them, they put out hundreds of rap records in the 90s and 00s.

———

Every one of these labels needed a way to sell their records, and while distribution in physical record stores like Fat Beats was crucial, the golden era of underground hip-hop coincided with the rise of e-commerce, as listeners started to buy vinyl and CDs online instead of in store.

Three websites in particular led the way: Sandbox Automatic, Hip Hop Site, and UGHH. Sandbox Automatic began in 1995 as a small-scale, Wikipedia-like database for underground hip-hop, named 'Mercer's Sandbox'. It was expanded in 1996 with a mail order service, including a distribution pipeline via Fat Beats, and editorial content to promote the latest releases. It now seems unfathomable that record labels faced barriers in operating their own websites, but such was the nature of the primitive web. Sandbox Automatic offered a solution by hosting individual pages for labels like Fondle 'Em Records, Rawkus Records and Guesswhyld. Amazingly, the website still exists today, still selling indie rap.

Hip Hop Site was started by Warren Peace and Mike Pizzo in 1996 as a rap news website. As a college radio deejay, Peace had industry connections and access to the latest promo records, and as an avid tape trader, Pizzo knew there was bubbling interest for underground hip-hop online. The move into mail order retail happened in 1997, and the site also included website creation services for artists under a business model that offered sites for free so long as the artist agreed to sell items exclusively through Hip Hop Site. Clients taking up the offer included MF DOOM, Kool Keith, and even Eminem. Artists could also pay to have tracks included on free sampler CDs shipped with every order. Business was good enough for a while to warrant the opening of a physical store in Las Vegas, but by 2007 the entire operation closed down.

Adam Walder started UGHH in 1997 from his dorm room at Northeastern University in Boston as a personal blog site named 'DJ Quest's Slammin' Hip Hop Page' (DJ Quest being Walder's stage name). The retail side ran in a similar fashion to Hip Hop Site, including a physical shop located in Boston's Back Bay neighborhood. The site also hosted a buzzing forum for many years. The business closed in 2016, and although there were attempts at a relaunch, they didn't last long.

7

WHAT'S GOLDEN

T he following is a deeper look at a selection of important indie albums released between 1995-2005, listed chronologically, and alphabetically where the same year includes more than one album. Some of the picks are obvious, others more obscure. It does not claim to be a list of the *best* albums, and some majorly important titles are not included. It is simply a selection of personal favorites of the author. Feel free to debate him on social media if you don't like the choices.

SAAFIR
Boxcar Sessions
(1994, Qwest)

Boxcar Sessions is the debut album by Oakland rhyme veteran and Hobo Junction member Saafir. It came out in 1994, and is therefore just out of scope for the timeline of this book, but it holds enough importance to be included. From the first bars of "Swig of The Stew" to the album closer "Joint Custody", the album is a relentless clinic in how to rap with confidence and conviction, with dense, abstract word play and layers of hidden meaning for the listener to unpack and decipher, all delivered in a deep voice that adds to the impact of each lyrical blow.

The greatest rappers often fall into one of two camps; those who make it look effortless, and those who sound like they are putting in a lot of effort. Saafir is somewhere in the middle on *Boxcar Sessions*, oftentimes spitting awkward, off-beat raps, while at the same time making it sound as natural as breathing.

All of this is backed up by slick production from Hobo Junction members DJ Jay-Z (an unfortunate choice of artist name in retrospect, and the reason why the more famous Jay-Z had an umlaut in his name earlier in his career), J Groove and Big Nose. While some tracks use sample sources that were already well-worn by 1994, the beats are deceptively multilayered, and very much in sync with the intricate rhymes coming out of Saafir's mouth.

Like the best underground hip-hop from California, there's also fun and lighter moments on the album, with g-funk elements soaking into some tracks, evoking images of sunshine, lowriders and clouds of weed smoke.

Incidentally, the legendary Hobo Junction versus Hieroglyphics emcee battle covered earlier has its roots in the track "Hype Shit" from *Boxcar Sessions*, as the original plan was to have guest lyrics by Casual (the album came out the same year as Casual's *Fear Itself*), but he never showed up to the studio when it was time to record, creating a rift between him and Saafir.

Although Hobo Junction never amounted to much, despite several impressive contributions to *Boxcar Sessions*, Saafir had an undeniable influence on his peers and contemporaries. *Boxcar Sessions* is a quintessential rapper's album, and a suitable textbook for any aspiring emcee, an album that showed how hip-hop could be complex and intellectual, without coming off as corny.

THE NONCE
World Ultimate

(1995, American)

The death of The Nonce member Yusef Afloat in 2000, and to an extent the mystery surrounding it, has overshadowed what they achieved as artists. The demise of a talented rapper at 28 is tragic, but that should not detract from the music. At a time when the west coast was more popular than ever thanks to the success of g-funk and other gangster rap, few albums capture more accurately what was happening in an alternate Los Angeles rap scene than *World Ultimate*.

Graduates of the Good Life Cafe and Leimert Park ciphers, Yusef and Nouka Basetype manage to make their rhymes complex but not complicated, challenging the listener but also not asking them to think too hard. It's tempting therefore to liken The Nonce to a group like A Tribe Called Quest, especially as the production on *World Ultimate* is jazz-infused but still rugged. Doing so also diminishes The Nonce's own unique style and delivery, however, which was very much their own.

World Ultimate covers a lot of ground, but mostly it should be remembered as an ode to the power and joy of hip-hop, and none more so than on "Mix Tapes", a single from the album, and The Nonce cut that most people heard first. The song is a nostalgic and reflective look back at a time we all experienced at the start of our journey into hip-hop, and a fine example of how, even in the often-too-serious, occasionally pretentious world of underground rap, simplicity is usually the way to go.

The Nonce didn't get to release another full album, and although Nouka Basetype still occasionally raps (under the name Sach lllpages), he has thus far not managed to make anything as impactful as *World*

Ultimate. We'll never get to find out what Yusef Afloat could have gone on to achieve. Irrespective of this, *World Ultimate* is the perfect reminder of the talent and skill coming out of a music scene running parallel to the huge commercial success of Dr. Dre, Snoop Doggy Dogg, 2Pac, and other big hitters representing the west coast.

DR. OCTAGON
Dr. Octagonecologyst
(1996, Bulk Recordings/Mo Wax)

It takes a special level of creative writing skill to conceive of an album about a space traveling, demented gynecologist with a penchant for murder. Fortunately, Kool Keith is a special artist.

What started off as a couple of tracks by Kool Keith and his long-time collaborator KutMasta Kurt – at a point in Keith's career when he wanted to move on from the Ultramagnetic MCs – developed into an epic, otherworldly concept album, with producer Dan The Automator orchestrating the soundtrack to Keith's twisted psyche, and DJ Q-Bert sprinkling his turntable wizardry on top.

This is an album that needs to be heard to be believed: a mash-up of many different musical, film and literary influences tied together with some of the most abstract lyrics ever committed to wax, many of which barely even make sense, but somehow still work. It is a brave and ballsy album, and far outside of what was happening in mainstream rap. The critical acclaim *Dr. Octagonecologyst* received helped reinvigorate Kool Keith's career, and finally elevated his reputation to a level never quite recognized during his time with the Ultramagnetic MCs.

Importantly, in addition to being a weird and wonderful master-piece, *Dr. Octagonecologyst* also left the door wide open for the next generation of unique, like-minded artists, giving them the confidence to take rap in any direction they wanted. It also inspired artists from the same previous generation as Kool Keith, including the transition of Daniel Dumile from Zev Love X to MF DOOM, and Del The Funky Homosapien, who four years later would create his own space odyssey with Dan The Automator on *Deltron 3030*.

It's also not coincidental that the only guest feature on the entire album is another mult-persona rap 'weirdo'. Sir Menlik appears on several cuts, and his contributions to the writing of the concept also deserve a lot of praise. Despite Kool Keith killing off the Dr. Octagon character on his Dr. Dooom albums, he reunited with Dan The Automator and DJ Q-Bert for a sequel in 2018, but *Moosebumps: An Exploration Into Modern Day Horripilation* has already largely been forgotten.

ATMOSPHERE
Overcast!
(1997, Rhymesayers Entertainment)

Before Atmosphere became just Slug and Ant, it was Slug, Ant and Spawn, plus peripheral members Stress and Beyond (aka fellow Rhymesayers Entertainment co-founders Sidiq and Musab). All of them were part of the wider Headshots collective, but *Overcast!* would turn out to be the only Atmosphere album where Spawn is credited as an official member.

While the music Slug and Ant make today has veered towards a different direction, their 1997 debut was firmly rooted in hip-hop. *Overcast!* is by far Atmosphere's most 'traditional' rap record, and quite different to how the group sounds now.

Briefly released as an EP before being expanded to a full album, *Overcast!* picked up steam thanks to heavy rotation on college radio, bringing Atmosphere to wider attention. As an emcee, Slug was already developing the soul-searching, introspective, blue collar every man persona that would later see Atmosphere tagged as making 'emo rap', but it somehow feels more organic on *Overcast!* than on later albums. It's also a shame that Spawn only ever appeared here, because he is a great rhyme partner for Slug.

Overcast! Includes artwork inspired by the 1964 *Judgement!* album from Andrew Hill, released via Blue Note Records. The catalog of the iconic jazz label has been used by countless hip-hop producers, but on *Overcast!*, Ant pulls samples from a huge array of other sources, including John Williams' scores for both *Jaws* and *Star Wars*. As Atmosphere's career progressed, and as he became the default producer for a lot of Rhymesayers releases, Ant began to use live instrumentation more and more, further widening his range. It's on *Overcast!* where you can find his hardest hip-hop beats, however, with piano keys and violin strings matching up to Slug's melancholy rhymes.

It's no overstatement to say that *Overcast!* and *The Dynospectrum* (released a year later) put Minnesota hip-hop on the map, and although their bigger breakout album was 2002's *God Loves Ugly*, *Overcast!* should be remembered as an important waypoint in Atmosphere's journey towards finding their identity as a group.

CENOBITES
Cenobites LP
(1997, Fondle 'Em Records)

There have been 11 *Hellraiser* movies, where the main characters are the Cenobites. There have been more than 40 Kool Keith albums, one of which is called the *Cenobites*. In both cases, the earlier releases were the best, with quality degrading as each new film and album has come out. First released in 1995 as an EP, the *Cenobites LP* project with Godfather Don marked the point where Kool Keith transitioned from golden era rhyme vet to indie rap hero.

By the time it was extended and re-released as a full album in 1997, Kool Keith was riding high on a wave of critical acclaim for *Dr. Octagonecologyst*. Whereas that album is weird and twisted, the *Cenobites LP* is much more of a straight hip-hop affair, with Kool Keith still using his faster-paced, Ultramagnetic MCs-era flow and stream of consciousness raps. It's a strong match for the dusty rhythms and hard drums of Godfather Don, who is on double-duty here as both producer and emcee. Some of the material for the *Cenobites LP* was recorded during the sessions for Ultramagnetic MCs *The Four Horsemen*, which Godfather Don produced on, hence the similarities to the feel of several tracks.

There's some genuinely hilarious moments on the *Cenobites LP*, in part thanks to Bobbito Garcia. The album came out on his Fondle 'Em Records, and he even raps on "Kick a Dope Verse". It all gets a bit immature and low-brow, but it was also very much on brand for a label with a name like this, and in fact some of the original EP's material was intended to be used as promos for Bobbito's radio show with Stretch Armstrong, which was known for goofy humor. The album also features Percee P, who like Kool Keith was also in the process of reinventing himself from early 90s emcee to underground darling.

The *Hellraiser* movies have been given the reboot treatment in recent years, with mixed results. Kool Keith and Godfather Don are still active today, and a reboot of their Cenobites partnership would be an intriguing proposition.

COMPANY FLOW
Funcrusher Plus
(1997, Rawkus Records)

Every one of the albums written about here encapsulated elements of this special time in hip-hop, but none quite as much as *Funcrusher Plus*. The hard beats, complex rhymes, and vicious cuts and scratches; the anti record industry stance; the paranoia and sci-fi dystopia; the low-budget, predecessor 12" EP; the nightmarish cover art (created by Matt Doo, who was also known for designing the cover of Organized Konfusion's classic album, *Stress: The Extinction Agenda*. He ended his life in 1998 aged 28); right down to El-P flipping the bird in a photo emblazoned with the words 'independent as fuck'. Everything about *Funcrusher Plus* screams underground rap, and the impact it had cannot be overstated.

As lyricists, Bigg Jus and El-P are a dynamic pairing, attacking each beat with ferocity, spitting out rapid-fire verses in a way that sounds complex and effortless at the same time. The highlights are many, but an obvious standout is the mesmerizing "The Fire in Which You Burn". It holds some of Bigg Jus and El-P's most scathing bars, and they get assisted perfectly by Breeze Brewin and J Treds, over a stripped-back, exotic beat and harsh scratches. It is a perfect rap song, and should be in any self-respecting hip-hop fan's top 10.

El-P deservedly gets the plaudits for production, ushering a new sound that he'd continue to evolve in the following years. That said, Bigg Jus and Mr. Len also had a hand in crafting the sound of *Funcrusher Plus*. Bigg Jus produces the graffiti tribute "Lune TNS", another standout cut, and Mr. Len gets to flex his production and deejay skills with "Lenorcism" and "Funcrush Scratch".

There's an ocean of difference between *Funcrusher Plus* and an album like *Mos Def & Talib Kweli are Black Star*, which speaks to how much of an identity crisis Rawkus Records had at this point as they tried to work out exactly what they wanted to be. Looked at from another perspective, the difference between the two albums showed just how wide reaching and all encompassing indie rap had gotten, and therefore how visionary Rawkus was for recognising the value at both ends of the spectrum. Either way, *Funcrusher Plus* is today remembered as a classic record not just in hip-hop, in all music.

MOOD
Doom
(1997, TVT/Blunt Recordings)

Main Flow, Dante and Jahson of Mood managed to put underground hip-hop from Ohio on the map with their *Doom* album from 1997, Cincinnati more specifically, slightly ahead of the MHz crew and Blueprint from nearby Columbus. In the wider context, it's worthy of being celebrated for more than just being the album that opened up fans to regional rap music from the Buckeye State.

In interviews published at the time of release, Mood talked about how being from the midwest and away from the east and west coasts meant their music was influenced by a bit of everything. There's a New York City feel to *Doom*, however, with Main Flow and Dante having traveled many times to the city to hone their skills at live shows. The album was also recorded there, at Platinum Island Studios, where many other significant hip-hop recording sessions took place in the 1990s.

There's some government conspiracy theory nonsense running through a lot of the album, which sounds very dated in retrospect, but Mood does at least manage to navigate this kind of subject matter better than other apocalyptic rap being released as the end of the millennium approached. *Doom*'s longest lasting impact is that it introduced the world to the talents of Hi-Tek, who produced half of the album (with group member Jahson handling the other half), demonstrating the skills that would mark him out as one of hip-hop's most creative beatmakers in the years that followed.

The album was also a turning point in the career of Talib Kweli. He guests on several tracks, including "Industry Lies", which was the first time he and Hi-Tek were credited together as the group Reflection Eternal. Talib Kweli and Hi-Tek are still around today (albeit as separate artists who no longer work together), but *Doom* was regrettably the one high point of Mood's career.

VARIOUS
Haze Presents...New York Reality Check 101, Mixed by DJ Premier
(1997, Payday)

New York Reality Check 101 was the ultimate shop window for everything the underground scene in the birthplace of hip-hop had to offer in 1997, and the entry point for many heads looking for something new. The fact it was hosted and mixed by one of the most beloved people in rap history, DJ Premier, who has always been a champion of good hip-hop no matter where it came from, was the icing on the cake.

A collaboration between the streetwear brand Haze and Payday Records, the compilation showcases every type of indie rap coming out at the time. From the hard-as-concrete beats and rhymes on tracks like "Metal Thangz" by Street Smartz, "Properties of the Steel" by Godfather Don, "8 Steps to Perfection" by Company Flow and "Off Balance" by Laster and Edo.G; to complex rhymers like J-Live on

"Braggin' Writes" and Choclair on "21 Years"; to thought-provoking storytelling like on "Change" by Shades of Brooklyn and "Inner City Blues" by Rezidue; to mellow, hypnotic joints such as "Feel The High, Pt. 2" by Finsta Bundy and "Head Over Wheels" by G-Depp, it gave a platform to several artists who emerged as the leading names in the indie rap movement.

DJ Premier mixing everything only adds to the dusty-fingered aesthetic, cutting up and beat juggling each track without getting in the way of the full listening experience. He also intersperses the proceedings with conversations with Payday A&R man Mr. Dave, where they discuss the state of the underground. Few people on this earth are as passionate about hip-hop as DJ Premier, and the story he tells on one of the skits about when he used to buy 12" records instead of buying food some weeks, only goes to prove it once again.

It came out the same year as *Soundbombing*, which probably explains why there's hardly any Rawkus artists on there (just Company Flow, in fact), but the collection is all the better for it, providing an alternative at the time to what was itself meant to be the alternative.

VARIOUS
Soundbombing
(1997, Rawkus Records)

If you wanted to get into underground hip-hop in 1997 there were no better starting points than the aforementioned *New York Reality Check 101*, and *Soundbombing*. In the case of the latter, it was also the ultimate way in which to discover everything that was great at the time about Rawkus Records. Those well versed in New York indie rap were already familiar with several of the tracks on *Soundbombing*, as Rawkus had steadily been dropping them as 12"s in the run up to the compilation's release, but having them presented in one mix added to their impact.

The man tasked with pulling everything together was DJ Evil Dee. As part of the legendary Da Beatninerz, who were integral to the rise of indie rap, he was the perfect person to host and mix, and his ubiquitous chant of "Evil Dee is on the mix, come on kick it" is remembered just as vividly as the music. DJ Evil Dee has stated in interviews how his mix was originally only meant to be a promotional tool, but the owners of Rawkus soon decided it was good enough for a full commercial release, especially after DJ Evil Dee had schooled them on the impressive number of units of independent records he had previously sold off his own back.

The mix is stacked high with gems and highlights, including records by the Indelible MCs (Company Flow, the Juggaknots and J Treds), Mos Def, Shabaam Sahdeeq, L-Fudge, Black Attack, Sir Menelik, Reflection Eternal, R.A. The Rugged Man, and more, plus freestyles recorded in the mix by Evil Dee at the famed D&D studios. It is 70 minutes of pure uncut hip-hop, and helped a lot of new fans to gravitate towards the burgeoning scene. It also sold well, and according to DJ Evil Dee was the first release from Rawkus Records to actually make money. The arguably even better *Soundbombing II* arrived two years later in 1999, followed by a third installment in 2002.

ACEYALONE
A Book of Human Language
(1998, Project Blowed)

Aceyalone's achievements as part of Freestyle Fellowship are of the utmost importance to the history of indie rap from California, but his best work came when he branched out as a solo artist. His

1995 debut, *All Balls Don't Bounce*, is a well executed album, but his second, *A Book of Human Language*, earned even greater plaudits. Two tracks from *All Balls Don't Bounce* were produced by Mumbles, who had been steadily learning the craft of beat making after observing his older brother DJ Marvski and Cut Chemist during their early days as part of the U.N.I.T.Y. Committee, before most group members later joined with the Rebels of Rhythm to form Jurassic 5.

Mumbles and Aceyalone had met in 1994, and by 1998 had formed a strong enough partnership to warrant a full album. It turned out to be a winning combination, with Mumbles' jazz-influenced instrumentals the ideal accompaniment to Aceyalone's vocals.

Delivered in short bursts resembling chapters of a novel and interspersed with spoken word, this is high-brow hip-hop for the intellectual listener. It is still grounded enough to be accessible to the casual listener, but those willing to invest time and give it their attention are rewarded with a lyrical masterclass from an emcee who doesn't get mentioned anywhere near as much as he should in those endless online debates about the greatest rappers. The kind of heavyweight, existential pondering that *A Book of Human Language* is concerned with would have risked coming off as too flowery by a lesser emcee, but Aceyalone excels at doing it, while still keeping the listener interested. Mumbles is fully in sync with Aceyalone – so much so that the cover art credits the album as being by 'Aceyalone accompanied by Mumbles' – but *A Book of Human Language* is still a solitary project for Aceyalone, deep in thought without any distractions from guest features. He's lazer-sharp focused, and although *A Book of Human Language* may not be as much fun to listen to as some of Aceyalone's other work, it is the kind of album that should be mandatory study material for every rapper.

BLACK STAR
Mos Def & Talib Kweli Are Black Star
(1998, Rawkus Records)

The image of Mos Def and Talib Kweli riding through Brooklyn in a minivan in the video for "Definition" – spitting rapid-fire verses and a hook about murdered emcees, over a Boogie Down Productions-sampling beat – is a well-remembered moment for anyone following underground hip-hop in 1998. It was the official coming out party for two major talents that had been causing excitement with several 12" singles. It was also the start of a major push by Rawkus Records to try and move from being a niche indie rap label to a major player, an endeavor that would ultimately not work out.

Regardless of Rawkus' long term goals, and despite some heads at the time scoffing at some of the more soulful moments, like "Brown Skin Lady", *Mos Def & Talib Kweli Are Black Star* is a bonafide underground record from back to front. Its packed with thick beats and slick flows, mainly down to Talib Kweli's Reflection Eternal partner, Hi-Tek, who contributes a career-best selection of instrumentals as the producer on "Definition", the follow-up "Re: Definition" ("Definition" and "Re: Definition" were actually meant to be one song with a beat switch midway, but Rawkus rejected the idea), the Common-featuring "Respiration", "Twice Inna Lifetime", and others.

As for Mos Def and Talib Kweli, their performances are impeccable, although the more exposure they got, the more the wider media decided it necessary to attach the 'conscious' rapper label to their names, which would soon become a term few emcees really wanted to be associated with. In many ways, *Mos Def & Talib Kweli Are Black Star* was a glimpse of what Mos Def would have in store on his solo debut a year later, where he'd get to showcase his entire range. For now though, he and Kweli made a great duo, and the partnership they formed here still endures today.

It would take 24 years for a second Black Star album to arrive, but due to a restrictive release that involved the album only being available on one streaming service, 2022's *No Fear of Time* was quickly forgotten about, even though it is fully produced by Madlib.

HIEROGLYPHICS
3rd Eye Vision
(1998, Hieroglyphics Imperium)

The close-knit Hieroglyphics crew have collaborated on many albums together, but when they all get together for an entire group album, it is extra special. *3rd Eye Vision* was their debut as a full unit, coming at a pivotal moment in the group's history as they transitioned to the independent route after various members had been messed around by major labels they had been signed to.

In a 2018 Instagram post marking the 20th anniversary of *3rd Eye Vision*, Domino describes the album as being a "get back up" record that taught the group how to be resilient, self-sufficient, and in control of their legacy. It turned out to be a wise decision from the business perspective, and creatively.

The album has a mix of tracks where multiple members feature, posse cut style, and others that are showcases for individual talents. Those solo tracks, short as they are, give each emcee a chance to demonstrate their skills in full, with Casual, Phesto, Tajai, Pep Love, A-Plus, Opio, and Del The Funkyhomosapian each getting their own spot. Del also gets his own full length song, understandable considering he's the one who brought together the crew in the first place, and the member with the longest career.

The group tracks are even better, as each of the emcees take turns to rip the microphone apart and get the best lines in. It's a whole lot of friendly competition, based on mutual respect and appreciation for the brotherhood of the group.

The production is also a family affair. Although the Hieroglyphics members with the most production credits across their entire catalog are Domino and Casual, those known primarily as emcees also produce tracks on *3rd Eye Vision*, including Del, Opio and A-Plus. It brings lots of variety to the album, and is also proof of how much trust and faith each member of Hieroglyphics has in each other.

Two more group albums came in subsequent years. Both were good, but nowhere near as thrilling as *3rd Eye Vision*.

JURASSIC 5
Jurassic 5
(1998, Pan)

Describing music as being a 'throwback' is not always complimentary, suggesting it is too much like what came before, without advancing anything. Calling Jurassic 5 a throwback is accurate, and a compliment. The group's style on 1998's *Jurassic 5* called back to a time many years before when rap crews performed together as ensembles, with call and response renditions, passing the mic back and forth. But at the same time, Jurassic 5 was also putting a thoroughly modern twist on an old classic, bringing the formula bang up to date.

Like Company Flow's *Funcrusher Plus*, *Jurassic 5* was an extended version of an original EP that came out the previous year. With extra tracks added, and a proper label and distribution behind it, the fuller edition introduced Jurassic 5 to a wider audience, and the group became busy touring artists on the strength of the album.

The track that best captures the spirit of the group is the superb "Concrete Schoolyard", where all four emcees – Chali 2na, Akil, Soup and Marc 7 – seamlessly go line for line, harmonize, and chant a chorus that perfectly sums them up with the line "Playground tactics, no rabbit in a hat tricks / Just that classic rap shit from Jurassic".

The back-to-basics approach of a track like "Concrete Schoolyard" is far from simplistic, however. It takes much collaborative writing skill to make this work cohesively. Rappers are also very competitive by nature, so it's also no mean feat to have four emcees willing to split verses between them all, instead of each one having full-length sections.

Much respect is also due to the other two members of Jurassic 5, producers DJ Numark and Cut Chemist, who share the work between them. Their experience as deejays made them perfect for soundtracking the live feel of the group, and they both get to flex their cutting and scratching skills and love for break beats and obscure vocal samples, on several interludes and full tracks.

RASCO
Time Waits for No Man
(1998, Stones Throw Records)

It's ironic that one of the best indie rap albums from the west coast was created by someone not even from California. Rasco is from Cleveland, but by the time his debut *Time Waits for No Man* came out in 1998 he was an integral part of the Bay Area underground scene. The album is significant for being one of the earliest full albums released by Stones Throw Records, helping to establish it as the go-to label for quality hip-hop for many years after.

Like his contemporaries Lootpack and Dilated Peoples, Rasco mostly concerns himself with bringing the pain to wack emcees on *Time Waits for No Man*, and raging against the mass commercialization of hip-hop. This is especially true of standout "Hip Hop Essentials", where Rasco takes rappers to task not just for the crassness of the shiny suit era, but also for how most of the extravagant displays of wealth in rap videos, like expensive cars and champagne bottle popping, was utterly faked. The Roots, De La Soul and Jeru The Damaja had been making this argument for a couple of years on the other side of the country, but Rasco adding to the rallying cry from out west was refreshing to hear.

Rasco's association with the Likwit Crew, and being on the Stones Throw roster, gave him his pick of many prominent indie artists in those orbits to collaborate with. Dilated Peoples appear on "Major League", as does Defari. Evidence also produces it, alongside frequent early Dilated Peoples producer Joey Chavez, while KutMasta Kurt also contributes a couple of tracks. Stones Throw owner Peanut Butter Wolf also produces several songs, as do Fanatik and DJ Paul Nice.

One of the KutMasta Kurt tracks, "Take It Back Home" is significant for being the first time Rasco and Planet Asia appeared together as the duo Cali Agents, and their *How The West Was Won* album came out two years later.

Rasco has released a ton of albums since *Time Waits for No Man*, but none of them have been as impactful as his debut.

SCARAMANGA
Seven Eyes, Seven Horns
(1998, Sun Large Music)

The beauty and challenge of listening to the multiple personas of MF DOOM and Kool Keith is how sometimes it's hard to know where one character ends and the next begins, if they are interchangeable, or even if there is a difference. It's the same with the music of Phill Collington, where the lines between Sir Menelik, Cyclops 4000 and Scaramanga get blurred and jumbled. *Seven Eyes, Seven Horns* is credited to Scaramanga, but could just as well have been any of his other aliases.

As an emcee, Scaramanga sounds like a cross between Ultramagnetic MCs era Kool Keith and 90s Ghostface Killah, which is by no means a bad thing (despite a few minor rumblings at the time that accused Scaramanga of biting). He spits words at a fast clip, and while his free-association, abstract lyrics don't always make a whole lot of sense, they are always entertaining.

Most of the beats on the album are provided by Scholarwise, Goldfingaz, and Scaramanga himself. Scholarwise and Scaramanga had known each other since high school but lost contact. After a couple of chance meetings in New York, they reconnected at a fortuitous time when Scaramanga was looking for beats for what would become *Seven Eyes, Seven Horns*. Scholarwise's production underpins the entire feel of the album, and he also lends his vocals to a few tracks. It's a shame, therefore, that Scholarwise is little remembered today.

There is also production on *Seven Eyes, Seven Horns* by Godfather Don, and even a track by the legendary Showbiz. A later version of the album from 2000 also includes a track produced by Showbiz' fellow D.I.T.C. member, Diamond D. Curiously, that later version also features the song "7XL", which was credited as being by Sir Menelik on 12" releases and on *Soundbombing II*, further complicating the multiverse of alter-egos.

Seven Eyes, Seven Horns is by far one of the rawest, dusty-fingered albums of the indie rap era, sustaining a hardcore aesthetic throughout, never trying to tone it down at all for any chance at radio play or commercial appeal. And for that, Scaramanga deserves a lot of respect.

VARIOUS
Lyricist Lounge, Volume One
(1998, Rawkus Records)

The Lyricist Lounge was a renowned club night in Manhattan's Lower East Side that began in 1991. By the late 90s it had become a place where rap legends and the hottest artists from the underground performed side by side. It was New York's version of the Good Life Cafe, a training group for various major talents from the indie rap scene that even branched off into a show on MTV.

Keen to capture the vibe of the event and recreate it on wax, Lyricist Lounge founders Danny Castro and Anthony Marshall partnered with Rawkus Records, who released *Lyricist Lounge, Volume One* in 1998.

The creators of the album make a good job of replicating the live experience, including having 'hosts' (De La Soul on Disc 1, Kool Keith and Sir Menelik on Disc 2); recording sessions with multiple emcees that mimicked the atmosphere of a rowdy cipher; and crowd participation sounds. It is a trip to listen to, and the closest most people ever got to the real thing.

The music on offer is a celebration of the cutting edge emcees coming from the underground and the generation of emcees that came before them, all at the same time. In addition to De La Soul and Kool Keith, we also get Q-Tip, KRS-One, O.C., Pharaohe Monch, Black Thought and Common as the elder statesman, holding their own against Jurassic 5, Company Flow, Mos Def, Mike Zoot, Natural

Elements, Shabaam Sahdeeq and many more elite indie rappers, catching wreck over production by Hi-Tek, Shawn J Period, 88-Keys and others. Add to that cameo appearances by Stretch and Bobbito, and you've got almost everyone who was anyone in the scene at that time (although mostly skewed towards New York artists).

A second Lyricist Lounge album came out in 2000 in a rush, reflecting the commercial appeal the owners of Rawkus were desperate to have by the start of the new millennium. Needless to say, it is nowhere near as good as the first edition.

ARSONISTS
As the World Burns
(1999, Matador Records)

It is tempting to wonder what might have become of the Arsonists had their label, Matador Records, actually been willing to promote them and take more seriously what was meant to be their move into hip-hop. But in all honesty, *As the World Burns* is way too underground to have crossed over into wider territory, and is all the better for it.

The Arsonists were like a cross between a mean-mugging crew from the early 90s and a lighter-hearted group like the Pharcyde. They could freestyle, breakdance, perform a wild show on stage, and then be just as comfortable in the studio. In other words they were the complete package, and *As the World Burns* showcased all of it.

It is a fun album to listen to with a lot of humor, both in the names of songs and the actual content. The crew clearly had a good time during the recording process and this comes through, in particular on tracks like the Looney Tunes-sounding, circus-esque "Pyromaniax". But just when you start to think the Arsonists are only about laughs, they hit you with a hardcore sureshot like "In Your Town".

Although they were no longer on Fondle 'Em Records by this point, *As the World Burns* includes the tracks the Arsonists dropped as 12"s on Bobbito's famed label, including one of their greatest songs, the powerful "Session". It was a nice callback to their earlier days, and a reminder that being signed to a larger, typically rock-focused label would in no way dilute their music.

Arguably the best track on the entire album comes midway through, when group member Freestyle pays tribute to all of the Arsonists' peers on "Underground Vandal", name-checking everyone who came up on the scene at the same time as them, from Eminem to MF DOOM. It is the ultimate homage to an exciting time in music, and an anthem for the entire movement.

Nothing the Arsonists did after *As the World Burns* lived up to the promise of their debut, but a repackaged version of the album reissued in 2018 did at least bring it to the attention of a newer generation of indie rap fans.

BLACKALICIOUS
Nia

(1999, Quannum Projects/Mo Wax)

When Gift of Gab died in 2021 there were tributes from all corners of the hip-hop world and further afield. A lot of this respect had been earned on his group Blackalicious' debut full-length album, *Nia*. Chief Xcel and Gift of Gab had been releasing music together since the early 90s, but reached wider acclaim on the strength of "Alphabet Aerobics" from their 1999 *A2G* EP. It upped the excitement levels for *Nia*, which actually came out in Europe a few months after *A2G*, before finally being released in the US in early 2000.

Nia is Gift of Gab at the very peak of his powers, tearing through all manner of themes and subjects over the sprawling and ambitious tracklist. It is positive and uplifting without being cliched or preachy, a balance that a lesser emcee would find hard to achieve. In fact, when *Nia* came out there was some pushback by certain factors of the underground community who considered the sentimental moments as having veered too far away from what is usually considered 'real' hip-hop, but thankfully Gift of Gab didn't care too much for pointless pigeonholing. *Nia* also includes a follow-up to "Alphabet Aerobics", "A to G", on which Gift of Gab once again makes it all look too easy.

Chief Xcel produces almost the entirety of *Nia* himself, pulling in styles from all manner of influences. The only tracks on *Nia* not produced by Chief Xcel were handled by other members of the SoleSides/Quannum Projects collective. Lyrics Born produces and features on "Do This My Way", while DJ Shadow handles the beat on "Cliffhangar". Having different beatmakers intervene could have been jarring, and indeed it is, albeit intentionally, when DJ Shadow goes electro for "Cliffhangar", but the crew have always been so well attuned to each other that any transitions end up feeling seamless.

Every album Blackalicious released was great, and the two albums that followed *Nia* – 2002's *Blazing Arrow* and 2005's *The Craft* – were just as influential during the period.

HANDSOME BOY MODELLING SCHOOL
So...How's Your Girl?
(1999, Tommy Boy)
Put two acclaimed hip-hop producers in the studio together – one of them known for having helped create some of the genre's most

loved albums, and both of them known for being experimental – and the result is something eclectic and off the wall.

So...How's Your Girl? by Handsome Boy Modelling School (aka DJ Prince Paul and Dan the Automator) is not strictly an indie album per se, seeing as it came out on Tommy Boy. It is also not strictly a rap album, but it shares many attributes with underground projects from the era, and is typical of what got tagged as 'alternative hip-hop'.

The album has crossovers between different types of music with surprising combinations – like pairing J-Live with singer Róisín Murphy on "The Truth" and the Beastie Boys' Mike D with Miho Hatori on "Metaphysical" – but there are also pure hip-hop tracks featuring some of the best. Highlights include "Magnetising" with Del the Funky Homosapien, "Waterworld" featuring Encore, and "The Projects (P Jays)" by Del and Trugoy. There's even a semi Brand Nubian reunion with Sadat X and Grand Puba both guesting on "Once Again", and hearing the much-missed Biz Markie channel the Bee Gees on "Calling the Biz" is a bonus treasure.

So...How's Your Girl was also crucial to the formation of Deltron 3030. With Del the Funky Homosapien appearing on two tracks and Kid Koala on "The Runaway Song", all three later toured together, where the idea for Deltron 3030 began to take shape.

In some ways *So...How's Your Girl* is overblown, self-indulgent and messy, and Prince Paul and Dan the Automator would go further away from hip-hop on their 2004 follow-up, *White People*. Handsome Boy Modelling School should be commended, however, for taking the average hip-hop listener out of their comfort zone. It's almost certainly the only album where you can find rhyme icons like Trugoy, Del the Funky Homosapien, El-P, Sadat X and Grand Puba share a track list with the son of a member of The Beatles.

LOOTPACK
Soundpieces: Da Antidote!
(1999, Stones Throw Records)

The overwhelming shadow of Madlib's legacy looms large over perceptions of Lootpack's *Soundpieces: Da Antidote!* It is a concrete fact that a big part of what makes the album so good is Madlib's exquisite production, but there's also plenty more to love about it, especially Wildchild's superb emcee performance, and even Madlib's own rapping.

Subject matter doesn't get very deep here, never deviating far from classic rap standards such as rallying against weak competition and the evils of the music business. And that is perfectly fine. Simplicity is often the key, and by keeping it light, Lootpack stays focused on delivering a timeless rap record.

As revered as he is as a producer, Madlib is the first to admit that he is not exactly the most technically gifted rapper. He has stated how he dislikes his rapping voice and never has much to say as himself, and this is partly why he developed the Quasimoto character. Nevertheless, his mic skills are underrated, and he holds his own throughout *Soundpieces: Da Antidote!* alongside the superior Wildchild. When Quasimoto then shows up on two tracks, Madlib's ability to perform as himself *and* Lord Quas at the same time is mind blowing stuff.

The combination of two emcees, including one who also produces, and a deejay (DJ Romes) saw Lootpack compared to Dilated Peoples. This helps make the Dilated Peoples featuring "Long Awaited" a highlight of the album, with the friendly competition bringing out the best in everyone. Lootpack also invites everyone else in their orbit to the party, including Oh No, M.E.D., Declaime, Defari, and an appearance by the group that gave them their original shot, Tha Alkaholiks. *Soundpieces: Da Antidote!* is a long album but never outstays its welcome, and is the ultimate reminder that before Quasimoto, before Jaylib, Madvillain, Yesterday's New Quintet and all the other great things he has achieved, Otis Jackson was just Madlib the Bad Kid from Oxnard, California.

MF DOOM
Operation: Doomsday
(1999, Fondle 'Em Records)

The MF DOOM origin story has become bigger than the actual content of his debut, *Operation: Doomsday*, and understandably so. The trauma, the heartbreak, and the transformational journey from Daniel Dumile to Zev Love X to the metal-fingered DOOM is an epic saga for the ages, but here we'll focus on the music itself.

It is no coincidence that when Dumile returned from the wilderness he chose to base his new rap persona on a comic book villain who lost everything and was now set on taking revenge against his enemies, while hiding his real identity behind a mask. The story mirrored Dumile's own real life struggles, but while Dr. Doom was aiming to destroy the world, Dumile just wanted to avenge his brother and his group KMD, by destroying the rap game. He states this very intention on "Doomsday", a song that encapsulates everything incredible about the MF DOOM persona. On "Doomsday" and other tracks, Dumile raps as MF DOOM but also makes reference to his brother's death and their family name, melding the real and the imagined, toying with the listener by challenging them to decipher what's what. "Doomsday" is also wonderfully low budget, raw and organic, with MF DOOM rapping over a basic loop of a Sade song with a beat and cuts laid on top, recorded on bare bones equipment.

It was an uncut return to basics, but there was nothing rudimentary about the way Dumile rapped, and how he wrote and structured his rhymes. It was revolutionary, different to how Zev Love X sounded, and most importantly, different to how everyone else sounded. The rest of the album is just as imperfectly perfect. Every song is a gem, but "Rhymes Like Dimes", "Dead Bent" and "Gas Drawls" are particularly beloved tracks in the MF DOOM canon.

The MF DOOM persona unleashed on *Operation: Doomsday* had a profound impact on hip-hop's underground scene and music in general. It continues to be a thrilling and captivating listen decades later, and will forever be remembered as the dawning of a new and exciting era for hip-hop.

MOS DEF
Black on Both Sides
(1999, Rawkus Records)

Black on Both Sides was the culmination of everything Mos Def had been promising each time he cut a 12" record or guest feature in the lead up to 1999. He leaves no stone left unturned, bringing something for every type of listener, from hard beats and rhymes on tracks like "Mathematics" and politics on "Mr. Nigga", to club bangers such as "Ms. Fat Booty" and "Do It Now", and the soulful "Umi Says", each one demonstrating an impressive range.

By 1999 Mos Def had become associated with the Soulquarians, a collective of like-minded artists centered around Questlove, Q-Tip, D'Angelo and J Dilla. The influence is strong throughout *Black on Both Sides*, which at the time was polarizing for some fans who were perhaps expecting something 'harder'.

It was a valid argument, but also a disservice to Mos Def. *Black* on *Both Sides* is actually packed with raw hip-hop, thanks not only to production by DJ Premier, Psycho Les of The Beatnuts, Diamond D, Ayatollah, and Ali Shaheed Muhammad, but also because of Mos Def's slick wordplay, confident swagger, and deep appreciation for what it takes to be a top-tier emcee.

His storytelling in particular helped elevate Mos Def to a level above his peers, whether that was spinning quick-fire stories in the space of only a few verses or whole narratives across entire songs. The album is also a tribute to Mos Def's native Brooklyn, celebrating the borough's storied history.

The critical and commercial success of the album brought a lot of new attention to Rawkus in what was already their major breakout year. Several years later *Black on Both Sides* was certified as having sold 500K copies, an epic sales number for an indie rap artist.

Black on Both Sides is way too long, and borders on self-indulgence in parts (this would be an even bigger problem on his disappointing follow up, *The New Danger*). These are minor gripes, however, and today *Black on Both Sides* is highly regarded as an album that plugged the ever-widening gap in 1999 between commercial rap and the underground. Mos Def was somehow able to be a jack of all trades, and master each one.

PEANUT BUTTER WOLF
My Vinyl Weighs a Ton
(1999, Stones Throw Records)

By the business end of the 1990s, Peanut Butter Wolf's original ambition for Stones Throw Records to be a platform for releasing the music he made with his lost partner Charizma had been fulfilled, and his focus could now move towards releasing his own solo records. *My Vinyl Weighs a Ton* is a showcase for the wide array of talent Stones Throw had to offer, but this was no mere compilation or promo piece. Peanut Butter Wolf produces the entire album, proving his worth as more than just the head of the label. His beats provide a solid base for many of California's finest underground emcees to shine, some making their first appearance of any real significance. Rasco, who had already released his own Stones Throw debut by now, and the group Lootpack, whose debut arrived on the label a few months later, both appear on *My Vinyl Weighs a Ton*, as does Madlib's Quasimoto character. Planet Asia and Kazi also put in strong vocal performances, and there is even a posthumous appearance by Charizma. Elsewhere, there are appearances by the lesser remembered Zest and Dave Dub, plus Capt. Funkaho, aka Stones Throw in-house designer, Jeff Jank.

All of the guest vocalists excel over Peanut Butter Wolf's top-tier production, and it's frustrating that he mostly stopped producing after *My Vinyl Weighs a Ton*.

Peanut Butter Wolf's origin story as a deejay made him an ally of the turntablist scene at the time, demonstrated by early Stones Throw releases including music by DJ Babu and Rob Swift. He also pays tribute to many of the genre's most talented deejays on *My Vinyl Weighs a Ton* track "Tale of Five Cities", which features cuts and scratches by, among others, A-Trak, Cut Chemist, Z-Trip, J Rocc, Kid Koala, DJ Rhettmatic, Rob Swift, and Shortkut.

When a documentary film about the history of Stones Throw Records came out in 2013 it was titled *Our Vinyl Weighs a Ton*, a nod to Peanut Butter Wolf's debut, and the importance it holds in the label's story.

QUANNUM
Spectrum
(1999, Quannum Projects)

When the SoleSides crew regrouped as Quannum Projects they decided to showcase how, despite the name change, the power-house collective of Gift of Gab, Chief Xcel, Lyrics Born, Lateef The Truthseeker, DJ Shadow, et al, was still as deadly as ever, both in front of the mic and behind it.

There are solo cuts from all the major players of the group, including Blackalicious, Latyrx, and Maroons, each one a reminder of what they were capable of. In order to enhance the appeal of the album, the crew also looked outside of their group dynamic to work with some of California's other premier indie rap artists. Jurassic 5 appears on "Concentration," while Souls of Mischief feature on "The Extravaganza". It is a genuine thrill to hear the self-styled Quannum MCs go toe-to-toe with their peers, making both of the tracks highpoints in the history of west coast hip-hop. There are also features by two artists from further afield. Former Rhyme Syndicate member Divine Styler drops by on the aptly-named "Divine Intervention", and for ""Looking Over a City", Lyrics Born and Lateef The Trutherseeker collaborate with El-P, providing another moment of indie rap royalty joining together.

At the halfway point of the album, Quannum Projects introduces a member of their extended family, Joyo Velarde (who also happens to be Lyrics Born's wife). This is followed by "I Changed My Mind", where a singing Lyrics Born collaborates with The Poets of Rhythm. To interrupt the hip-hop with a soul and funk track could have derailed the whole album, but it works as a nice reprise before the high-energy kicks back in on the next song.

The final full track of the album has the Quannum MCs together with no outside features. "Bombonyall" is a treat, with intertwined verses and some vicious putdowns aimed at anyone brave enough to step to them.

Interspersed among the tracks are some skits ("Mic Break" parts 1 and 2) where group members discuss the change from SoleSides, and the meaning of the word 'Quannum' (something about energies combining, apparently). Even though skits were played out by 1999, they give some rare, albeit short insight into the background of an extremely important collective of artists.

BINARY STAR
Masters of The Universe
(2000, Subterraneous Records)

Turning a negative into a positive, emcees OneManArmy (now better known as One Be Lo) and Senim Silla met in prison, got out, formed the duo Binary Star, and made an entire album for just a few hundred dollars. Although *Waterworld* was intended to be a stepping stone to a more substantial project, it was more than just a demo. The extremely tight budget ($500 to be exact) taught the group to be fully prepared for the studio, recording tracks in one take. It was a disciplined, methodical way to make music that served Binary Star well when it came to make the more grandiose *Masters of The Universe*, essentially an expanded and rearranged version of *Waterworld*.

Masters of The Universe covers familiar underground territory, like the poor state of commercial rap and the perils of the music biz, but there's also a lot of introspection, with both emcees evaluating mistakes made and wrong turns taken. This was refreshing, and not seen all that often in rap music, where the goal is usually to project yourself as being the greatest, without flaws.

The definitive highlight is "New Hip-Hop", where the group introduces their manifesto, dropping slick wordplay as producer Decompoze cuts up a sample of KRS-One. It's simple but effective, as most of the best hip-hop is.

Today, *Masters of The Universe* feels forgotten about. Coming from Pontiac, Michigan, they were outliers at the time, but more so today, when the history of rap music from the state is dominated by the legacies of J Dilla and Eminem (former Slum Village emcee Elzhi appears on the posse cut "The KGB", but other than that the album is disconnected from the Detroit scene). It also doesn't help that One Be Lo has diluted the brand by continuing to use the Binary Star name as a solo artist ever since Senim Silla left the group. This is a shame, because they worked great as a duo, and *Masters of The Universe* deserves to be remembered by everyone.

DELTRON 3030
Deltron 3030
(2000, 75 Ark)

After touring together at festivals around the world, Del The Funky-homosapien introduced Dan The Automator and Kid Koala to the futuristic character who'd been living rent free in his head for years, Deltron Zero. The trio fleshed this out into a full concept, formed the group Deltron 3030, and created an epic, self-styled 'rap opera'.

Del's music has always been a celebration of the bizarre side of hip-hop, but this was something different. Del took the paranoia and madness of the new millennium here on earth and wrote a foreboding saga about what life in a distant future would be like if we fail to take heed of what is happening now. It was hardly a new idea in sci-fi, but was breaking new ground in hip-hop, prefacing similar dystopian, post-apocalyptic themes explored in the years that followed by emcees such as Mr. Lif and El-P.

In short, the plot of *Deltron 3030* concerns the human race having been banished from Earth to the depths of space, where the planets are controlled by oppressive, government-like forces. Deltron Zero is a soldier who leads the resistance and fights enemies in rap battles. It is a bleak scenario, but Del's skillful writing not only sustains interest, it does so with wit and humor.

Dan The Automator had already proven to be a master at concept albums, in particular with *Dr. Octagonecologyst*. He excels again here, giving Del a sci-fi movie soundtrack beamed live and direct from the future. Where DJ Q-Bert enhanced Automator's creations with cuts and scratches for Dr. Octagon, here we get the equally precise and deadly Kid Koala doing the same, adding the final flourishes to cap the whole thing off.

Deltron 3030 is the kind of album only fully appreciated years after release, achieving cult status when those who dismissed it at the time finally get round to listening to it, and those who were down from the start finally understanding what it all means. It also resonates now more than ever when you consider that some of the disastrous scenarios that Del predicted could happen, have.

DILATED PEOPLES
The Platform
(2000, Capitol)

Moving on from the false start of what would have originally been their debut in 1995, Dilated Peoples were at long last able to drop an album in 2000. The journey took a while (album track "Work

The Angles" came out as a 12" two years prior), and this is eluded to a few times on the album, but *The Platform* finally marked the breakout moment for a group that was truly one of the innovators of indie rap from the period, and it still sounds just as fresh today.

All three members of the crew bring their a-game, with Evidence and Rakaa perfectly in sync throughout. In the intervening years, Evidence has been open about how in the 90s he rapped in a vocal tone that wasn't how he really talked, lowering his voice to make himself sound 'harder'. Today he raps how he sounds in real life, and comparing his vocals now and on *The Platform* is a fun exercise, although in all honesty, both versions of Evidence are dope.

As for Rakaa Iriscience, he's one of hip-hop's most underrated emcees, a true master of the microphone who makes it look effortless. DJ Babu, meanwhile, adds the cuts and scratches, and also produces one track. Other production is handled by frequent Dilated Peoples collaborators KutMasta Kurt, Joey Chavez, and unofficial fourth member Alchemist. Several tracks are also produced by Evidence himself, including highlights such as "Ear Drums Pop" and "Triple Optics". It's only in recent years that Evidence has been applauded for the quality and range of his production skills, but *The Platform* is a reminder that he's actually been doing it for years.

The Platform is also a celebration of indie rap from the west coast, with Tha Alkaholiks and Aceyalone stopping by to pass the torch to a newer generation (on "Right On" and "The Shape of Things to Come"), and a platform for wider crew members like Planet Asia, Phil da Agony and Defari. There's even appearances from two of the west's most famous OGs, B-Real and Everlast, the latter using his verse on the "Ear Drums Pop" remix to diss Eminem. That, however, is just a footnote in the story of what is undoubtedly one of rap's most crucial albums.

SLUM VILLAGE
Fantastic, Vol. 2
(2000, Barak Records/Goodvibe)

The career of J Dilla was filled with mesmerizing, genre-bending moments, and several of them can be found on 2000's *Fantastic, Vol. 2* by his group Slum Village. The album had been recorded several years previous but got delayed due to record label drama. It turned out to be a blessing in disguise, as by the time *Fantastic, Vol. 2* was finally released, J Dilla had become one of hip-hop's most respected producers, thus bringing wider attention to the album and Slum Village as a group. The album is stacked with J Dilla favorites, including "Climax", "Fall in Love", "Get Dis Money" and "Raise It Up", songs that have been studied ever since by musicians and musicologists trying to figure out exactly how J Dilla made them.

Fantastic, Vol. 2 is a Detroit album through and through, from the track named after the Conant Gardens neighborhood where Slum Village grew up, to the heavy basslines that rattled the speakers at any number of J Dilla's beloved local strip clubs. The line-up of Slum Village has changed many times over the years, but the recording of *Fantastic, Vol. 2* was made during the era of the original line-up of T3, Baatin and J Dilla, and although T3 and Baatin were never the most technically gifted emcees, they knew better than most when to let Dilla's beats do most of the talking. It would be a disservice to T3 and Baatin to suggest that their verses are superfluous, but *Fantastic, Vol. 2* is most enjoyable for the music, not the lyrical content.

A few months after Dilla died, The Roots released their *Game Theory* album, which included a heartfelt tribute from Black Thought where he proclaims J Dilla as being the best producer-rapper. This is perhaps a little overstated, but it is true that the focus on Dilla as a producer means his skills as a rapper are often overlooked. He was indeed a great emcee, and arguably the best out of all three members in Slum Village at the time.

It is a tragedy that two of the three Slum Village members who made *Fantastic, Vol. 2* are no longer with us, but the high regard in which the album is held is a fitting tribute to them both.

AESOP ROCK
Labor Days
(2001, Definitive Jux)

A concept album about working a job, the thing we all have to do but few of us enjoy, sounds mundane on paper. Handled by a writer and emcee as skilled as Aesop Rock, however, and it becomes very exciting. Aesop Rock had already impressed on *Music For Earthworms*, *Appleseed* and *Float*, but they were merely appetizers for what was coming with *Labor Days*, his first album on Definitive Jux.

Few rappers are better at taking the everyday things in life and turning them into entertaining stories than Aesop Rock. When he describes the average person's commute to work on "9-5"s Anthem" you can picture him having written this after doing that same commute himself. It makes his lyrics throughout *Labor Days* seem totally relatable, and therein lies the appeal of an artist like Aesop Rock, especially to the kind of listener who has never experienced the highs and lows often found in other rapper's music. He is not quite yet the fully-formed lyrical monster here, but very close, and by now had already cracked the formula of how to pack many words and a lot of intellect into a verse without getting too highfalutin.

Like the majority of his previous work, production on *Labor Days* is split between self-produced tracks, and contributions by

Omega One and Blockhead. On this occasion, Omega One only has one credit ("Coma", one of the singles), and after this he and Aesop Rock never really worked together again. Blockhead does most of the lifting, and really came into his own on this record.

There are obvious parallels between *Labor Days* and another influential Definitive Jux album from the same year, Cannibal Ox's *The Cold Vein*. Both albums are stark and desolate, but whereas *The Cold Vein* evokes images of gray concrete, *Labor Days* feels more earthy, perhaps partly thanks to Blockhead's heavy use of flute samples. *Labor Days* kicked off an important set of releases by Aesop Rock on Definitive Jux, including the follow-up *Daylight* EP in 2002.

CANNIBAL OX
The Cold Vein
(2001, Definitive Jux)

Vast Aire and Vordul Mega emerged from the Atoms Family collective to record one of the first hip-hop classics of the new millennium. Eager fans first got an early taste of what was to come from Cannibal Ox when two songs that would eventually feature on *The Cold Vein* were included on the *Def Jux Presents* EP. Anticipation was therefore high, but few could have expected the duo would deliver something so impactful.

Eerily released just a few months before 9/11 but sounding more like it was recorded directly after, *The Cold Vein* depicts a bleak, forsaken New York City as the backdrop for some incredibly vivid storytelling, with both Vast Aire and Vordul Mega bending and shaping the English language as they pleased. They each give a stellar performance full of pain and honesty, among the finest in all of hip-hop.

Company Flow member and Definitive Jux leader El-P was like the third member of Cannibal Ox for *The Cold Vein*, his production just as integral to the power of the album as Vast Aire and Vordul Mega's bars. Some of the beats on *The Cold Vein* were originally intended to be used by El-P on his own albums (he even alludes to this in the intro to "Ridiculoid"), yet they still align completely.

A couple of decades worth of think pieces on *The Cold Vein* dictate that it is impossible to describe the album without using words like claustrophobic, dystopian, intense, post-apocalyptic, futuristic and unsettling. All of them are accurate ways to describe El-P's beats, but the instrumentals are also indicative of his complex, multi-layered production technique, reminiscent of The Bomb Squad's famed 'wall of noise' approach.

The critical success of *The Cold Vein* was a key factor in the ascendance of Definitive Jux as the the new destination for quality underground hip-hop in the early aughts. It was to be Cannibal Ox's one and only album on El-P's label, but one not easily forgotten.

J-LIVE
The Best Part
(2001, Triple Threat Productions)

When an album includes production by Pete Rock, DJ Premier, DJ Spinna, DJ Prince Paul and 88-Keys, you know it's probably going to be good. But the reason why *The Best Part* is so good is less about the people making the beats and more about the man rapping on top of them. After the acclaim of his "Braggin Writes" 12", and after a lot of label problems, J-Live was finally able to drop his debut album in 2001 to an audience that had been ready for a while.

What we get on *The Best Part* is a lesson in emceeing from

one of the nicest of all time. J-Live possesses that rare ability to educate and enlighten while still remembering to keep the listener entertained. There are some heavy subjects addressed, but J-Live's wit and overall positivity never allows the album to get bogged down too deeply into politics or socioeconomic issues.

The exalted list of producers ensure the beats throughout *The Best Part* are immaculate. For the title track, J-Live not only got a DJ Premier beat, he got a unique DJ Premier beat, on which the famed producer uses the sound of someone blowing into a jug to build the beat around. And when the beat drops out for a period for J-Live to rap acapella, and then drops back in perfectly in time, it's abundantly clear this is an occasion where producer and rapper could not have been any more in sync.

There are plenty of other moments on *The Best Part* where J-Live gels perfectly with the soundtrack from the producer, especially DJ Spinna, who he worked with a lot more on his next albums. There's also a reason J-Live named his own label, which released *The Best Part*, Triple Threat Productions. He could rap, deejay, and also produce, evidenced by the final track on the album, "The Epilogue", where he demonstrates beatmaking skills that have since become a common feature of his work.

J-Live delivered his second masterwork just a year later with *All of The Above*, and continues to release quality hip-hop to this day.

VARIOUS
Farewell Fondle 'Em
(2001, Definitive Jux)

It was indicative of how quickly musical subgenres and trends can change and evolve that Bobbito Garcia looked at the demise of his Fondle 'Em Records and the rise of El-P's Definitive Jux as the bridge between two generations of emcee, despite there being hardly any daylight between the label's respective runs, and even some overlap, and despite most of the Fondle 'Em roster still being active way beyond the end of the label. Regardless of the true context, *Farewell Fondle 'Em* worked as a symbolic passing of the torch from the gritty, vinyl-only, DIY nature of Bob's label, to the futuristic and often dystopian sounds of El's. It was also the perfect excuse to unleash some excellent, timeless indie rap.

Farewell Fondle 'Em is a tribute to what made Fondle 'Em great, and a celebration of the diverse but cohesive group of artists it put out, featuring freestyle sessions – some from Stretch & Bobbito's radio show – by Kool Keith, Cage, J-Treds (plus El-P for good measure) and the Arsonists, and nuggets like the original version of MF DOOM's "Dead Bent" and an alternative mix of "The Session" by the Arsonists.

Farewell Fondle 'Em ends with an epic posse cut, "Fondle 'Em Fossils", that is a veritable wet dream for any fan of New York underground hip-hop, featuring the once-in-a-lifetime line-up of MF DOOM, Godfather Don, Breeze Brewin, J-Treds and Q-Unique, providing the ultimate sign off from a hugely influential label. The album is credited as being a Definitive Jux release, and comes with artwork by Dan Ezra Lang, who also designed the covers for most of the label's iconic albums (the liner notes are also a treat, with Bob providing a potted history of Fondle 'Em). El-P paid homage to Bobbito's humor and low-budget aesthetic on the record sleeve of the "Fondle 'Em Fossils" 12", which simply consists of a note written by Bob to El-P about how he's never had proper artwork before, complete with corrected typos, and a message asking if El-P wanted to go see a movie.

CAGE
Movies For The Blind
(2002, Eastern Conference)

Making funny rap turn out good is hard, and at the complete opposite end of the spectrum, so is horrorcore. Do it right and it can resonate in the same way horror movies do, tapping into our collective psyche. Get it wrong, and it comes across as corny, and shocking for the sake of being shocking. A select few did get it right, including Cage. *Movies For The Blind* is no easy listen and not for the faint hearted, an unfiltered, drug-induced, nightmarish journey through a horrific set of events.

Perhaps most shocking is how some of it is inspired by Cage's real life experiences of an awful childhood, hardcore drug abuse and major struggles with mental health. Knowing that some of the themes were lived-in experiences for Cage makes it even more harrowing, but like the 80s video nasties *Movies For The Blind* evokes, such issues are also a reflection of society and dare us to enjoy them, making us question why we find it entertaining.

Unlike Eminem, who also did this kind of rap but usually for cheap laughs, Cage is able to spin tales of anger, hatred and debauchery with literary precision and charisma (incidentally, Cage accused Eminem of stealing his whole style during their short beef).

Cage assembled a formidable group of producers to enhance his luridly vivid verses, with El-P, Camu Tao, J-Zone, DJ Mighty Mi, and RJD2 each providing soundscapes to complement the madness.

He has distanced himself from *Movies For The Blind* in the intervening years, choosing instead to make the Cage persona less of an extreme character. It was a wise artistic decision, because more than one album like this would have been overkill. In isolation, however, like Cage's equally fucked up concept albums

Nighthawks and *Waterworld* (with Camu Tao and Tame One, respectively), *Movies For The Blind* packs a punch.

EDAN
Primitive Plus
(2002, Lewis Recordings)

While Jay Mumford was in New York making funny, creative hip-hop as the J-Zone character that didn't take itself too seriously, Edan was doing similar things in Boston, further blurring the lines between character and real person by rapping under his real government name. Edan's second album, *Beauty and the Beat*, is widely accepted to be his best, but *Primitive Plus* was the beginning, when a small indie label from the other side of the Atlantic ocean unlocked the potential of a one-of-one talent.

Like J-Zone, the funny raps and song titles all come from a place of deep love and appreciation of hip-hop, so when Edan talks about how emcees smoke crack while he smokes aluminum, the aim is not to humiliate hip-hop or exploit it. It's tribute and pastiche, not parody, and Edan does it expertly. Again like J-Zone, Edan has the double-threat skills to do this kind of music properly and elevate it to a level above mere comedy, with well-crafted bars and storytelling. Take for instance the track "Run That Shit!". A three verse tale about a work-shy man who gets everything he needs in life by stealing it, the song is witty and laugh-out-loud funny, but the storytelling is delivered on a par with Slick Rick and rap's other great narrators.

The love letter to rap continues throughout thanks mainly to the production, handled in full by Edan himself, giving hat tips to the late 80s and early 90s while bringing the sound up to date with fresh innovation. *Primitive Plus* is clearly a pet project that took a lot of time and intricate effort to make (in addition to production, Edan also provides the cuts, mixing and mastering). This is probably why there's only two featured guests on the album, Mr. Lif and Father Time. Mr. Lif fully understands the assignment, syncing with Edan effortlessly on one of the many standouts, "Rapperfection".

EL-P
Fantastic Damage
(2002, Definitive Jux)

Not one to rest on laurels, El-P followed *The Cold Vein* with his own album a year later. The Twin Towers had by now fallen, adding an even darker dimension to the image of New York City depicted in similar detail on both *The Cold Vein* and *Fantastic Damage*, but again, like the Cannibal Ox album, El-P had written and recorded most of the album before 9/11. El-P has stated in interviews that only "Accidents Don't Happen" directly references the September 11 attacks, having been recorded after, and how the weird connections and premonitions even freaked him out, especially as he found out after 9/11 that a couple of years earlier he'd left a message on a friend's phone while high, ranting about how one day soon the Twin Towers would come crashing down. It is all just a set of peculiar coincidences, but it speaks equally to how close our world has come to a nightmarish world of dystopia, and how good El-P is at channeling this and communicating it back to us.

One of the highest of many high points is the much-talked about "Stepfather Factory". The song is El-P reflecting on the horrific trauma he experienced living with an abusive stepdad in his pre-teens, and is a companion piece to "Last Good Sleep" from Company Flow's *Funcrusher Plus*. As a piece of writing, it epitomizes El-P's skill at being able to take an incredibly painful memory and turn it into an engrossing fantasy narrative, echoing the great sci-fi writers who influenced him throughout *Fantastic Damage*.

Despite all of the deep meaning that can be drawn, like *The Cold Vein*, *Fantastic Damage* is first and foremost a dope hip-hop album and can be enjoyed at face value just as easily as those interested in delving deeper.

Simultaneously running the label *and* being a flagship artist would eventually take a toll on El-P's artistry, culminating in the demise of Definitive Jux. But in 2002, this was a man fully in control of both his business and his creative oeuvre.

NON PHIXION
The Future Is Now
(2002, Uncle Howie)

It wasn't always easy for underground artists to make the transition from 12" singles to full albums. Hitting the listener with a blast of energy over the duration of a big record and a b-side is one thing, but sustaining that enthusiasm and attention is another. Brooklyn's Non Phixion managed to nail it with their full length debut in 2002. The firepower drafted in to collaborate with on *The Future Is Now* felt impressive at the time, and even more so decades on. There are guest features from MF DOOM and The Beatnuts, and production by the holy trinity of DJ Premier, Pete Rock, and Large Professor, each one a connection likely forged thanks to group members Ill Bill and DJ Eclipse's association with the Fat Beats record store.

But all of this was just an extra sweetener, as Non Phixion had more than enough talent on their own. The political, conspiratorial and paranoid nature of their breakthrough 12"s is maintained (although a lot of the rhetoric is dumb, ill conceived and offensive, especially in retrospect), mostly reserved for the dark and brooding tracks produced by honorary member Necro. Thankfully, Non Phixion puts the beats from the masters to good use by writing about more accessible and familiar hip-hop subjects instead: their love of the music and its history, social issues, memories of family lost, and their lyrical prowess as emcees.

Each emcee from the group makes an impact, with Sabac Red and Goretex going pound for pound with the dominant Ill Bill, and DJ Eclipse enhances proceedings with devastating cuts and scratches throughout.

In the midst of so many great producers the lesser-known Dave One deserves a special commendation. The Obscure Disorder member (and brother of A-Trak, who provides the scratches) produces just a single song on the album, "Cult Leader", but it's a special one that has him masterfully flipping a Jackson 5 sample to make it sound far removed from the original source.

The Future Is Now turned out to be the only proper album we'd get from Non Phixion. It was definitely a memorable one.

PEOPLE UNDER THE STAIRS
O.S.T.

(2002, Om Records)

People Under The Stairs (aka Thes One and the late Double K) never once put out a bad album. Several of them are influential, but *O.S.T.* was where they started to earn wider recognition. Many groups never even make it to a third album. If they do, they'll often struggle to rekindle the same magic of their earlier work. That Thes One and Double K were able to be this good on their third album is a testament to their enduring chemistry and friendship.

One of the most impressive aspects of People Under The Stairs as a group is how they managed to be almost completely self-contained, producing all of their albums themselves, and hardly ever having features. *O.S.T.* is no exception, with only the odd guest here and there. It makes for a refreshing change in a genre where albums often come full of features as standard. And besides, People Under The Stairs had enough talent between them to not need anyone else to lean on. Their production skills are in full effect on *O.S.T.*, each track intricately put together with multiple sample sources from digging sessions on tour around the world.

The jewel of the album is their most famous track, the sublime "Acid Raindrops". Simultaneously mellow and hard-as-fuck, the fluidity of the verses over the calming and exotic beat truely makes this one of hip-hop's absolute best songs.

Recorded at a time when underground hip-hop was arguably starting to get too complicated and borderline pretentious, *O.S.T.* provides the antidote. This is pure hip-hop, simple but never basic; respectful to the classics without being a throwback. From the very beginning of their career to the end of it, the only thing People Under The Stairs ever wanted to do was make unadulterated rap music and have fun doing it with good weed and a few drinks, and *O.S.T.* is the perfect manifestation of that mission statement. The album is joyful to listen to, and a poignant reminder of what the rap world lost when Double K died in 2021.

INI
Center of Attention (released as part of the *Lost & Found: Hip Hop Underground Soul Classics* compilation)
(2003, BBE)

Attempting to rank the best songs created by Pete Rock is a fool's errand. As the producer of so many important and beloved records from the past three decades, there's just too many contenders to choose from. But Rock's work on *Center of Attention* would indisputably be near the top of such a ranking. Considered a 'lost' classic for years (despite being bootlegged to death), when it was finally released – first as part of the aptly named *Lost & Found: Hip Hop Underground Soul Classics* collection and later as an individual album – the world at last got to experience some of the finest examples of Pete Rock's famed piano and horn chops, smooth jazz loops, and speaker-rattling drums.

There's some contention about the final 'legit' release of the album. Pete Rock was unhappy with how BBE Records bundled Centre of Attention as a package with the similarly 'lost' *The Original Baby Pa* by Deda, and Grap Luva has discussed in interviews how the album was actually supposed to be called *The Life I Live*, and have a different song sequence and instrumental interludes.

Drama aside, the music itself has a timeless feel, exemplified by a single all rap heads remember fondly, "Fakin Jax", on which Pete Rock, Rob-O, Grap Luva and Ras G catch serious wreck over a sublime beat by Rock.

Mid-way through the runtime, *Center of Attention* also blesses the listener with a mighty posse cut, where Grap Luva and Rob-O are joined by Q-Tip and Large Professor. A collaborative effort involving three of rap's greatest producers was always destined to be special, and "To Each His Own " lives up to expectation.

It remains to be seen what impact Inl could have made long-term had they been able to continue making music together. The chemistry may not have been as strong as that between Rock and his partner CL Smooth, but Inl had enough potential to keep standing out at a time when New York was stacked with extremely talented groups.

JUGGAKNOTS
Re: Release
(2003, Matic Records)

Originally released as *Clear Blue Skies* on Bobbito Garcia's Fondle 'Em Records and expanded with several extra tracks, *Re: Release* is one of the finest examples of everything great about underground hip-hop

The song that sticks in most people's mind even years later, deservedly, is the original album's title track, "Clear Blue Skies". The song is a masterful performance by the group, and one of the most thought-provoking records about racial tension in all of rap's history. Based on a real scenario Breeze Brewin experienced when a white friend of his got some ugly pushback from his mum for dating Black girls, the song is a conversation between a father and son, with the father disproving of his offspring being with a Black girl. It takes a lot of skill and sensitivity to deliver subject matter such as this without resorting to cliche, but the Juggaknots pull it off remarkably, breaking down every type of hateful and stereotypical opinion that people of color have to deal with on a daily basis.

There's also plenty more to love about *Re: Release*, and not least the production, most of which is handled by the group themselves, with some tracks credited to them as a whole, some co-produced with Chris Liggio, and others to Breeze Brewin or Buddy Slim on their own.

Elsewhere, "Who Makes It Hot" is produced by The Obvious Wonder of the group Adagio, who also appear on the song. Despite this multitude of producers the sound is even across the whole album, with an aesthetic that is rough and hard-edged but also bright and breezy, simultaneously complementing and contrasting with the heavy subject matter.

Breeze Brewin stands out as a top notch narrative storyteller throughout *Re: Release*, and this was no doubt a factor in his being sought out by DJ Prince Pau to play the lead character in his epic *A Prince Among Thieves* album in 1999. In a perfect world, Breeze Brewin would be known today on a much wider scale, but with *Re: Release* and *A Prince Among Thieves* he does at least have two classic albums attached to his name.

LITTLE BROTHER
The Listening
(2003, ABB)

The creation of Little Brother's *The Listening* captured the DIY spirit of hip-hop and brought it up to date at the same time (or at least what classed as up to date in 2003). While producers in the late 80s and early 90s were discovering workarounds to get the most out of short memory banks on primitive samplers, the challenge for 9th Wonder in the early aughts was to push basic audio editing and sequencer software to the limits in order to create beats that dripped with soul, but still made necks snap with sampled drums.

It was a transitional period for rap production, where a new generation was now using computers to make music, much to the chagrin of an older generation that was used to physical hardware and studio gear. 9th Wonder was able to straddle both eras, however, using the new technology while also staying true to the foundational principles of cutting up samples and drums. He was also recording vocals by his fellow Little Brother members Phonte and Rapper Big Pooh on cheap microphones in makeshift vocal booths constructed in dorm rooms at North Carolina Central University, or in the houses of their Justus League cohorts.

The result of all of this could have been amateurish, but the high level of skill from all three members resulted in an album that sounds professional while still maintaining the organic feel of what happens when creatively hungry people get together and make the best of what they have.

The Listening also broke ground in other ways. By the 2000s, so-called 'southern rap' was a phenomenon that had taken the attention of the rap world away from the east and west coasts. Most of this was brash, loud club music, but the North Carolina-dwelling Little Brother were proving that the south could also be a place to find good indie rap. Lastly, *The Listening* is remembered for having come of age online, the group gaining traction via online music forums, with their tracks getting shared across the internet instead of via the more traditional routes of radio play, videos, or magazine coverage.

Most importantly, *The Listening* is musically brilliant, heralding the full arrival of three very special talents.

VIKTOR VAUGHN
Vaudeville Villain
(2003, Sound-Ink Records)

Vaudeville Villain came together in the middle of another period of rampant creativity by Daniel Dumile. It was released the same year as *Take Me To Your Leader*, and recorded during the time MF

DOOM and Madlib were on hiatus from their Madvillain album. But this is no throwaway side project. This time Dumile is under the alter ego Viktor Vaughn, which further blurs the lines between his array of characters in that 'Viktor Vaughn' is a play on the name of Victor Von Doom, who itself was an alter ego of Dr. Doom. It's all very confusing, but it really doesn't matter, because Dumile is again on top form throughout, delivering another exceptional performance full of sharp rhymes, mind boggling wordplay, and pop culture references.

Vaudeville Villain was a departure for Dumile in the sense that he doesn't produce any of it himself. Whereas previous albums were mostly self-produced (often using beats from the *Special Herbs* series), here Dumile fully hands the reins to the in-house production team of the relatively obscure label he chose to put *Vaudeville Villain* out on, Sound-Ink Records. Consisting of producers Heat Sensor, Max Bill and King Honey, their non-hip-hop background could have been a gamble, but it pays off with a rich selection of beats well suited to Viktor Vaughn, who accepts the challenge of maneuvering such a varied selection of instrumentals.

In another change from his earlier work, Dumile also has way more guest features on *Vaudeville Villain* than usual. Louis Logic, Lord Sear and M. Sayyid from Antipop Consortium are among those that appear, but the highlight is when Apani B. Fly goes line for line with Viktor Vaughn on "Let Me Watch." Despite these differences, *Vaudeville Villain* has all the elements of a Dumile album, including sampled dialogue from Spider-Man episodes.

Operation: Doomsday, Mm..Food and *Madvillainy* tend to get all the attention, but *Vaudeville Villain* is a superb Daniel Dumile album, and there's a section of MF DOOM's fanbase who consider it to be his best.

MADVILLAIN
Madvillainy
(2004, Stones Throw Records)

There's a moment, thirty-three seconds into "Money Folder", a track that appears exactly halfway through *Madvillainy*, where MF DOOM spits the line "He flipped it like Madlib did a old jazz standard", at which point Madlib does indeed flip the track to play twelve seconds of a jazz standard. The track then reverts back to the beat, with MF DOOM continuing his verse with "Don't mind me". It is a small moment, but perfectly captures the relationship between Madlib and MF DOOM, aka the two geniuses behind Madvillain. They refused to be bound by the normal conventions of hip-hop, or music in general, breaking all manner of musicality rules and structure to create a sound that is all their own.

You can already find entire books out there covering the making of *Madvillainy*, but in summary: The ever-elusive MF DOOM was handed a batch of Madlib instrumentals in 2001, and liked them enough to want to work with the producer on a full project. Some of the tracks that eventually appeared on *Madvillainy* were created together in Madlib's L.A. studio, where recording sessions were interspersed with copious amounts of weed and magic mushrooms.

Madlib worked on other songs during a trip to Brazil, during which a demo version of *Madvillainy* was stolen and uploaded online. It left Madvillain disillusioned, but they regrouped, and a new, tweaked version of *Madvillainy* was finally released in 2004.

The album is a tour de force in emceeing by MF DOOM and production by Madlib. It was a meeting of two kindred spirits, two masters of their disciplines who were not in it for fame or fortune, and just wanted to make good hip-hop. *Madvillainy* has inspired generations of artists since, not just in hip-hop, and is arguably the highest point in the careers of two artists who have experienced way more high points than most.

There has been talk of a follow-up being semi-complete, or possibly even fully completed, for years (there was an official follow-up of sorts with *Madvillainy 2: The Madlib Remix* where Madlib reworked tracks from the original). Since MF DOOM's death in 2020, however, it is unclear if this will ever get released.

———

As with the choices of albums in the previous pages, the following list of 12"s gives a selection of some of the author's favorites, in order of year, and alphabetically if more than one of them came out in the same year. The only rule was that a 12" could not be included if it was on one of the albums listed earlier. Again, you are encouraged to debate him on socials.

BREEZ EVAHFLOWIN
"Forsaken" b/w "Dip...Dip"
(1996, Hot Wax)

Seasoned New York City battle rapper Breez Evahflowin – who was also a member of the Stronghold collective with Immortal Technique, C-Rayz Walz and Poison Pen – made an impactful debut with the infectious "Forsaken" 12" in 1996, produced by Cashus Clay, along with "Dip...Dip" on the b-side. Although the record came out on the obscure Sound Plus Rhythm Records, "Forsaken" gained a lot of momentum when it was included on the *5 Deadly Venoms of Brooklyn* mixtape in 1997, and on the Kenny Dope hosted *Hip-Hop Forever* compilation and an edition of Wreck Records' *Hip-hop Independence Day* series, both in 1998.

LACE DA BOOMS
"Cut That Weak Shit" b/w "Ain't No Secret"
(1996, Guesswhyld)

A number of rap songs had already sampled "I'll Play The Blues For You" by Albert King when it was used on "Cut That Weak Shit" by Lace Da Booms, but this is one of the best interpolations of it. The Guesswhyld (misspelled on the label as Guesswild!) 12" also features guest vocals by Royal Flush and Quasi Modo (not to be confused with Madlib's Quasimodo character), and includes a darker, more sinister remix by Buckwild, who keeps the same vocal samples of Slick Rick and KRS-One as the original.

SIAH AND YESHUA DAPOED
The Vizualz (EP)
(1996, Fondle 'Em Records)

Before it was expanded with extra tracks in 2008, *The Vizualz* by New York's Siah and Yeshua DapoED was a six-track, vinyl-only EP, and one of the jewels of Bobbito's Fondle 'Em Records catalog. The whole EP is highly regarded, in particular the title track and "Gravity". The final track, "A Day Like No Other" is especially powerful. The 11-minute opus is a feast for the ears, full of multiple beat changes and creative storytelling by two raw talents who never quite got the attention they deserved.

DUTCHMIN
"Get Your Swerve On" b/w "Surrounded"
(1997, Dolo Records)

Released the same year that The Notorious B.I.G. was murdered,

Dutchmin lift Biggie Smalls' "I'm surrounded by criminals / Heavy rollers, even the sheisty individuals" line from Junior M.A.F.I.A.'s "Player's Anthem" and turn in into a rowdy hook on "Surrounded", released on the Stretch Armstrong-affiliated Dolo Records. It is produced by Jeff Brown, who also works in a subtle snippet of Biz Markie's voice from Big Daddy Kane's "Just Rhymin' With Biz". "Surrounded" is actually the b-side to "Get Your Swerve On", which is also great.

KRUMB SNATCHA
"Gettin Closer To God"
(1997, M.I.A. Recording Corp)

Krumb Snatcha's rap career never amounted to much, but his association with Gang Starr Foundation gifted him one of DJ Premier's most spellbinding beats. "Gettin Closer To God" is a cautionary tale about the devastating impact of guns, based on Krumb Snatcha's own personal experience. It is thought provoking stuff, but this song is all about the beat, on which Premier flips a Jackson 5 sample, adds a touch of A Tribe Called Quest, and then creates a hook by cutting up bars from Prodigy of Mobb Deep, Rakim, and Snoop Doggy Dogg.

THE HIGH & MIGHTY
"B-Boy Document" b/w "Mind, Soul & Body"
(1998, Eastern Conference)

El-P and Mos Def were at polar ends of what Rawkus Records had to offer. Mos Def was soulful and spiritual, El-P brash and anti-establishment, but both were lyrical masters at the very top of their game in 1998. To have them on the same record was a rare treat, brought together with Mike Zoot by The High & Mighty for a cut from the *Eastern Conference All Stars* compilation via their Eastern Conference label. It is loud and rambunctious, and very enjoyable.

MHZ
"World Premier" b/w "Camu"
(1998, Fondle 'Em Records)

Another classic Fondle 'Em Records 12", "World Premier" was most people's introduction to Columbus' MHZ crew, including Copywrite, and an artist who would become one of indie rap's most beloved artists, Camu Tao. Over a simple but blistering beat that takes a haunting sample from "Monkey Man" by The Rolling Stones, Copyright goes after wack emcees, while Camu Tao spits a verse packed with complexity and hidden meaning. On the b-side, simply named "Camu", the late rapper gets to flex over a more upbeat instrumental, further setting out his store for what was to come.

SMUT PEDDLERS
"One By One" b/w "The Hole Repertoire"
(1998, Eastern Conference)

When The High & Mighty linked up with Cage to form Smut Peddlers, the idea of hearing Cage and Mr. Eon – two talented emcees with unique voices and twisted rhymes – go line for line over DJ Mighty Mi production was an exciting proposition. They delivered in spades with "One By One", a full three years before a 'revamped' version of the track appeared on the 2001 Smut Peddlers album, *Porn Again*. The group has had a complicated relationship since, but decades on this remains a definitive high point.

DA GRASSROOTS
"Thematics" b/w "Price of Livin"
(1999, Conception Records)

Toronto's Da Grassroots released *Passage Through Time* in 1999. The album includes "Thematics" and "Price of Livin", which had a 12" release the same year via the Seattle based Conception Records. Both tracks are mellow but hard-edged productions, courtesy of group member Mr. Attic. The record brought wider attention to the group outside of the Canadian underground, and to Arcee, who features on "Thematics". Both songs hit harder today in light of the death of group member Swiff in 2018.

MASS INFLUENCE
"Analyze" b/w "All Out"
(1999, Non Stop Music Works)

Planets away from everything else coming out of Atlanta in 1999, Mass Influence dropped a head nodding 12" that sounded more like it was made in New York City. Fat Beats got in on the hype over ATL's hip-hop scene by labeling the "Analyze" b/w "All Out" 12" as being on 'Fat Beats Atlanta', but the NYC feel was enhanced by Company Flow's Mr. Len providing cuts on "Analyze". The production is credited to Underground Science, which was also the name of a Mass Influence album released the same year, although neither track from the 12" features on *The Underground Science*.

MASTERS OF ILLUSION
"Partnas Confused" b/w "Magnum Be I"
(1999, Copasetik Recordings)

The 1999 "Partnas Confused" b/w "Magnum Be I" 12" by Masters of Illusion presented two of the many standout tracks from the self-titled album by Kool Keith, Motion Man and KutMasta Kurt's group, complete with all three wearing freaky luchador masks on the cover. There's many great things about this record, but a highlight is hearing Kool Keith spit the line "Them handicapped raps get smacked back in the wheelchair / Tuck in your anus piece / we catch crews with rectum grease", whatever that means.

SCREWBALL
"F.A.Y.B.A.N." b/w "Seen It All"
(1999, Tommy Boy/Hydra)

For the unenlightened, F.A.Y.B.A.N. stands for "fuck all you bitch ass niggas", an eyebrow raising song title even in the profanity-riddled world of hip-hop. Another DJ Premier production, the neck-snapping beat and hardcore rhymes were the perfect introduction to Screwball, setting up their debut project with backing from Tommy Boy, *Y2K: The Album*. It was the kind of record that caused drama in the club, a year before M.O.P. would do the same with their smash "Ante Up". The b-side, "Seen It All" is also produced by Premier, rounding off one of Hydra Entertainment's toughest vinyl releases.

7L & ESOTERIC
"Speaking Real Words" b/w "Bound To Slay"
(1999, Direct Records)

In 2013, Boston's 7L & Esoteric teamed up with Wu-Tang Clan's Inspectah Deck to form the group Czarface, but they first connected many years before when Deck featured on the "Speaking Real Words" 12" (b/w "Bound To Slay"), taken from 7L & Esoteric's EP of the same name. The chemistry between Esoteric and Inspectah Deck is already recognizable here, and sets up what they'd build on years later. Each emcee lays impressive verses over 7L's beat, which sample's Deck's vocals from Wu-Tang's "Bring Da Ruckus" for good measure.

JIGMASTAS
"Lyrical Fluctuation Remix" b/w "Lyrical Fluctuation"
(2000, Beyond Real Recordings)

The original version of "Lyrical Fluctuation" is a Joc Max produced banger from the Jigmastas' *Grass Roots: Lyrical Fluctuations* album, with guest verses from the all-star line up of Pharoahe Monce, Talib Kweli, Shabaam Sahdeeq and Mr. Complex. The 12" single release came with a remix by DJ Spinna as the a-side, with Mos Def added for extra kick, and was just one of many excellent pieces of wax from DJ Spinna's Beyond Real Recordings. Ironically, every single one of the guest emcees was primarily known for their connection to Rawkus Records.

K-OTIX
"Mind Over Matter" b/w "Frequencies"

(2000, Bronx Science)

While Mass Influence were busy in Atlanta making music unlike anything else coming out of their city, K-Otix were doing something similar in Houston. "Mind Over Matter" is a fast-paced, high-energy joint with decent verses by Micah and Damien, while the b-side "Frequencies" has a rugged beat. Both tracks are produced by crew member The Are, and sound dramatically different to most other rap songs from the home of the Geto Boys and DJ Screw. It is no surprise, therefore, that the record came out on New York label Bronx Science.

8

THE FUTURE IS NOW

Like the rappers and producers from the early-mid 90s that inspired them, the artists from the indie rap era of 1995-2005 have themselves inspired generations of artists since. Many from the era are still active today – including Madlib, Alchemist, Blueprint, Planet Asia, Evidence, Aesop Rock, Breeze Brewin, Little Brother, 9th Wonder, Apathy, Ill Bill, El-P, The High & Mighty, Jedi Mind Tricks and countless others – but more recent waves of rappers and producers have taken the blueprint, carried the torch, and broken their own new ground. Some have gone on to carve out modest but dedicated fan bases, others have transitioned to mainstream commercial success, and some have even been elevated to cultural icon status, but all of them are indebted at least in some way to the pioneers of underground hip hop that came before them.

New York indie rap is still alive and as vibrant as before, despite the death of Fat Beats, Lyricist Lounge, and various other pillars of the local underground scene. In Queens, Action Bronson has built a career that spans music, TV and film, after dropping a couple of releases on tiny indie labels before making a bigger splash with the *Mr. Wonderful* album in 2015. After dabbling with major labels he has mostly returned to releasing albums independently in recent years. Frequent Action Bronson collaborator and fellow Queens native Mayhem Lauren has also released several quality albums since the late aughts, with highlights including 2014's *Silk Pyramids* with producer Buckwild, and 2016's *Piatto D'Oro*. Mayhem Lauren and Action Bronson were also both members of the short-lived The Outdoorsmen.

Queens emcee Heems released his acclaimed debut, *Eat Pray Thug*, in 2015, and was also a member of the group Das Racist, with another artist from Queens, Dapwell, and Kool A.D. They released the *Relax* album in 2011. Heems is close with Despot, whose indie rap credentials go back as far as the final years of Definitive Jux, where he released a few records and was scheduled to drop a full album. That never happened, but Despot has continued to work with El-P since then.

Arguably the most respected indie rapper from Queens in recent years is Homeboy Sandman. He has released many albums and EPs since 2007, some on Stones Throw Records, others fully independently. His catalog includes solo work, plus collaborations with Aesop Rock, Edan, and more.

————

In an ironic twist, one of the most influential independent artists of the last two decades – a man who birthed a style that has now fathered countless imitators – actually got his start via a huge commercial rap star. Roc Marciano, from Long Island, New York, had his first act as part of Busta Rhymes' Flipmode Squad. This never amounted to much more than a few appearances, and by 2001 Roc Marciano had moved on. The next phase of his career came as a member of The U.N., who released the acclaimed *UN or U Out* album in 2004. It was here where Roc Marciano began making music akin to the golden era of indie rap, with complex rhymes and hardcore beats that were very different to the kind of rap associated with Busta Rhymes.

It was in 2010, however, that Marciano changed the game in a similar way to how MF DOOM, Mos Def, El-P and others did several years before. The Fat Beats-released *Marcberg* album sounded like what would happen if you took the best street rap and crossed it with the finest word association rappers, but Roc Marciano's style was also distinctly his own. *Marcberg* is full of visceral, cinematic stories and scenarios, like a gritty New York City movie from the 1970s in hip-hop form. It was also influential for popularizing so-called 'drumless' production, where sparse percussion takes the place of hard drum breaks.

In the proceeding years Marciano has only gotten better, releasing many finely-crafted albums, some self-contained with few features and mostly self-produced, others full collaborations with carefully chosen counterparts. His impact on recent generations of underground hip-hop has been huge, and you can hear his influence all over the indie rap scene of today.

—

One of the select few artists Roc Marciano consistently worked with was Ka. After leaving Natural Elements just before their brief heyday, Ka made music on his own and alongside Kev in the group Nightbreed, but his breakout moment came courtesy of an emcee who himself had inspired the 1990s indie rap revolution of which Ka had originally been part of. Ka was featured on "Firehouse" from GZA's 2008 *Pro Tools* album after being sought out by the Wu-Tang Clan veteran, immediately catching the attention of rap heads hungry for more.

Ka released his official solo debut in 2008, and like his close collaborator Marciano, he proved to be a rare talent, writing dense and evocative rhymes that use chess theory, history, religion, spirituality, philosophy and other subjects as metaphors for the harsh realities of street life in his native Brooklyn, all delivered in a distinctive, gravel and grit voice.

A flawless collection of albums followed, each one highly acclaimed, especially projects such as *The Night's Gambit*, *Honor Killed the Samurai*, and *Descendants of Cain*, the joint project *Orpheus and the Sirens* with producer Animoss as Hermit and the Recluse, and the *Days with Dr. Yen Lo* album as Dr. Yen Lo with producer Preservation.

In between each release Ka was fiercely private, creating an enigmatic persona. Outside of rap Ka was also a decorated fire chief, and a first responder on 9/11. It all added to the intrigue of one of hip-hop's most interesting figures, and if you ever needed proof of just how beloved Ka was, you'd only need look at social media posts of the huge lines of people who gathered to speak to him each time Ka arranged one of his pop up events to meet and greet fans any time he released a new album.

And then, at the height of his career, Ka suddenly died in October 2024. There was an outpouring of sadness from multiple generations of indie rap artists and fans, who still hadn't yet fully processed the loss of MF DOOM, Gift of Gab, Double K, Dave from De La Soul and several other artists gone too soon in quick concession.

There was hype for many years about a full Roc Marciano and Ka album, named *Metal Clergy*. In light of Ka's death, we're unlikely to ever get this.

———

Elsewhere in Brooklyn, several other rappers have kept the underground aesthetic alive. Skyzoo has gotten better with every album he's released since 2006, dropping impressive solo projects and one-producer albums such as 2016's *The Easy Truth* with Apollo Brown, and *Retropolitan* with Pete Rock in 2019. Skyzoo also released the *Barrel Brothers* album in 2014 as a collaboration with another Brooklyn emcee, Torae. Since the release of his *Daily Conversation* mixtape in 2008, Coney Island's Torae has recorded many acclaimed albums, including his debut, *For the Record*, in 2011, 2009's *Double Barrel* with producer Marco Polo, and 2016's *Entitled*. These projects and others have seen him work with many of hip-hop's most revered producers, in particular DJ Premier.

Ukrainian-born, Brooklyn-raised Your Old Droog emerged onto the scene in 2014, and after a rocky start in which he was inexplicably rumored to be Nas incognito – despite barely sounding like him at all – he has since released a huge body of work, building a solid reputation that has seen him gain respect from some of the genre's biggest names.

Skyzoo, Torae, and Your Old Droog have all worked with Marco Polo, and although he is Canadian, he has been based in New York for many years. He is one of indie rap's most active producers, releasing albums including *Port Authority* in 2007, and two acclaimed projects with Masta Ace.

Crown Heights emcee Mr. Muthafuckin' eXquire has had brief stints on major labels, but is mostly known for his independently released projects, including the *Lost in Translation* mixtape from 2011, notable for the anthemic "The Last Huzzah!" featuring El-P, Despot, Danny Brown, and Das Racist.

When Brooklyn emcee Joey Badass broke through with his *1999* mixtape in 2012, he brought his Pro Era crew with him, and the wider

Beast Coast collective that also included The Underachievers and the Flatbush Zombies. Pro Era boasted several talented members, including Capital STEEZ, who had a promising career ahead of him before he tragically ended his life in 2012 at only 19 years of age.

Artists from other parts of New York to have impressed in recent years include Hempstead, Long Island's Hus Kingpin, and Orange Country duo The Dopplegangaz. From over the water in New Jersey, rappers Rasheed Chappell and Crimeapple have also both established themselves with solid releases.

El-P is himself still a major presence having found huge success with Run The Jewels alongside Killer Mike, releasing several albums and becoming a fixture of the live festival circuit. Rapper and producer Uncommon Nasa – an engineer on many albums released by El-P's Definitive Jux label – has carved out his own career since 2014 via his label, Uncommon Records.

———

Two current New York indie rap labels in particular embody the 90s spirit of being 'independent as fuck'. The first is Backwoodz Studioz, founded and operated by billy woods, who came up under the wing of Vordul Mega from Cannibal Ox. His first solo album – and the first Backwoodz Studioz release – was 2003's *Camouflage*. He also released early albums as one half of the duo Super Chron Flight Brothers (with Privilege). woods has since released a long run of acclaimed solo albums, including *History Will Absolve Me* (2012), *Known Unknowns* (2017), and *Hiding Places* (2019). He is also a member of Armand Hammer, with Elucid, and they have dropped numerous revered albums, among them *Rome* (2017), *Paraffin* (2018), and *Haram* in 2021, fully produced by Alchemist. Elucid has an equally impressive solo catalog, including highlights such as 2016's *Save Yourself* and 2022's *I Told Bessie*. In addition to being one half of Armand Hammer, Elucid is also in the duo Nostrum Grocers (with R.A.P. Ferreira) and Small Bills (with producer The Lasso).

Backwoodz Studioz has additionally released progressive hip-hop albums by other New York based artists including AKAI Solo, Steel Tipped Dove, ShrapKnel, and Henry Canyons.

The other label is Griselda Records, founded upstate in Buffalo by Westside Gunn. While Backwoodz Studioz specializes in what used to get called 'alternative rap', Gunn's music, and that of his brother Conway The Machine, cousin Benny The Butcher, and their producer Daringer, is like a harder-edged version of the street raps of peak-era The Lox and G-Unit, with an ear for the classic boom bap era of the early-mid 90s.

It is a powerful combination that has earned the crew acclaim from all levels of the genre, and helped Westside Gunn start an empire of business interests. In an act of true dedication to being independent, Westside Gunn walked away from a distribution deal Griselda Records had with Eminem's Shady Records, preferring to release music on his own terms.

The label has also dropped music by Queens based emcee Rome Streetz, and albums by the enigmatic Mach-Hommy, based in New Jersey. Though not on Griselda, the label's success has additionally opened doors for more rappers from Buffalo and other cities across upstate New York, including Stove God Cooks, Che Noir, 38 Spesh and Eto.

———

On the west coast, collectives like Project Blowed, Hieroglyphics and Quaanum Projects, who wrote the manual on how to operate as both an independent record label and as a group, have continued to inspire others to do the same, spawning major stars like Kendrick Lamar and Tyler, The Creator.

Lamar has his roots in the group Black Hippy from Los Angeles, with Jay Rock, Schoolboy Q and Ab-Soul. They were signed to the now hugely successful indie label Top Dawg Entertainment (TDE), founded by Anthony "Top Dawg" Tiffith in 2004. Each Black Hippy member has gone on to have solo success, but Lamar in particular has risen to god-like status, releasing several forward-thinking and progressive hip-hop albums.

Tyler, The Creator was a co-founder of Odd Future; a collective of emcees, producers and R&B artists from Los Angeles that included Earl Sweatshirt, Domo Genesis, Frank Ocean and Syd from the group The Internet. Tyler, The Creator has built his own multi-media empire, and makes music that is both beloved and polarizing. Earl Sweatshirt has become an indie rap icon since his debut album, *Doris*, especially via his frequent work with Alchemist.

Project Blowed itself has continued to birth the careers of new rappers and producers. Originally from Chicago but based in Los Angeles for many years, Open Mike Eagle has built a loyal fanbase and critical acclaim for several albums since his 2010 debut, *Unapologetic Art Rap*. Producer Dibiase has amassed a sizable catalog of albums and EPs in recent years, as had Ras G, who put out a lot of music – including for labels like Brainfeeder, owned by fellow Los Angeles producer Flying Lotus – until his death in 2019.

The Low End Theory club night was also an incubator of unique Los Angeles talent for several years, including emcee and producer Jonwayne, who has self-released many projects, and gained wider exposure with 2013's *Rap Album One* on Stones Throw, and the follow-up *Rap Album Two* in 2017.

Blu has amassed a revered discography since he and Exile blew listeners away with *Below the Heavens* in 2007, both solo and in collaboration with Madlib, Oh No, Evidence, and Nottz among others, in addition to touring and still releasing music with Exile. Their circle extends to Fresno rapper Fashawn, who has himself released many acclaimed projects, including albums with Murs and Alchemist. Another Los Angeles native who has released quality indie rap in the last twenty years is producer and emcee Georgia Anna Muldrow, releasing music on a host of labels including Stones Throw Records, and on SomeOthaShip Connect, which she co-founded with her ex husband Dudley Perkins.

One of the biggest Los Angeles-based supporters of underground rap in recent years is someone from a previous era. Decades after major success as a member of Cypress Hill and his work with groups like House of Pain, DJ Muggs has racked up collaborative albums with luminaries of the indie rap era, such as Ill Bill and Planet Asia, but also the latest generation, including Roc Marciano, Eto, Mach-Hommy, Crimeapple, Tha God Fahim, Rome Streetz, and Rigz.

———

In Chicago, Naledge joined together with Double-O (who is from New York) in the year 2000 to form Kidz In The Hall. Their 2006 debut, *School Was My Hustle*, came out on Rawkus Records when it relaunched years after its original run, but by 2008's *The In Crowd* the duo were signed to Duck Down Records.

The In Crowd included a collaboration with another group from Chicago, The Cool Kids, aka Sir Michael Rocks and Chuck Inglish. They created a buzz with several mixtape drops, and have gone on to have a long career since their debut album in 2001, *When Fish Ride Bicycles*. Emcee Vic Spencer has dropped a monster amount of albums in the last decade, and works hard to promote other talented artists from the city. The Windy City is also home to Serengeti, who has released some of the most quirky hip-hop of the last two decades.

Kanye West aside, the two other artists from Chicago who started independently and have found big success are Lupe Fiasco and Chance The Rapper, the former gaining critical acclaim for his *Food & Liquor* debut in 2006, the latter for 2013's *Acid Rap* mixtape.

———

In Boston, 7L & Esoteric have found a new lease of life that has given them the most success they've ever had, connecting with Inspectah Deck to form Czarface. The group has released many projects since their self-titled debut in 2013, including full album collaborations with MF DOOM, and Inspectah Deck's fellow Wu-Tang Clan member, Ghostface Killah.

Other Massachusetts based artists of note are Termanology, who has a huge number of albums under his belt – often in collaboration with other members of his ST. Da Squad crew, and with producer Statik Selektah – and Estee Nack, who has made waves both as a solo artist and as part of the Tragic Allies collective.

———

The city of Gary, Indiana was the birthplace of Michael Jackson and the rest of the Jackson Five, but it was hardly known for having much hip-hop pedigree. Freddie Gibbs was therefore fighting an uphill career battle from the start, not helped by several shitty record deals that fizzled out and almost deaded his chances of ever making it.

It was only when Gibbs tapped into the underground by working with an indie rap hero that he was finally able to reach new heights. Gibbs released a series of EPs with Madlib between 2011 and 2013, culminating with their renowned *Piñata* album in 2014. It was swiftly anointed as a new classic among listeners and critics alike, and widened Gibbs's career with two distinct sets of fans; those who remembered his more mainstream music who were now checking for him again, and the indie rap heads who dug him for his association with Madlib.

The fruitful relationship led to another album in 2019, *Bandana*, and there are set to be several more in the years to come. Incidentally, *Bandana* coincided with Gibbs and Madlib signing to a major label, showing that independent hip-hop can still be a pipeline to bigger things, even in a modern music industry where being independent can often be more lucrative for an artist than being signed.

And Madlib isn't the only underground legend Gibbs has channeled. He has also worked consistently with Alchemist, including on the *Fetti* album alongside another artist who likes to tap into both the mainstream and the underground, Currensy. Gibbs and Alchemist's most high profile release was 2020's Grammy-nominated *Alfredo*.

———

In Detroit, emcees and producers who were just starting to make noise circa 2005 have since flourished into accomplished artists. Black Milk has racked up a catalog of solo albums and collaborations, with highlights that include 2007's *Popular Demand*, 2013's *No Poison No Paradise*, and *If There's a Hell Below* the year after. He also recorded the *Random Axe* album in 2011 with Guilty Simpson and Sean Price, the same year he connected with fellow Detroit rapper Danny Brown for the *Black & Brown!* EP.

Guilty Simpson, now an elder statesman of Detroit hip-hop, released several albums on Stones Throw Records, including *Ode to the Ghetto* in 2008, *O.J. Simpson* in 2010, and *The Simpson Tape* with Oh No in 2014.

Danny Brown has himself earned much success, getting respect from both the underground and the mainstream for albums such as 2011's *XXX*, 2013's *Old*, and 2016's *Atrocity Exhibition*.

Since his time as a member of Slum Village, Elzhi has become one of the most respected emcees working today. His debut *The Preface* came out in 2008, and among his other acclaimed releases is 2011's *Elmatic*, on which Elzhi created a tribute to Nas' classic debut.

Detroit rapper Quelle Chris has also notched up a significant collection of acclaimed releases since 2011, as has producer Apollo Brown, who has dropped several instrumental projects, and vocal albums with Ghostface Killah, O.C., Planet Asia, Skyzoo, and Guilty Simpson.

Although the label is not from Detroit, most of Quelle Chris and Apollo Brown's music has been released by Mello Music Group. The Arizona-based company has become the premier independent label since it was founded in 2007, releasing scores of albums and EPs from artists across the country, including most material released by Oddisee.

Other Detroit artists to have made an impact post-2005 include producer Bronze Nazareth, the groups Clear Soul Forces, Lawless Element and Wisemen, and the emcees Nolan The Ninja, Fat Ray, Fatt Father, Marv Won, Denmark Vessey, and Finale. Deejay and producer House Shoes, one of the biggest supporters of hip-hop from his native Detroit, released his debut album in 2012 with *Let It Go*, featuring all manner of artists from the city.

———

In Washington D.C., in addition to the success of Oddisee – who has released many acclaimed albums, including *People Hear What They See* in 2012, *The Good Fight* in 2025, plus two albums with fellow D.C. artists XO and yU as the group Diamond District – the city is home to acclaimed producer Damu The Fudgemunk. He has amassed a wide range of albums, most of which came out on the label he co-founded, Redefinition Records.

———

In North Carolina, 9th Wonder has continued to develop local artists via his independent label, Jama Records. The biggest success story from the label so far is Rapsody, who released projects on the label before being signed to a major label. Khrysis, a producer who served his tenure as a protege of 9th Wonder, has also released many renowned projects, and collaborated with Detroit rapper Elzhi in 2018 under the name Jericho Jackson.

———

As with the many outliers who broadcasted underground hip-hop from far away places across the US map during the golden period, there are artists doing the same today. Although originally from Chicago, emcee R.A.P. Ferreira is something of a nomad, making music in places as varied as Kenosha, Wisconsin, Los Angeles, and Nashville, Tennessee. He has released music as R.A.P. Ferreira, milo, and Scallops Hotel, and earned positive reviews for 2015's *So The Flies Don't Come*, produced by Kenny Segal.

Most of R.A.P. Ferreira's music has come out on his own indie label, Ruby Yacht, and via Alpha Pup Records, founded by Daddy Kev. He was also a member of the defunct Hellfyre Club collective, an off-shoot of Project Blowed founded by Nocando, which also included Open Mike Eagle and Busdriver. Kenny Segal has earned a reputation as one of the underground's go to talents himself, working with many different artists. He has also released two albums with Freestyle Fellowship member Self Jupiter as The Kleenerz, bringing together artists from two generations of Project Blowed.

The influential Okayplayer message board forums brought together two artists from different parts of the country, who took full advantage of the rise of digital music production software, file sharing and internet speeds. Donwill is from Cincinnati and Von Pea is from Brooklyn, but they connected online to form the group Tanya Morgan in 2003, also with an original third member, Illyas, who later left but continues to make sporadic contributions to their music. The group scored rave reviews for the 2009 *Brooklynati* concept album, and Donwill and Von Pea are also members of The Lessondary, another crew spawned from the message boards that also includes Elucid and Rob Cave.

Last but by no means least there was Mac Miller, who achieved the rare distinction of having a completely independent album reach the Billboard charts with 2011's *Blue Slide Park*. After first starting out with a more commercial, 'white boy' rapper style, Miller earned praise with the release of *Watching Movies With the Sound Off* in 2013, and went from strength to strength after that, before his untimely death at only 26 in 2018.

———

Hip-hop, therefore, is going to be ok. The summary above is a mere surface scratch of the many rappers and producers making good rap, regardless of what is happening in the mainstream. There's quality music coming out every day, and while the ease and accessibility of music creation tools and streaming sites have made everyone a musician, creating an internet packed full of terrible music, the good still manages to filter through the noise, especially if you know where to look.

The entire landscape of the music industry has changed, and it's no longer necessary for an artist to even be on a record label. They can now make and distribute music by themselves, promote it across many social media platforms, and even get it manufactured as a physical product, all without needing to sign a contract with anyone. Record labels large and small still have their place, but the stronghold they had on the music business for most of the 20th century has been significantly diminished. Power and autonomy is now with musicians, who are able to achieve more freely what the underground hip-hop artists of the mid-late 90s and early aughts wanted: to focus on their craft and earn a living from doing it. Regardless of the genre they work in, and whether they even realise it or not, artists across the world are as close as possible to being able to write, record, produce, distribute, promote, and book shows by themselves on their own terms, and truly be independent as fuck.

ENDNOTES

The following websites, articles, videos, books and podcast episodes were used for research:

GENERAL

Independent As Fuck: 20 Essential Underground Hip-hop Releases From 1997, Medium https://festivalpeak.com/independent-as-fuck-20-essential-underground-hip-hop-releases-from-1997-db1c5206a99e

Independent As Fuck 2: 25 Essential Underground Hip-hop Releases From 1998, Medium https://dartadams.medium.com/independent-as-fuck-2-25-essential-underground-hip-hop-releases-from-1998-c4fd5ccb26af

Independent As Fuck 3: 32 Essential Underground Hip-hop Releases From 1999, Medium https://dartadams.medium.com/independent-as-fuck-3-32-essential-underground-hip-hop-releases-from-1999-a3c3a87ab486

Top 25 Underground Hip Hop Albums, HHGA https://hiphopgoldenage.com/list/top-25-underground-hip-hop-albums-of-all-time/

100 Essential Underground Hip Hop Albums, HHGA https://hiphop-goldenage.com/list/100-essential-underground-hip-hop-albums/

100 Great Hip Hop Albums You Have Never Heard, HHGA https://hiphopgoldenage.com/list/100-great-hip-hop-albums-you-have-never-heard/

Check The Technique: Liner Notes for Hip-Hop Junkies, Brian Coleman

Check The Technique Volume 2: More Liner Notes for Hip-Hop Junkies, Brian Coleman

https://www.discogs.com/

https://www.whosampled.com/

https://en.wikipedia.org/

CHAPTER 1 - FROM 93 TIL

Goin' Off: The Story of The Juice Crew, Ben Merlis

CHAPTER 2 - STRESS RAP

A Walk Through The Avant-Garde World of 'Art Rap' Music, Bandcamp
https://daily.bandcamp.com/lists/art-rap-artists-guide

The Apocalypse in 1990s Hip-hop, Red Bull Music Academy https://
daily.redbullmusicacademy.com/2019/03/the-apocalypse-in-1990s-
hip-hop

CHAPTER 3 - THE FIRE IN WHICH YOU BURN

Episode 87 – Kool Keith Interview, Dad Bod Rap Pod https://
dadbodrappod.com/2019/09/26/dbrp87/

The Many Faces of Kool Keith, Def Goldbloom https://www.youtube.
com/watch?v=5W8dGONL4kM

Stepfather Factory, Vice https://www.vice.com/en/article/stepfa-
ther-v9n2/

El-P Lecture, Red Bull Music Academy https://www.redbullmusica-
cademy.com/lectures/el-p-lecture

El-P: The Overly Dramatic Truth, Drowned in Sound https://drowne-
dinsound.com/in_depth/2443202-el-p--the-overly-dramatic-truth

Episode 83 – Mr. Len Interview, Dad Bod Rap Pod https://dadbodrappod.
com/2019/08/22/dbrp83/

Episode 36 – Mr. Len, The Cipher Show https://theciphershow.com/
episode/36/

The Mask of Doom, The New Yorker https://www.newyorker.com/
magazine/2009/09/21/the-mask-of-doom

Godfather Don – The Unkut Interview, Unkut https://unkut.com/2024/03/
godfather-don-the-unkut-interview/

Six Essential Juggaknots Albums on Bandcamp, Bandcamp https://
daily.bandcamp.com/lists/juggaknots-discography-guide

Breeze Brewin From Juggaknots Interview, Unkut https://unkut.
com/2007/11/breeze-brewin-from-juggaknots-interview/

The Real Story About Why Non Phixion Broke Up, And Why They Reunited, The Village Voice https://www.villagevoice.com/the-real-story-about-why-non-phixion-broke-up-and-why-they-reunited/

R.A. The Rugged Man – The Unkut Interview, Unkut https://unkut.com/2013/04/r-a-the-rugged-man-the-unkut-interview/

Recommended Listening: Siah and Yeshua Dapoed The Visualz Anthology, Rhymesayers https://rhymesayers.com/blogs/fifth-element/6417088-recommended-listening-siah-and-yeshua-dapoed-the-visualz-anthology-circa-96-98

Episode 105 – Dopest Opus With Guest Yesh, Dad Bod Rap Pod https://dadbodrappod.com/2020/02/13/dbrp105/

Episode 198 – Self Mythologizing With Guest Siah, Dad Bod Rap Pod https://dadbodrappod.com/2021/12/09/dbrp198/

How The Atoms Family Became a Force in Hip-Hop, Bandcamp https://daily.bandcamp.com/features/the-atoms-family-feature

Episode 138.5 – I Can See Alaska From My House, Dad Bod Rap Pod https://dadbodrappod.com/2020/10/15/dbrp1385/

Episode 166 – Nothing is Gonna Be Normal With Guest Vast Aire, Dad Bod Rap Pod https://dadbodrappod.com/2021/04/22/dbrp166/

The Largest Vocabulary in Hip-hop, The Pudding https://pudding.cool/projects/vocabulary/

Episode 197 – Sonic Boom With Guest Rob Sonic, Dad Bod Rap Pod https://dadbodrappod.com/2021/12/02/dbrp197/

How The Antipop Consortium Dragged Rap Into The Millenium, Bandcamp https://daily.bandcamp.com/features/antipop-consortium-feature

The Highs & Lows of Hip-Hop Legend, Masta Ace, Forbes https://www.forbes.com/sites/passionoftheweiss/2015/12/30/the-highs-lows-of-hip-hop-legend-masta-ace/

InI – The Life I Live, Boom Bap Reviews https://boombapreviews.blogspot.com/2016/08/ini-life-i-live-bootlegged-as-center-of.html

Swigga aka L-Swift Interview, Unkut https://unkut.com/2007/04/swigga-aka-l-swift-interview/

Anthony Cruz AKA A-Butta Interview, Unkut https://unkut.com/2005/10/anthony-cruz-aka-a-butta-interview/

Holdin' New Cards – Scaramanga Interview, Unkut https://unkut.com/2005/06/holdin-new-cards-scaramanga-interview/

CHAPTER 4 - CALI AGENTS

This Is the Life, Variety https://variety.com/2009/film/markets-festivals/this-is-the-life-1200474226/

The Good Life: L.A. Hip-Hop's Untold Story, HipHopWired https://hiphopwired.com/2734/the-good-life-l-a-hip-hops-untold-story/

Where We're From: Rise of L.A. Underground Hip-hop, Ghetto Blaster Magazine https://ghettoblastermagazine.com/film/where-were-from-filmology-with-spoken-nerd/

How LA Proved Hip-hop Could Go Global – By Staying Thoroughly Local, NPR https://www.npr.org/2023/08/10/1192466118/hip-hop-50-los-angeles

Figures of Speech – The Last Word, Fake For Real https://english.fakeforreal.net/index.php/post/2017/FIGURES-OF-SPEECH-The-Last-Word

Meet The Godmother of LA Hip-hop – Medusa The Gangsta Goddess, Hip Hop and Politics https://hiphopandpolitics.com/2008/03/08/meet-the-godmother-of-la-hip-hop-medusa-the-gangsta-goddess/

An Oral History of Low End Theory, Passion of The Weiss https://www.passionweiss.com/2018/06/06/an-oral-history-of-low-end-theory/

Bio, Mumbles https://www.mumbles.online/bio

Access All Areas With Abstract Rude, Rhymesayers https://rhymesayers.com/blogs/news/access-all-areas-with-abstract-rude

Extra Prolific's Debut Album 'Like It Should Be' Anniversary, Albumism *https://albumism.com/features/extra-prolific-debut-album-like-it-should-be-album-anniversary*

The Nonce Were One of L.A.'s Greatest 90's Rap Groups – Until Tragedy Intervened, Passion of The Weiss https://www.passionweiss.com/2018/06/11/the-nonce/

Episode 143 – Mystidious Mixtapes with Guests Sach and Laurent Fintoni, Dad Bod Rap Pod https://dadbodrappod.com/2020/11/12/dbrp143/

An Oral History of Souls of Mischief's 93 Til Infinity, Spin https://www.spin.com/2013/03/souls-of-mischief-20-years-93-til-infinity-oral-history/

93 'Til Now – An Oral History With Souls of Mischief, Esquire https://www.esquire.com/entertainment/music/a28043/oral-history-souls-of-mischief/

Souls of Mischief: Eclipsing The Infinite, Red Bull Music Academy https://daily.redbullmusicacademy.com/2014/09/souls-of-mischief-feature

How Hip-hop Crew Hieroglyphics Created Its Sound Out of Friendship, Westworld https://www.westword.com/music/how-hip-hop-crew-hieroglyphics-created-its-sound-out-of-friendship

Hip-Hop Hippies, The Culture Crush https://www.theculturecrush.com/hip-hop-hippies

Casual vs Saafir Wake Up Show Battle, Random Rap Radio https://randomrapradio.com/2019/11/18/casual-hieroglyphics-vs-saafir-hobo-junction-sway-tech-wake-up-show-kmel-18-november-1994/

Casual vs Saafir: Battle of The Bay, Hip Hop Nostalgia https://www.hiphopnostalgia.com/2021/01/casual-vs-saafir-battle-of-bay.html

Sleep Light: A Requiem for Saafir, Passion of The Weiss https://www.passionweiss.com/2024/11/22/saafir-eulogy-rip-boxcar-sessions/

Dilated Peoples – Neighbourhood Watch, Exclaim https://exclaim.ca/music/article/dilated_peoples-neighbourhood_watch

Dilated Peoples, Back in Focus, Los Angeles Times https://www.latimes.com/archives/la-xpm-2006-feb-16-wk-pop16-story.html

Evidence Interview, Grown Up Rap https://grownuprap.com/2018/01/26/interview-evidence/

CHAPTER 5 - UNIVERSAL MAGNETIC

Reflection of the City: The Story of Boston Hip-hop, Medium https://medium.com/@ebonygill/the-story-of-boston-hip-hop-and-its-reflection-of-the-city-4c8cde576145

Boston and Hip-hop: An Overlooked History, Rock The Bells https://rockthebells.com/articles/boston-and-hip-hop-an-overlooked-history/

Exploring the Rich and Vibrant Hip-hop History of Philadelphia, Philadelphia Freeway https://www.philadelphiafreeway.com/where-can-i-find-information-about-upcoming-newspaper-articles-featuring-hip-hop-artists-in-philadelphia-pa

10 Essential Songs From the 90s Hip-hop Scene in Philly, XPN https://xpn.org/2022/12/01/10-essential-songs-from-the-90s-hip-hop-scene-in-philly/

The High & Mighty Interview, MV Remix https://mvremix.com/urban/interviews/highandmighty.shtml

Low Budget Collective, Academic https://en-academic.com/dic.nsf/enwiki/5000993

North Carolina Hip-hop: Oral History, Indy Week https://indyweek.com/music/north-carolina-hip-hop-oral-history/

Episode 86 – Little Brother Interview, Dad Bod Rap Pod https://dadbodrappod.com/2019/09/19/dbrp86/

The History of MHz, The Crypt https://thecryptonline.com/v4/the-history-of-mhz-2/

MHz: Legacy, The Real Hip-hop https://therealhip-hop.com/mhz-legacy/

Amp Fiddler Interview, Red Bull Music Academy https://daily.redbullmusicacademy.com/2017/06/interview-amp-fiddler

Dilla Time, Dan Charnas

The 'Fantastic' Origin Story of J Dilla & Slum Village, Cuepoint https://medium.com/cuepoint/the-fantastic-origin-story-of-j-dilla-slum-village-818cc795cb0f

Interview: Brother Ali – Shadows on The Sun, Wordplay https://www.wordplaymagazine.com/blog-1/2019/2/28/interview-brother-ali-shadows-on-the-sun-15th-anniversary

One Brilliant Eyedea, Def Goldbloom https://www.youtube.com/watch?v=92D7MB_eMX0

The Fall and Rise of Canadian Hip-hop, Same Page Team https://samepageteam.com/2012/09/21/the-fall-and-rise-of-canadian-hip-hop/

CHAPTER 6 - THE ANTIPOP CONSORTIUMS

Little Brother Ask Fans Not to Buy Minstrel Show Reissue Because They Haven't Been Paid, HipHop DX https://hiphopdx.com/news/id.64676/title.little-brother-ask-fans-not-to-buy-minstrel-show-reissue-because-they-havent-been-paid

Little Brother Explains the Conflict With ABB Records, Rock The Bells https://rockthebells.com/articles/little-brother-mic-drop/

The Best of Def Jux, The Dowsers https://www.the-dowsers.com/the-dowser-posts/best-def-jux

Def Jux, Center of The Indie Label Universe https://indieuniverse.wordpress.com/2009/06/22/def-jux/

A History of Definitive Jux, Extraordinary Nobodies https://extraordinarynobodies.net/2018/01/07/a-history-of-definitive-jux/

The Rise and Fall of Def Jux, Def Goldbloom https://www.youtube.com/watch?v=b6JPwynZmNY

Uncommon Records, Uncommon Nasa https://www.uncommonnasa.com/uncommonrecords

Dru-Ha Looks Back on 20 Years of Duck Down Music, XXL https://www.xxlmag.com/dru-ha-duck-down-music-20-year-anniversary/

Hip-Hop Label 101: Duck Down Music, Rock The Bells https://rockthebells.com/articles/duck-down-music/

DJ Mighty Mi – The Unkut Interview, Unkut https://unkut.com/2024/08/dj-mighty-mi-the-unkut-interview/

Fat Beats: An Oral History, Red Bull Music Academy https://daily.redbullmusicacademy.com/2016/05/fat-beats-oral-history

Uncommon Approach: RIP To Fat Beats, The Find Mag https://www.thefindmag.com/features/stories-articles/uncommon-approach-r-i-p-fat-beats/

DJ Jab Interview, The Find Mag https://thefindmag.com/features/hip-hop-interviews/fat-beats-interview-joseph-abajian-hip-hop/

The Story of Fat Beats Told Through These Eight Iconic Records, Okayplayer https://www.okayplayer.com/originals/the-best-fat-beat-records-of-all-time-time-joseph-abajian.html

How Fat Beats Became a New York Institution, Bandcamp https://daily.bandcamp.com/label-profile/fat-beats-records-history

The Closing of New York's Fat Beats Store, The Couch Sessions https://www.thecouchsessions.com/articles/featured/quoted-the-closing-of-new-yorks-fat-beats-store

DJ Eclipse Interview, Grown Up Rap https://grownuprap.com/2019/08/06/25-years-of-fat-beats-dj-eclipse-interview/

Episode 79 – Fat Beats Retrospective With Guest DJ Eclipse, Dad Bod Rap Pod https://dadbodrappod.com/2019/07/25/dbrp79/

Bobbito Garcia Interview, Who Mag https://www.whomag.net/bobbito-garcia/

Fondle 'Em: A Legacy of Dopeness, Above Average Hip-hop http://aboveaveragehiphop.com/fondle-em-a-legacy-of-dopeness/

Bobbito Garcia Lecture, Red Bull Music Academy https://www.redbullmusicacademy.com/lectures/bobbito-garcia

Bobbito The Barber & His Multiple Personalities, YRB https://yrbmag.com/bobbito-the-barber-his-multiple-personalities-by-erika-hamilton-koolboblove-tbt/

Matt Fingaz – The Unkut Interview, Unkut https://unkut.com/2014/04/non-rapper-dudes-series-matt-fingaz-interview-guesswyld-records/

Episode 249 – Mike Heron, The Cipher Show https://theciphershow.com/episode/249/

Hydra Special – Mike Heron Interview, Unkut https://unkut.com/2007/05/hydra-special-mike-heron-interview/

Hydra Special – Jerry Famolari Interview, Unkut https://unkut.com/2007/04/hydra-special-jerry-famolari-interview/

The Mighty V.I.C. – The Unkut Interview, Unkut https://unkut.com/2014/11/the-mighty-v-i-c-the-unkut-interview/

When James Murdoch Was a Hip-hop Mogul, The Guardian https://www.theguardian.com/media/2011/jul/11/james-murdoch-hip-hop

James Murdoch: Hip-hop Head, The Atlantic https://www.theatlantic.com/entertainment/archive/2011/07/james-murdoch-hip-hop-head/242235/

Evil Dee Details What Led To The Demise of Rawkus Records, Ambrosia For Heads https://ambrosiaforheads.com/2019/04/rawkus-records-end/

The Best Albums From Rawkus Records, HHGA https://hiphopgoldenage.com/list/bring-rawkus-best-releases-rawkus-records/

Memory Lane – Rawkus Records, HHGA https://hiphopgoldenage.com/memory-lane-rawkus-records/

Smut Peddlers: A Failed Oral History, Cabbages Hip-hop https://www.cabbageshiphop.com/smut-peddlers-oral-history/

How Rawkus' Soundbombing II Launched a New Era of Independent Rap, Okayplayer https://www.okayplayer.com/originals/soundbombing-11-impact-mos-def-talib-kweli-black-star-1999.html

A Beginner's Guide to Rawkus Records, Pigeons & Planes https://www.complex.com/pigeons-and-planes/a/pigeons/rawkus-records-history

Hip-hop Label 101: Rawkus Records, Rock The Bells https://shop.rockthebells.com/blogs/articles/rawkus-records

Counting Down Our 10 Favorite Rawkus Records Albums, The Hundreds https://thehundreds.com/blogs/content/counting-10-favorite-rawkus-records-albums

A Brief History of Rawkus Records, The Hundreds https://www.youtube.com/watch?v=qKtqLlg_qus

The Rise and Fall of Rawkus Records, Def Goldbloom https://www.youtube.com/watch?v=DBjNi4z4-Os&t=7s

Lyricist Lounge: An Oral History, Red Bull Music Academy https://daily.redbullmusicacademy.com/2015/06/lyricist-lounge-oral-history

Write Lines: Adventures In Rap Journalism, Andrew Emery

Talib Kweli and El-P Talk Run The Jewels 4, Killer Mike, Company Flow & Rawkus, People's Party With Talib Kweli https://www.youtube.com/watch?v=klta75ld4Kc

We're Samplers So We Listen To Everything: An Interview With Da Beatminerz, Passion of The Weiss https://www.passionweiss.com/2024/04/02/da-beatminerz-mr-walt-dj-evil-dee-interview-stifled-creativity/

Kool G Rap's The Giancana Story: An Oral History, Red Bull Music Academy https://daily.redbullmusicacademy.com/2015/07/kool-g-rap-giancana-oral-history

Remembering the Kaleidoscopic Vision of Matt Doo, DJ Booth https://djbooth.net/features/2020-02-17-matt-doo-visual-artist-denzel-curry-kenny-beats-album-covers-vision/

Stressed: The Life & Art of Matt Reid, Red Bull Music Academy https://daily.redbullmusicacademy.com/2014/08/matt-reid-feature

Rhymesayers At 20: An Oral History, Forbes https://www.forbes.com/
sites/shawnsetaro/2015/11/30/rhymesayers-20-an-oral-history/

Stones Throw Records: The Label That Changed Hip-hop, The Guardian
https://www.theguardian.com/music/musicblog/2014/apr/03/stones-
throw-records-an-education-in-hip-hop

Micro-Chopping Stones Throw Records, Micro-Chop https://medium.com/
micro-chop/micro-chopping-stones-throw-records-d558c19f77cb

*For Stones Throw Records, A Love of Hip-hop Sparked 20 Years of
Musical Conversations*, Fader https://www.thefader.com/2016/11/14/
stones-throw-peanut-butter-wolf-interview

Interview With Peanut Butter Wolf, LA Taco https://lataco.com/inter-
view-peanut-butter-wolf

VMP Interview With Peanut Butter Wolf, Vinyl Me Please https://www.
vinylmeplease.com/blogs/magazine/vmp-interview-with-peanut-
butter-wolf-founder-of-stones-throw-records

Interview With Stones Throw's Peanut Butter Wolf, Stones Throw https://
www.stonesthrow.com/news/interview-pbw-archive/

Everybody's Got a Story, Here's Mine, Stones Throw https://www.
stonesthrow.com/about

Under The Covers: Stones Throw, Red Bull https://www.redbull.com/
gb-en/under-the-covers-stones-throw-jeff-jank-interview

Peanut Butter Wolf Interview, Stones Throw https://www.stonesthrow.
com/news/peanut-butter-wolf-bona-fide/

Peanut Butter Wolf Interview, Acclaim https://acclaimmag.com/music/
interview-peanut-butter-wolf/

Nervous Records: 30 Years of New York's Pioneering House Label, DJ
Mag https://djmag.com/longreads/nervous-records-30-years-new-
york-s-pioneering-house-label

The Birth of Battle Axe: The Business End of Swollen Members, Faze
https://faze.ca/battle-axe-business-end-of-swollen-members/

About Bomb Hip-hop, Bomb Hip-hop http://www.bombhiphop.com/
newbomb/bombpages/intro.html

Brick Records: Not Giving a Fuck Since 1996, Sound of Boston https://
soundofboston.com/brick-records-not-giving-a-fuck-since-1996/

Still Diggin': An Oral History of D.I.T.C., Cuepoint https://medium.com/cuepoint/still-diggin-an-oral-history-of-d-i-t-c-b91d44360a8e

Raw Shack Productions Interview, Blackout Hip-hop https://black-outhiphop.com/blog/blackout-rap-show-raw-shack-productions-interview-w-g-sulmers-yeshua-da-poed-25-03-1998/

Mr. Complex Interview, Old To The New https://oldtothenew.wordpress.com/2012/02/18/old-to-the-new-qa-part-two-mr-complex/

About 7 Heads, 7 Heads https://web.archive.org/web/20010321000845/http://www.sevenheads.com/2/4.htm

"I Left With Nothing": Eddie James, Tru Criminal Records, And The Making of AK Skills' "East Ta West", Micro-Chop https://medium.com/micro-chop/i-left-with-nothing-eddie-james-tru-criminal-records-and-the-making-of-ak-skills-east-ta-4506a3615685

DJ Pizzo – The Unkut Interview, Unkut https://unkut.com/2015/11/non-rapper-dudes-dj-pizzo-interview-hiphopsite-com/

UGHH, A Stalwart of The Hip-hop Scene, Is Closing Down, Boston Globe https://www.bostonglobe.com/metro/2016/12/28/ughh-com-stalwart-hiphop-scene-closing-down/QQpacMpK9VVKfAuVRaCNKP/story.html

CHAPTER 7 - WHAT'S GOLDEN

Saafir's Debut Album 'Boxcar Sessions' Anniversary, Albumism https://albumism.com/features/saafir-debut-album-boxcar-sessions-album-anniversary

The Nonce's 'World Ultimate' Anniversary, Albumism, https://albumism.com/features/the-nonce-debut-album-world-ultimate-turns-25-anniversary-retrospective

20 Years of Funcrusher: Looking Back on Company Flow, The Mad Geniuses of Underground Rap, Vice https://www.vice.com/en/article/20-years-of-funcrusher-looking-back-on-company-flow-the-mad-geniuses-of-underground-rap/

Soundbombing II Review, Pitchfork https://pitchfork.com/reviews/albums/various-artists-soundbombing-ii/

Aceyalone's 'A Book of Human Language' Anniversary, Albumism https://albumism.com/features/aceyalone-a-book-of-human-language-album-anniversary

Episode 171 – A Podcast of Human Language, Dad Bod Rap Pod https://dadbodrappod.com/2021/05/27/dbrp171/

Black Star's 'Mos Def & Talib Kweli Are Black Star' Anniversary, Albumism https://albumism.com/features/black-star-mos-def-talib-kweli-are-black-star-album-anniversary

Episode 9 – Black Star and Hidden Gems, Dad Bod Rap Pod https://dadbodrappod.com/2018/02/23/dbrp9/

Hieroglyphics's '3rd Eye Vision' Anniversary, Albumism https://albumism.com/features/hieroglyphics-debut-album-3rd-eye-vision-album-anniversary

3rd Eye Vision 20th Anniversary Retrospective, Yameen https://yameenmusic.com/blog/2018/03/3rd-eye-vision-20th-anniversary-retrospective-hieroglyphics/

Jurassic 5's Eponymous Debut EP 'Jurassic 5' Anniversary, Albumism https://albumism.com/features/jurassic-5-debut-jurassic-5-ep-anniversary

Rasco's Debut Album 'Time Waits For No Man' Anniversary, Albumism https://albumism.com/features/rasco-debut-album-time-waits-for-no-man-album-anniversary

Supply And Demand – Scholarwise Interview, Unkut https://unkut.com/2010/05/supply-and-demand-scholarwise-interview/

Blackalicious's Debut Album 'Nia' Anniversary, Albumism https://albumism.com/features/blackalicious-debut-album-nia-album-anniversary

Twenty Year Later – Blackalicious' Nia, Across The Margin https://acrossthemargin.com/twenty-years-later-blackalicious-nia/

MF DOOM "Operation: Doomsday" A 25th Anniversary Retrospective, Medium https://dartadams.medium.com/mf-doom-operation-doomsday-a-25th-anniversary-retrospective-d716143cdf66

Peanut Butter Wolf's Debut Album 'My Vinyl Weighs a Ton' Anniversary, Albumism https://albumism.com/features/peanut-butter-wolf-debut-album-my-vinyl-weighs-a-ton-album-anniversary

Mastermind: How Deltron 3030 Predicted The Future, Passion of The Weiss
https://www.passionweiss.com/2023/08/22/deltron-3030-review/

Deltron 3030: An Oral History, Red Bull Music Academy https://daily.
redbullmusicacademy.com/2014/08/deltron-3030-oral-history

Dilated Peoples' Debut Album 'The Platform' Anniversary Retrospective,
Albumism https://albumism.com/features/dilated-peoples-debut-al-
bum-the-platform-turns-20-anniversary-retrospective

The Platform: Dilated Peoples' Decades-in-the-making Debut, U
Discover Music https://www.udiscovermusic.com/stories/dilat-
ed-peoples-the-platform/

Cannibal Ox – The Cold Vein Review, HHGA https://hiphopgoldenage.
com/cannibal-ox-the-cold-vein-2001-review/

How El-P and Cannibal Ox Crafted a Cult Classic, Cuepoint https://
medium.com/cuepoint/how-el-p-and-cannibal-ox-crafted-a-cult-
classic-4d17ccb5a93b

Cannibal Ox's Debut Album 'The Cold Vein' Anniversary, Albumism https://albumism.com/features/cannibal-ox-debut-al-
bum-the-cold-vein-turns-20-anniversary-retrospective

Edan's 'Primitive Plus' Anniversary Retrospective, Albumism https://albu-
mism.com/features/tribute-celebrating-20-years-edan-primitive-plus

Season 2 Episode 4: Fantastic Damage, What Had Happened Was
https://www.youtube.com/watch?v=HNwiOxJyt8k

People Under The Stairs 'OST' Anniversary Retrospective, Albumism
https://albumism.com/features/tribute-celebrating-20-years-of-
people-under-the-stairs-ost

The Making of Clear Blue Skies by The Juggaknots, Passion of The
Weiss https://www.passionweiss.com/2020/04/07/the-making-of-
clear-blue-skies-by-the-juggaknots/

Little Brother on 20 Years of The Listening, Rolling Stone https://www.
rollingstone.com/music/music-features/little-brother-the-listening-
big-pooh-phonte-9th-wonder-1234685925/

*Nearly 20 Years Later, Little Brother's The Listening Continues to
Shape Hip-hop*, Rolling Stone https://www.rollingstone.com/music/
music-features/little-brother-influence-1392279/

Little Brother Looks Back on 20 Years of The Listening, GQ https://www.gq.com/story/little-brother-the-listening-album-20-years

Little Brother's Debut Album 'The Listening' Anniversary, Albumism https://albumism.com/features/little-brother-debut-album-the-listening-album-anniversary

Viktor Vaughn's 'Vaudeville Villain' Anniversary, Albumism https://albumism.com/features/viktor-vaughn-vaudeville-villain-album-anniversary

Madvillainy, Will Hagle

Madvillain Turns 20, Stereogum https://www.stereogum.com/2256094/madvillainy-turns-20/reviews/the-anniversary/

Searching For Tomorrow: The Story of Madlib and DOOM's Madvillain, Pitchfork https://pitchfork.com/features/article/9478-searching-for-tomorrow-the-story-of-madlib-and-dooms-madvillainy/

11 Artists and Creatives on The Enduring Influence of Madvillainy, Crack Magazine https://crackmagazine.net/article/lists/madvillainy-20th-anniversary/

CHAPTER 8 - THE FUTURE IS NOW

Roc Marciano: The Godfather of Underground Hip-hop, Def Goldbloom https://www.youtube.com/watch?v=_JmsFB42X0s

How Tanya Morgan Became a Rap Group And Sustained Itself Over The Years, Bandcamp https://daily.bandcamp.com/features/tanya-morgan-oral-history

Estee Nack Gives the Boom-bap Sound a Psychedelic Edge, Bandcamp https://daily.bandcamp.com/features/estee-nack-al-divino-interview

Hus Kingpin's Beautiful, Evocative, Grimy New York Rap, Stereogum https://www.stereogum.com/1922362/hus-kingpins-beautiful-evocative-grimy-new-york-rap/columns/status-aint-hood/

ACKNOWLEDGMENTS

Thanks to my wife Louise for all the support, and for giving me the time I needed to work on the book when there were so many other things that needed to be done. Thanks to Florence and Frances and the rest of my family and friends, and a special shoutout to my parents for never complaining when I played indie rap music out loud from my bedroom growing up. Thanks to Dart Adams for giving the book a thorough fact-check, to Matt Diamond from Coalmine Records for being someone to bounce ideas off, and to the legendary Chuck D for giving me the perfect quote for the cover. Thanks to Colin Steven at Velocity Press for the opportunity, and for everyone who helped promote the book. Love and solidarity to all the journalists who write about underground hip-hop, several of whom wrote articles, books, podcasts and social media posts that provided research material for what you have just read: Abe Beame, Andre Gee, Andrew Barber, Andrew Emery, Dan Charnas, Dart Adams (again!), David Ma, Demone Carter, Dylan Green, Gary Suarez, Gino Sorcinelli, Jeff Weiss, Jeff Mao, Jessie Ducker, John Morrison, Jonathan Abrams, Justin Tinsley, Lance Scott Walker, Max Bell, Mike Pizzo, Nate LeBlanc, Open Mike Eagle, Paul Thompson, Phillip Mlynar, Robbie Ettelson, Ryan Proctor, S.H. Fernando, Shawn Setaro, Soren Baker, Ta-Nehisi Coates, Thomas Hobbs, Tim Fish, Tom Breihan, Will Hagle, William E. Ketchum III, and others I'm likely forgetting. Lastly, thank you to everyone who pre-ordered the book in advance, including several dedicated followers of Grown Up Rap. You are very much appreciated.

———

ACKNOWLEDGMENTS

Thanks one more time to the following people who pre-ordered the book: Kevin Anderson, Gonzalo Arilla, Luke Bailey, Timothy Baker, Dawid Bartkowski, Paul Binning, Dan Bowen, Bas Braamhaar, Fiona Broom, Tim Burke, James Capaldi, Thomas Clover, David Michael Coleman, David Da Silva, Miguel Da Silva, Charles Dobson, Matthew Dolan, Morten Flobakk, Martyn Flyn, Timo Gaab, Stephen Goalby, Jon Green, Ian Gregory, Alex Harrison, Calum Haswell, Sted Hellvis, James Henderson, Matt Heneghan, Victor Holm, Ben Jones, Mike Justin, Andrew Kay, Chris Kovarik, Mr Lawson, Francisco López Hernández, Farid Joubbi, Garry Maltman, Tim Meaden, Bert Middendorp, Leon Mize, Joerg Mueller-Kindt, Jim Munchow, Matt Northam, Alan Nutton, Sigurdur Palmarsson, Donovan Parrish, Barnaby Ridge, Enzo Rodrigo Rabe, Damien Ratcliffe, Nick Rowe, Vojtech Rozsival, Dino Schweiger, The Segura Brothers, Jonathan Shaw, Christy Small, Nick Stebbing, Djordje Stojadinovic, Vladimir Stojadinovic, David Taylor, Olly Thomas, P Turner, Jeffrey u, Verbz MC, Dan Whittle, Barry Wood, Martin Zuidema.